NOTHING TO BE
FRIGHTENED OF

NOTHING TO BE FRIGHTENED OF

Julian Barnes

WINDSOR
PARAGON

First published 2009
by Vintage
This Large Print edition published 2013
by AudioGO Ltd
by arrangement with
The Random House Group Ltd

Hardcover   ISBN: 978 1 4713 4561 6
Softcover   ISBN: 978 1 4713 4562 3

Extracts from 'Aubade' from *Collected Poems* by Philip Larkin edited by Anthony Thwaite (Faber & Faber 2003); extracts from 'Church Going' and 'Wants' by Philip Larkin are reprinted from *The Less Deceived* by permission of The Marvell Press, England and Australia. Extracts from *Chasing Daylight* by Eugene O'Kelly (© Eugene O'Kelly 2006) reproduced by kind permission of McGraw-Hill Companies, Inc.

British Library Cataloguing in Publication Data available

Printed and bound in Great Britain by
TJ International Ltd

to P.

I don't believe in God, but I miss Him. That's what I say when the question is put. I asked my brother, who has taught philosophy at Oxford, Geneva and the Sorbonne, what he thought of such a statement, without revealing that it was my own. He replied with a single word: 'Soppy.'

The person to begin with is my maternal grandmother, Nellie Louisa Scoltock, née Machin. She was a teacher in Shropshire until she married my grandfather, Bert Scoltock. Not Bertram, not Albert, just Bert: so christened, so called, so cremated. He was a headmaster with a certain mechanical dash to him: a motorcycle-and-sidecar man, then owner of a Lanchester, then, in retirement, driver of a rather pompously sporty Triumph Roadster, with a three-person bench seat in front, and two bucket seats when the top was down. By the time I knew them, my grandparents had come south to be near their only child. Grandma went to the Women's Institute; she pickled and bottled; she plucked and roasted the chickens and geese that Grandpa raised. She was petite, outwardly unopinionated, and had the thickened knuckles of old age; she needed soap to get her wedding ring off. Their wardrobe was full of home-knitted cardigans, Grandpa's tending to feature more masculine cable stitch. They had regular appointments with the chiropodist, and were of that generation advised by dentists to have all their teeth out in one go. This was a normal rite of passage then: from being rickety-gnashered to fully porcelained in one leap, to all that buccal sliding and clacking, to social embarrassment and

1

the foaming glass on the bedside table.

The change from teeth to dentures struck my brother and me as both grave and ribald. But my grandmother's life had contained another enormous change, never alluded to in her presence. Nellie Louisa Machin, daughter of a labourer in a chemical works, had been brought up a Methodist; while the Scoltocks were Church of England. At some point in her young adulthood, my grandmother had suddenly lost her faith and, in the smooth narration of family lore, found a replacement: socialism. I have no idea how strong her religious faith had been, or what her family's politics were; all I know is that she once stood for the local council as a socialist and was defeated. By the time I knew her, in the 1950s, she had progressed to being a communist. She must have been one of the few old-age pensioners in suburban Buckinghamshire who took the *Daily Worker* and—so my brother and I insisted to one another—fiddled the housekeeping to send donations to the newspaper's Fighting Fund.

In the late 1950s, the Sino-Soviet Schism took place, and communists worldwide were obliged to choose between Moscow and Peking. For most of the European faithful, this was not a difficult decision; nor was it for the *Daily Worker*, which received funding as well as directives from Moscow. My grandmother, who had never been abroad in her life, who lived in genteel bungalowdom, decided for undisclosed reasons to throw in her lot with the Chinese. I welcomed this mysterious decision with blunt self-interest, since her *Worker* was now supplemented by *China Reconstructs*, a heretical magazine posted direct

2

from the distant continent. Grandma would save me the stamps from the biscuity envelopes. These tended to celebrate industrial achievement— bridges, hydroelectric dams, lorries rolling off production lines—or else show various breeds of dove in peaceful flight.

My brother did not compete for such offerings, because some years previously there had been a Stamp-Collecting Schism in our home. He had decided to specialize in the British Empire. I, to assert my difference, announced that I would therefore specialize in a category which I named, with what seemed like logic to me, Rest of the World. It was defined solely in terms of what my brother didn't collect. I can no longer remember if this move was aggressive, defensive, or merely pragmatic. All I know is that it led to some occasionally baffling exchanges in the school stamp club among philatelists only recently out of short trousers. 'So, Barnesy, what do you collect?' 'Rest of the World.'

My grandfather was a Brylcreem man, and the antimacassar on his Parker Knoll armchair—a high-backed number with wings for him to snooze against—was not merely decorative. His hair had whitened sooner than Grandma's; he had a clipped, military moustache, a metal-stemmed pipe and a tobacco pouch which distended his cardigan pocket. He also wore a chunky hearing aid, another aspect of the adult world—or rather, the world on the farther side of adulthood—which my brother and I liked to mock. 'Beg pardon?' we would shout satirically at one another, cupping hands to ears. Both of us used to look forward to the prized moment when our grandmother's

3

stomach would rumble loudly enough for Grandpa to be roused from his deafness into the enquiry, 'Telephone, Ma?' An embarrassed grunt later, they would go back to their newspapers. Grandpa, in his male armchair, deaf aid occasionally whistling and pipe making a hubble-bubble noise as he sucked on it, would shake his head over the *Daily Express*, which described to him a world where truth and justice were constantly imperilled by the Communist Threat. In her softer, female armchair—in the red corner—Grandma would tut-tut away over the *Daily Worker*, which described to her a world where truth and justice, in their updated versions, were constantly imperilled by Capitalism and Imperialism.

Grandpa, by this time, had reduced his religious observance to watching *Songs of Praise* on television. He did woodwork and gardened; he grew his own tobacco and dried it in the garage loft, where he also stored dahlia tubers and old copies of the *Daily Express* bound with hairy string. He favoured my brother, taught him how to sharpen a chisel, and left him his chest of carpentry tools. I can't remember him teaching (or leaving) me anything, though I was once allowed to watch while he killed a chicken in his garden shed. He took the bird under his arm, stroked it into calmness, then laid its neck on a green metal wringing machine screwed to the door jamb. As he brought the handle down, he gripped the bird's body ever more tightly against its final convulsions.

My brother was allowed not just to watch, but also participate. Several times he got to pull the lever while Grandpa held the bird. But our memories of the slaughter in the shed diverge into

4

incompatibility. For me, the machine merely wrung the chicken's neck; for him, it was a junior guillotine. 'I have a clear picture of a small basket underneath the blade. I have a (less clear) picture of the head dropping, some (not much) blood, Grandpa putting the headless bird on the ground, its running around for a few moments . . .' Is my memory sanitized, or his infected by films about the French Revolution? In either case, Grandpa introduced my brother to death—and its messiness—better than he did me. 'Do you remember how Grandpa killed the geese before Christmas?' (I do not.) 'He used to chase the destined goose round its pen, flailing at it with a crowbar. When he finally got it, he would, for good measure, lay it on the ground, put the crowbar across its neck, and tug on its head.'

My brother remembers a ritual—never witnessed by me—which he called the Reading of the Diaries. Grandma and Grandpa each kept separate diaries, and of an evening would sometimes entertain themselves by reading out loud to one another what they had recorded on that very week several years previously. The entries were apparently of considerable banality but frequent disagreement. Grandpa: 'Friday. Worked in garden. Planted potatoes.' Grandma: 'Nonsense. "Rained all day. Too wet to work in garden."'

My brother also remembers that once, when he was very small, he went into Grandpa's garden and pulled up all the onions. Grandpa beat him until he howled, then turned uncharacteristically white, confessed everything to our mother, and swore he would never again raise his hand to a child. Actually, my brother doesn't remember any of

5

this—neither the onions, nor the beating. He was just told the story repeatedly by our mother. And indeed, were he to remember it, he might well be wary. As a philosopher, he believes that memories are often false, 'so much so that, on the Cartesian principle of the rotten apple, none is to be trusted unless it has some external support'. I am more trusting, or self-deluding, so shall continue as if all my memories are true.

Our mother was christened Kathleen Mabel. She hated the Mabel, and complained about it to Grandpa, whose explanation was that he 'had once known a very nice girl called Mabel'. I have no idea about the progress or regress of her religious beliefs, though I own her prayer book, bound together with *Hymns Ancient and Modern* in soft brown suede, each volume signed in surprising green ink with her name and the date: 'Dec: 25th. 1932.' I admire her punctuation: two full stops and a colon, with the stop beneath the 'th' placed exactly between the two letters. You don't get punctuation like that nowadays.

In my childhood, the three unmentionable subjects were the traditional ones: religion, politics and sex. By the time my mother and I came to discuss these matters—the first two, that is, the third being permanently off the agenda—she was 'true blue' in politics, as I would guess she always had been. As for religion, she told me firmly that she didn't want 'any of that mumbo-jumbo' at her funeral. So when the undertaker asked if I wanted the 'religious symbols' removed from the crematorium wall, I told him I thought that this is what she would have wanted.

The past conditional, by the way, is a tense of

6

which my brother is highly suspicious. Waiting for the funeral to start, we had, not an argument—this would have been against all family tradition—but an exchange which demonstrated that if I am a rationalist by my own standards, I am a fairly feeble one by his. When our mother was first incapacitated by a stroke, she happily agreed that her granddaughter C. should have the use of her car: the last of a long sequence of Renaults, the marque to which she had maintained a francophiliac loyalty over four decades. Standing with my brother in the crematorium car park, I was looking out for the familiar French silhouette when my niece arrived at the wheel of her boyfriend R.'s car. I observed—mildly, I am sure— 'I think Ma would have wanted C. to come in *her* car.' My brother, just as mildly, took logical exception to this. He pointed out that there are the wants of the dead, i.e. things which people now dead once wanted; and there are hypothetical wants, i.e. things which people would or might have wanted. 'What Mother would have wanted' was a combination of the two: a hypothetical want of the dead, and therefore doubly questionable. 'We can only do what *we* want,' he explained; to indulge the maternal hypothetical was as irrational as if he were now to pay attention to his own past desires. I proposed in reply that we should try to do what she would have wanted, a) because we have to do *something*, and that something (unless we simply left her body to rot in the back garden) involves choices; and b) because we hope that when we die, others will do what we in our turn would have wanted.

I see my brother infrequently, and so am often

7

startled by the way in which his mind works; but he is quite genuine in what he says. As I drove him back to London after the funeral, we had a—to me—even more peculiar exchange about my niece and her boyfriend. They had been together a long time, though during a period of estrangement C. had taken up with another man. My brother and his wife had instantly disliked this interloper, and my sister-in-law had apparently taken a mere ten minutes to 'sort him out'. I didn't ask the manner of the sorting out. Instead, I asked, 'But you approve of R. ?'

'It's irrelevant,' my brother replied, 'whether or not I approve of R.'

'No, it's not. C. might want you to approve of him.'

'On the contrary, she might want me *not* to approve of him.'

'But either way, it's not irrelevant to *her* whether or not you approve or disapprove.'

He thought this over for a moment. 'You're right,' he said.

You can perhaps tell from these exchanges that he is the elder brother.

* * *

My mother had expressed no views about the music she wanted at her funeral. I chose the first movement of Mozart's piano sonata in E flat major K282—one of those long, stately unwindings and rewindings, grave even when turning sprightly. It seemed to last about fifteen minutes instead of the sleeve-noted seven, and I found myself wondering at times if this was another Mozartian repeat or the crematorium's CD player skipping backwards. The previous year I had appeared on *Desert Island Discs*, where the Mozart I had chosen was the *Requiem*. Afterwards, my mother telephoned and picked up on the fact that I had described myself as an agnostic. She told me that this was how Dad used to describe himself—whereas she was an atheist. She made it sound as if being an agnostic was a wishy-washy liberal position, as opposed to the truth-and-market-forces reality of atheism. 'What's all this about death, by the way?' she continued. I explained that I didn't like the idea of it. 'You're just like your father,' she replied. 'Maybe it's your age. When you get to my age you won't mind so much. I've seen the best of life anyway. And think about the Middle Ages—then their life expectancy was really short. Nowadays we live seventy, eighty, ninety years . . . People only believe in religion because they're afraid of death.' This was a typical statement from my mother: lucid, opinionated, explicitly impatient of opposing views. Her dominance of the family, and her certainties about the world, made things usefully clear in childhood, restrictive in adolescence, and grindingly repetitive in adulthood.

After her cremation, I retrieved my Mozart CD from the 'organist' who, I found myself reflecting, must nowadays get his full fee for putting on and taking off a single CD track. My father had been despatched, five years earlier, at a different crematorium, by a working organist earning his money honestly from Bach. Was this 'what he would have wanted'? I don't think he would have objected; he was a gentle, liberal-minded man who wasn't much interested in music. In this, as in most

9

things, he deferred—though not without many a quietly ironical aside—to his wife. His clothes, the house they lived in, the car they drove: such decisions were hers. When I was an unforgiving adolescent, I judged him weak. Later, I thought him compliant. Later still, autonomous in his views but disinclined to argue for them.

The first time I went to church with my family— for a cousin's wedding—I watched in amazement as Dad dropped to his knees in the pew, then covered his forehead and eyes with one hand. Where did *that* come from, I asked myself, before making some half-heartedly imitative gesture of piety, attended by furtive squinting through the fingers. It was one of those moments when your parents surprise you—not because you've learnt something new about them, but because you've discovered a further area of ignorance. Was my father merely being polite? Did he think that if he simply plonked himself down he would be taken for a Shelleyan atheist? I have no idea.

He died a modern death, in hospital, without his family, attended in his final minutes by a nurse, months—indeed, years—after medical science had prolonged his life to a point where the terms on which it was being offered were unimpressive. My mother had seen him a few days previously, but then suffered an attack of shingles. On that final visit, he had been very confused. She had asked him, characteristically, 'Do you know who I am? Because the last time I was here, you didn't know *what* I was.' My father had replied, just as characteristically, 'I think you're my wife.'

I drove my mother to the hospital, where we were given a black plastic bag and a creamy holdall. She sorted through both very quickly, knowing exactly what she wanted and what was to be left for—or at least with—the hospital. It was a shame, she said, that he never got to wear the big brown slippers with the easy Velcro fastenings that she'd bought him a few weeks earlier; unaccountably, to me, she took these home with her. She expressed a horror of being asked if she wanted to see Dad's body. She told me that when Grandpa died, Grandma had been 'useless' and had left her to do everything. Except that at the hospital, some wifely or atavistic need had kicked in, and Grandma had insisted on seeing her husband's body. My mother tried to dissuade her, but she was unbudgeable. They were taken to some mortuary viewing space, and Grandpa's corpse was displayed to them. Grandma turned to her daughter and said, 'Doesn't he look awful?'

When my mother died, the undertaker from a nearby village asked if the family wanted to see the body. I said yes; my brother no. Actually, his reply—when I telephoned through the question—was, 'Good God, no. I agree with Plato on that one.' I didn't have the text he was referring to immediately in mind. 'What did Plato say?' I asked. 'That he didn't believe in seeing dead bodies.' When I turned up alone at the undertaker's—which was merely the rear extension to a local haulage business—the funeral director said apologetically, 'I'm afraid she's only in the back room at the moment.' I looked at him questioningly, and he elaborated: 'She's on a trolley.' I found myself replying, 'Oh, she didn't stand on ceremony,' though couldn't claim to guess what she would, or wouldn't, have wanted in the circumstances.

She lay in a small, clean room with a cross on the wall; she was indeed on a trolley, with the back of her head towards me as I went in, thus avoiding an instant face-to-face. She seemed, well, very dead: eyes closed, mouth slightly open, and more so on the left side than the right, which was just like her—she used to hang a cigarette from the right corner of her mouth and talk out of the opposite side until the ash grew precarious. I tried to imagine her awareness, such as it might have been, at the moment of extinction. This had occurred a couple of weeks after she was moved from hospital into a residential home. She was quite demented by this time, a dementia of alternating kinds: one in which she still believed herself in charge of things, constantly ticking off the nurses for imaginary mistakes; the other, acknowledging that she had lost control, in which she became a child again, with all her dead relatives still alive, and what her mother or grandmother had just said of pressing importance. Before her dementia, I frequently found myself switching off during her solipsistic monologues; suddenly, she had become painfully interesting. I kept wondering where all this stuff was coming from, and how the brain was manufacturing this counterfeit reality. Nor could I now feel any resentment that she only wanted to talk about herself.

I was told that two nurses had been with her at the moment of death, and were engaged in turning her over, when she had just 'slipped away'. I like to imagine—because it would have been characteristic, and people should die as they have lived—that her last thought was addressed to herself and was something like, Oh, get on with it then. But this is sentimentalism—what she would have wanted (or rather, what I would have wanted for her)—and perhaps, if she was thinking anything, she was imagining herself a child again, being turned in a fretful fever by a pair of long-dead relatives.

At the undertaker's, I touched her cheek several times, then kissed her at the hairline. Was she that cold because she'd been in the freezer, or because the dead are naturally so cold? And no, she didn't look awful. There was nothing overpainted about her, and she would have been pleased to know that her hair was plausibly arranged ('Of course I never dye it,' she once boasted to my brother's wife, 'It's all natural'). Wanting to see her dead came more, I admit, from writerly curiosity than filial feeling; but there was a bidding farewell to be done, for all my long exasperation with her. 'Well done, Ma,' I told her quietly. She had, indeed, done the dying 'better' than my father. He had endured a series of strokes, his decline stretching over years; she had gone from first attack to death altogether more efficiently and speedily. When I picked up her bag of clothes from the residential home (a phrase which used to make me wonder what an 'unresidential home' might be), it felt heavier than I expected. First I discovered a full bottle of Harvey's Bristol Cream, and then, in a square cardboard box, an untouched birthday cake, shop-bought by village friends who had visited her on her final, eighty-second birthday.

My father had died at the same age. I had always imagined that his would be the harder death,

13

because I had loved him the more, whereas at best I could only be irritatedly fond of my mother. But it worked the other way round: what I had expected to be the lesser death proved more complicated, more hazardous. His death was just his death; her death was their death. And the subsequent house-clearing turned into an exhumation of what we had been as a family—not that we really were one after the first thirteen or fourteen years of my life. Now, for the first time, I went through my mother's handbag. Apart from the usual stuff, it contained a cutting from the *Guardian* listing the twenty-five greatest post-war English batsmen (though she never read the *Guardian*); and a photo of our childhood dog Max, a golden retriever. This was inscribed on the back in an unfamiliar hand '*Maxim: le chien*', and must have been taken, or at least annotated, in the early 1950s by P., one of my father's French *assistants*.

P. was from Corsica, an easy-going fellow with what seemed to my parents the typically Gallic trait of blowing his month's salary as soon as it arrived. He came to us for a few nights until he could find lodgings, and ended up staying the whole year. My brother went into the bathroom one morning and discovered this strange man in front of the shaving mirror. 'If you go away,' the foam-clad face informed him, 'I will tell you a story about Mr Beezy-Weezy.' My brother went away, and P. turned out to know a whole series of adventures that had befallen Mr Beezy-Weezy, none of which I can remember. He also had an artistic streak: he used to make railway stations out of cornflakes packets, and once gave my parents— perhaps in lieu of rent—two small landscapes he had painted. They hung on the wall throughout my childhood, and struck me as unimaginably skilful; but then, anything remotely representational would have done so.

As for Max, he had either run away or—since we could not imagine him wishing to abandon us—been stolen, shortly after the photo was taken; and wherever he had gone, must have been dead himself for more than forty years. Though my father would have liked it, my mother would never have another dog after that.

*   *   *

Given my family background of attenuated belief combined with brisk irreligion, I might, as part of adolescent rebelliousness, have become devout. But neither my father's agnosticism nor my mother's atheism were ever fully expressed, let alone presented as exemplary attitudes, so perhaps they didn't justify revolt. I might, I suppose, if it had been possible, have become Jewish. I went to a school where, out of 900 boys, about 150 were Jewish. On the whole, they seemed both socially and sartorially more advanced; they had better shoes—one contemporary even had a pair of elastic-sided Chelsea boots—and they knew about girls. They also got extra holidays, an obvious advantage. And it would have usefully shocked my parents, who had the low-level anti-Semitism of their age and class. (As the credits rolled at the end of a TV play and a name like Aaronson occurred, one or other of them might observe wryly, 'Another Welshman.') Not that they behaved any differently towards my Jewish friends, one of

15

whom was named, rightly it seemed, Alex Brilliant. The son of a tobacconist, Alex was reading Wittgenstein at sixteen, and writing poetry which pulsed with ambiguities—double, triple, quadruple, like heart bypasses. He was better than me at English, and took a scholarship to Cambridge, after which I lost sight of him. Down the years I would occasionally imagine his presumed success in one of the liberal professions. I was over fifty when I learnt that such biography-giving was an idle fantasy. Alex had killed himself—with pills, over a woman—in his late twenties, half my life ago.

So I had no faith to lose, only a resistance, which felt more heroic than it was, to the mild regime of God-referring that an English education entailed: scripture lessons, morning prayers and hymns, the annual Thanksgiving service in St Paul's Cathedral. And that was it, apart from the role of Second Shepherd in a nativity play at my primary school. I was never baptised, never sent to Sunday school. I have never been to a normal church service in my life. I do baptisms, weddings, funerals. I am constantly going into churches, but for architectural reasons; and, more widely, to get a sense of what Englishness once was.

My brother had marginally more liturgical experience than I did. As a Wolf Cub, he went to a couple of regular church services. 'I seem to recall being mystified, an infantile anthropologist among the anthropophagi.' When I ask how he lost his faith, he replies, 'I never lost it since I never had it to lose. But I realized it was all a load of balls on 7 Feb 1952, at 9.00. Mr Ebbets, headmaster of Derwentwater Primary School, announced that the

King had died, that he had gone to eternal glory and happiness in Heaven with God, and that in consequence we were all going to wear black armbands for a month. I thought that there was something fishy there, and How Right I Was. No scales fell from my eyes, there was no sense of loss, of a gap in my life, etc. etc. I hope,' he adds, 'that this story is true. It is certainly a very clear and lasting memory; but you know what memory is.'

My brother would have been just nine at the time of George VI's death (I was six, and at the same school, but have no memory of Mr Ebbets' speech, or of black armbands). My own final letting go of the remnant, or possibility, of religion, happened at a later age. As an adolescent, hunched over some book or magazine in the family bathroom, I used to tell myself that God couldn't possibly exist because the notion that He might be watching me while I masturbated was absurd; even more absurd was the notion that all my dead ancestors might be lined up and watching too. I had other, more rational arguments, but what did for Him was this powerfully persuasive feeling—a self-interested one, too, of course. The thought of Grandma and Grandpa observing what I was up to would have seriously put me off my stroke.

As I record this now, however, I wonder why I didn't think through more of the possibilities. Why did I assume that God, if He *was* watching, necessarily disapproved of how I was spilling my seed? Why did it not occur to me that if the sky did not fall in as it witnessed my zealous and unflagging self-abuse, this might be because the sky did not judge it a sin? Nor did I have the imagination to conceive of my dead ancestors

17

equally smiling on my actions: go on, my son, enjoy it while you've got it, there won't be much more of that once you're a disembodied spirit, so have another one for us. Perhaps Grandpa would have taken his celestial pipe out of his mouth and whispered complicitly, 'I once knew a very nice girl called Mabel.'

*   *   *

At primary school, we had our voices tested. One by one, we went up to the front of the class and tried to sing an easy tune to the teacher's accompaniment. Then we were placed into one of two groups: The High Voices or The Low Voices (a musical Rest of the World). These labels were kindly euphemisms, given that our voices were years away from breaking; and I remember my parents' indulgence when I reported, as if it were an achievement, the group into which I had been put. My brother was also a Low Voice; though he had a greater humiliation in store. At our next school, we were tested again, and divided—my brother reminds me—into groups A, B and C by 'a repulsive man called Walsh or Welsh'. The reason for my brother's continuing animus more than half a century on? 'He created group D especially for me. It took me some years to stop hating music.'

At this school, music came every morning attached to a thunderous organ and nonsensical hymns. 'There is a green hill far away / Without a city wall / Where the dear Lord was crucified / Who died to save us all.' The tune was less dreary than most; but why would anyone want a city wall built around a green hill anyway? Later, when I understood that 'without' meant 'outside', I switched my puzzlement to the 'green'. There is a *green* hill? In Palestine? We didn't do much geography now that we were in long trousers (if you were clever you gave it up), but even I knew it was all sand and stones out there. I didn't feel an anthropologist among the anthropophagi—I was now part of a quorum of scepticism—but I certainly sensed a distance between words familiar to me and meanings attached to them.

Once a year, on Lord Mayor's Prize Day, we would sing 'Jerusalem', which had been adopted as the school song. It was a tradition among the rowdier boys—a posse of unreformed Low Voices—to launch at a given moment into an unmarked and frowned-upon fortissimo: 'Bring me my arrows [*slight pause*] OF-DEE-SIRE.' Did I know the words were by Blake? I doubt it. Nor was there any attempt to promote religion through the beauty of its language (perhaps this was regarded as self-evident). We had an elderly Latin master who liked to stray from the script into what posed as private musings but which were, I now realize, a calculated technique. He came on like a prim and sober clergyman, but would then mutter, as if it had just occurred to him, something like, 'She was only an Arab's daughter, but you should have seen Gaza strip,' a joke far too risqué to retail to my own school-teaching parents. On another occasion, he grew satirical about the absurd title of a book called *The Bible Designed to be Read as Literature*. We chuckled along with him, but from a contrary angle: the Bible (boring) was obviously *not* designed to be read as literature (exciting), QED.

Among us nominal Christians, there were a few

19

boys who were devout, but they were regarded as slightly weird, as rare—and as weird—as the master who wore a wedding ring and could be made to blush (he was devout too). In late adolescence, I had an out-of-body experience once, possibly twice: the sense of being up near the ceiling looking down at my untenanted flesh. I mentioned this to the schoolfriend with the elastic-sided boots—but not to my family; and while I found it a matter for mild pride (something's happening!), I didn't deduce anything significant, let alone religious.

It was probably Alex Brilliant who passed on Nietzsche's news that God was officially dead, which meant we could all wank away the merrier for it. You made your own life, didn't you—that was what Existentialism was all about. And our zestful young English master was implicitly against religion. At least, he quoted the Blake that sounded like the opposite of 'Jerusalem': 'For Old Nobodaddy aloft / Farted & Belch'd & cough'd.' God farted! God belched! That proved He didn't exist! (Again, I never thought to take these human traits as arguments for the existence, indeed the sympathetic nature, of the deity.) He also quoted to us Eliot's bleak summary of human life: birth, and copulation, and death. Half-way into his own natural span, this English master, like Alex Brilliant, was to kill himself, in a pills-and-drink suicide pact with his wife.

I went up to Oxford. I was asked to call on the college chaplain, who explained that as a scholar I had the right to read the lesson in chapel. Newly freed from the compulsions of hypocritical worship, I replied, 'I'm afraid I'm a happy atheist.'

Nothing ensued—no clap of thunder, loss of scholar's gown, or rictus of disapproval; I finished my sherry and left. A day or two later, the captain of boats knocked on my door and asked if I wanted to try out for the river. I replied—with perhaps greater boldness, having faced down the chaplain—'I'm afraid I'm an aesthete.' I wince now for my reply (and rather wish I'd rowed); but again, nothing happened. No gang of hearties broke into my room looking to smash the blue china I did not possess, or to thrust my bookish head down a lavatory bowl.

I was able to state my position, but too shy to argue it. Had I been articulate—or crass—I might have explained to both cleric and oarsman that being an atheist and being an aesthete went together: just as being Muscular and being Christian once had for them. (Although sport might still provide a useful analogy: hadn't Camus said that the proper response to life's meaninglessness was to invent rules for the game, as we had done with football?) I might have gone on—in my fantasy rebuttal—to quote them Gautier's lines: *'Les dieux eux-mêmes meurent. / Mais les vers souverains / Demeurent / Plus forts que les airains.'* [The Gods themselves die out, but Poetry, stronger even than bronze, survives everything.] I might have explained how religious rapture had long ago given way to aesthetic rapture, and perhaps topped it off with a cheesy sneer about St Teresa manifestly not seeing God in that famous ecstatic sculpture but enjoying something altogether more corporeal.

When I said that I was a happy atheist, the adjective should be taken as applying to that noun

21

and no further. I was happy not to believe in God; I was happy to have been academically successful so far; and that was about it. I was consumed with anxieties I tried to hide. If I was intellectually capable (while suspecting myself of being merely a trained exam-passer), I was socially, emotionally and sexually immature. And if I was happy to be free of Old Nobodaddy, I wasn't blithe about the consequences. No God, no Heaven, no afterlife; so death, however distant, was on the agenda in quite a different way.

*   *   *

While I was at university, I spent a year in France, teaching at a Catholic school in Brittany. The priests I lived among surprised me by being as humanly various as civilians. One kept bees, another was a Druid; one bet on horses, another was anti-Semitic; this young one talked to his pupils about masturbation; that old one was addicted to films on television, even if he liked to dismiss them afterwards with the lofty phrase 'lacking both interest and morality'. Some of the priests were intelligent and sophisticated, others stupid and credulous; some evidently pious, others sceptical to the point of blasphemy. I remember the shock around the refectory table when the subversive Père Marais started baiting the Druidical Père Calvard about which of their home villages got a better quality of Holy Ghost coming down at Pentecost. It was also here that I saw my first dead body: that of Père Roussel, a young teaching priest. His corpse was laid out in an anteroom by the school's front entrance; boys and staff were encouraged to visit him. I did no more than gaze through the glass of the double doors, telling myself that this was tact; whereas in all probability it was only fear.

The priests treated me in a kindly way, a little teasing, a little incomprehending. 'Ah,' they would say, stopping me in the corridor, touching my arm and offering a shy smile, *'La perfide Albion.'* Among their number was a certain Père Hubert de Goësbriand, a dim if good-hearted fellow who might have acquired his grand, aristocratic Breton name in a raffle, so little did it fit him. He was in his early fifties, plump, slow, hairless and deaf. His main pleasure in life was to play practical jokes at mealtimes on the timid school secretary, M. Lhomer: surreptitiously stuffing cutlery into his pocket, blowing cigarette smoke in his face, tickling his neck, shoving the mustard pot unexpectedly under his nose. The school secretary displayed a truly Christian endurance to these tedious daily provocations. At first, Père de Goësbriand used to poke me in the ribs or pull my hair every time he passed me, until I cheerfully called him a bastard and he stopped. During the war he had been wounded in the left buttock ('Running away, Hubert!' 'No, we were surrounded'), so travelled cheap-rate and had a subscription to a magazine for *Anciens Combattants*. The other priests treated him with head-shaking indulgence. *'Pauvre Hubert'* was the most common remark heard at mealtimes, whether as a muttered aside or shouted directly into his face.

De Goësbriand had just celebrated twenty-five years as a priest, and took his faith very

23

straightforwardly. He was shocked when, listening in on my conversation with Père Marais, he discovered that I hadn't been baptised. *Pauvre Hubert* became immediately concerned on my behalf, and spelled out to me the dire theological consequences: that without baptism I had no chance of getting to heaven. Perhaps because of my outcast status, he would sometimes admit to me the frustrations and restrictions of the priestly life. One day, he cautiously confided, 'You don't think I'd go through all this unless there was heaven at the end of it, do you?'

At the time, I was half impressed by such practical thinking, half appalled at a life wasted in vain hope. But Père de Goësbriand's calculation had a distinguished history, and I might have recognized it as a workaday version of Pascal's famous wager. The Pascalian bet sounds simple enough. If you believe, and God turns out to exist, you win. If you believe, and God turns out not to exist, you lose, but not half as badly as you would if you chose not to believe, only to find out after death that God does exist. It is, perhaps, not so much an argument as a piece of self-interested position-taking worthy of the French diplomatic corps; though the primary wager, on God's existence, does depend on a second and simultaneous wager, on God's nature. What if God is not as imagined? What, for instance, if He disapproves of gamblers, especially those whose purported belief in Him is dependent on some acorn-beneath-the-cup mentality? And who decides who wins? Not us: God might prefer the honest doubter to the sycophantic chancer.

The Pascalian bet echoes down the centuries,

always finding takers. Here is an extreme, action-man version. In June 2006, at the Kiev zoo, a man lowered himself by rope into the island compound where the lions and tigers are kept. As he descended, he shouted across to the gawping crowds. One witness quoted him as saying, 'Who believes in God will be unharmed by lions'; another, the more challenging, 'God will save me, if He exists.' The metaphysical *provocateur* reached the ground, took off his shoes, and walked towards the animals; whereupon an irritated lioness knocked him down, and bit through his carotid artery. Does this prove a) the man was mad; b) God does not exist; c) God does exist, but won't be lured into the open by such cheap tricks; d) God does exist, and has just demonstrated that He is an ironist; e) none of the above?

And here is the bet made to sound almost not like a bet: 'Go on, believe! It does no harm.' This weak-tea version, the weary murmur of a man with a metaphysical headache, comes from Wittgenstein's notebooks. If you were the Deity, you might be a little unimpressed by such lukewarm endorsement. But there are times, probably, when 'it does no harm'—except for not being true, which some might find irreducible, unnegotiable harm.

As an example: some twenty years before he wrote this note, Wittgenstein worked as a schoolmaster in several remote villages of lower Austria. The locals found him austere and eccentric, yet devoted to his pupils; also willing, despite his own religious doubts, to begin and end each day with the paternoster. While teaching at Trattenbach, Wittgenstein took his pupils on a

25

study trip to Vienna. The nearest station was at Gloggnitz, twelve miles away, so the trip began with a pedagogic hike through the intervening forest, with the children being asked to identify plants and stones they had studied in class. In Vienna, they spent two days doing the same with examples of architecture and technology. Then they took the train back to Gloggnitz. By the time it arrived, night was falling. They set off on their return twelve-mile hike. Wittgenstein, sensing that many of the children were frightened, went from one to the other, saying quietly, 'Are you afraid? Well, then, you must think only about God.' They were, quite literally, in a dark wood. Go on, believe! It does no harm. And presumably it didn't. A non-existent God will at least protect you from non-existent elves and sprites and wood demons, even if not from existent wolves and bears (and lionesses).

A Wittgenstein scholar suggests that while the philosopher was not 'a religious person', there was in him 'in some sense, the *possibility* of religion'; though his idea of it was less to do with belief in a creator than with a sense of sin and a desire for judgement. He thought that 'Life can educate one to a belief in God'—this is one of his last notes. He also imagined himself being asked the question of whether or not he would survive death, and replying that he couldn't say: not for the reasons you or I might give, but because 'I haven't a clear idea of what I am saying when I'm saying "I don't cease to exist".' I shouldn't think many of us do, except for fundamentalist self-immolators expecting very specific rewards. Though what it means, rather than what it might imply, is surely within our grasp.

*   *   *

If I called myself an atheist at twenty, and an agnostic at fifty and sixty, it isn't because I have acquired more knowledge in the meantime: just more awareness of ignorance. How can we be sure that we know enough to know? As twenty-first-century neo-Darwinian materialists, convinced that the meaning and mechanism of life have only been fully clear since the year 1859, we hold ourselves categorically wiser than those credulous knee-benders who, a speck of time away, believed in divine purpose, an ordered world, resurrection and a Last Judgement. But although we are more informed, we are no more evolved, and certainly no more intelligent than them. What convinces us that our knowledge is so final?

My mother would have said, and did say, that it was 'my age'—as if, now that the end was nearer, metaphysical caution and brute fear were weakening my resolve. But she would have been wrong. Awareness of death came early, when I was thirteen or fourteen. The French critic Charles du Bos, friend and translator of Edith Wharton, created a useful phrase for this moment: *le réveil mortel*. How best to translate it? 'The wake-up call to mortality' sounds a bit like a hotel service. 'Death-knowledge', 'death-awakening'?—rather too Germanic. 'The awareness of death'?—but that suggests a state rather than a particular cosmic strike. In some ways, the (first) bad translation of du Bos's phrase is the good one: it *is* like being in an unfamiliar hotel room, where the alarm clock

27

has been left on the previous occupant's setting, and at some ungodly hour you are suddenly pitched from sleep into darkness, panic, and a vicious awareness that this is a rented world.

My friend R. recently asked me how often I think about death, and in what circumstances. At least once each waking day, I replied; and then there are the intermittent nocturnal attacks. Mortality often gatecrashes my consciousness when the outside world presents an obvious parallel: as evening falls, as the days shorten, or towards the end of a long day's hiking. A little more originally, perhaps, my wake-up call frequently shrills at the start of a sports event on television, especially, for some reason, during the Five (now Six) Nations rugby tournament. I told R. all this, apologizing for what might seem a self-indulgent dwelling on the subject. He replied: 'Your death-thoughts seem HEALTHY. Not sicko like [our mutual friend] G. Mine are v. v. sicko. Always have been = DO IT NOW type. Shotgun-in-mouth. Much improved since Thames Valley Police came and removed my twelve-bore because they'd heard me on *Desert Island Discs*. Now have only [his son's] airgun. No good. No blasto. So we WILL HAVE AN OLD AGE TOGETHER.'

People used to talk more readily about death: not death and the life to come, but death and extinction. In the 1920s, Sibelius would go to the Kämp restaurant in Helsinki and join the so-called 'lemon table': the lemon being the Chinese symbol of death. He and his fellow-diners—painters, industrialists, doctors and lawyers—were not just permitted, but required to talk about death. In Paris, a few decades previously, the loose group of

28

writers at the Magny dinners—Flaubert, Turgenev, Edmond de Goncourt, Daudet and Zola—would discuss the matter in an orderly and companionable way. All were atheists, or serious agnostics; death-fearing but not death-avoiding. 'People like us,' Flaubert wrote, 'should have the religion of despair. One must be equal to one's destiny, that's to say, impassive like it. By dint of saying "That is so! That is so!" and of gazing down into the black pit at one's feet, one remains calm.'

I have never wanted the taste of a shotgun in my mouth. Compared to that, my fear of death is low-level, reasonable, practical. And one problem with gathering some new lemon table or Magny dinner to discuss the matter might be that some of those present would turn competitive. Why should mortality be less a matter for male boasting than cars, income, women, cock size? 'Night sweats, screaming—*Ha!*—that's primary-school stuff. You wait till you get to . . .' And so our private anguish might be shown up as not just banal but under-powered. MY FEAR OF DEATH IS BIGGER THAN YOURS AND I CAN GET IT UP MORE OFTEN.

On the other hand, this would be one occasion when you would happily lose out in a male boasting session. One of the few comforts of death-awareness is that there is always—almost always—someone worse off than yourself. Not just R., but also our mutual friend G. He is the long-time holder of the thanatophobes' gold medal for having been woken by *le réveil mortel* at the age of four (*four! you bastard!*). The news affected him so profoundly that he spent his childhood in the presence of eternal non-existence and terrible infinity. In adulthood, he remains much more death-haunted than me; also, liable to much deeper depressions. There are nine basic criteria for a Major Depressive Episode (from Depressed Mood Most of the Day, via Insomnia and Feelings of Worthlessness, up to Recurrent Thoughts of Death and Recurrent Suicidal Ideation). Hosting any five over a two-week period is sufficient for a diagnosis of depression. About a decade ago, G. checked himself into hospital after managing to score a full nine out of nine. He told me this story without any competitive edge (I have long stopped competing with him), though with a certain sense of grim triumph.

Every thanatophobe needs the temporary comfort of a worst-case exemplar. I have G., he has Rachmaninov, a man both terrified of death, and terrified that there might be survival after it; a composer who worked the *Dies Irae* into his music more times than anyone else; a cinema-goer who ran gibbering from the hall during the opening graveyard scene of *Frankenstein*. Rachmaninov only surprised his friends when he *didn't* want to talk about death. A typical occasion: in 1915, he went to visit the poet Marietta Shaginyan and her mother. First he asked the mother to tell his fortune at cards, in order (of course) to find out how much longer he had to live. Then he settled down to talk to the daughter about death: his chosen text that day being a short story by Artsybashev. There was a dish of salted pistachio nuts to hand. Rachmaninov ate a mouthful, talked about death, shifted his chair to get nearer the bowl, ate another mouthful, talked about death. Suddenly, he broke off and laughed. 'The pistachio nuts have made my fear go away. Do you know where to?' Neither the poet nor her mother could answer this question; but when Rachmaninov left for Moscow, they gave him a whole sack of nuts for the journey 'to cure his fear of death'.

If G. and I were playing Russian composers, I would match (or raise) his bet with Shostakovich, a greater composer and just as much of a brooder on death. 'We should think more about it,' he said, 'and accustom ourselves to the thought of death. We can't allow the fear of death to creep up on us unexpectedly. We have to make the fear familiar, and one way is to write about it. I don't think writing and thinking about death is characteristic only of old men. I think that if people began thinking about death sooner, they'd make fewer foolish mistakes.'

He also said: 'Fear of death may be the most intense emotion of all. I sometimes think that there is no deeper feeling.' These views were not publicly expressed. Shostakovich knew that death—unless it came in the form of heroic martyrdom—was not an appropriate subject for Soviet art, that it was 'tantamount to wiping your nose on your sleeve in company'. He could not have the *Dies Irae* blaze from his scores; he had to be musically covert. But increasingly, the cautious composer found the courage to draw his sleeve across his nostrils, especially in his chamber music. His last works often contain long, slow, meditative invocations of mortality. The violist of the Beethoven Quartet was once given the following advice about the first movement of the fifteenth quartet by its composer: 'Play it so that the flies drop dead in mid-air.'

31

When my friend R. talked about death on *Desert Island Discs*, the police took away his shotgun. When I did so, I received various letters pointing out that my fears would be cured if I looked within, opened myself up to faith, went to church, learnt to pray, and so on. The theological bowl of pistachio nuts. My correspondents weren't exactly patronizing—some were soppy, some were stern— but they did seem to imply that this solution might come as news to me. As if I were a member of some rainforest tribe (not that I wouldn't have had my own rituals and belief system in place if I were), rather than one speaking at a point when the Christian religion is approaching extinction in my country, partly because families like mine have been not believing it for a century and more.

*   *   *

That century is about as far as I can trace my family back. I have become, by default, our archivist. In a shallow drawer, a few yards from where I am writing, sits the entire corpus of documentation: the certificates of birth and marriage and death; the wills and grants of probate; the professional qualifications, references and testimonials; the passports, ration cards, identity cards (and *cartes d'identité*); the scrapbooks and notebooks and keepsakes. Here are the texts of patter songs my father wrote (to be performed in dinner jacket, leaning against the piano while a school or service colleague provided a languid nightclub accompaniment), his signed menus, theatre programmes and half-filled-in cricket scorecards. Here is my mother's hostess book, her Christmas card lists and tabulations of stocks and shares. Here are the telegrams and wartime aerogrammes between them (but no letters). Here are their sons' school reports and physical development cards, their prize-day programmes, swimming and athletics certificates— I see that in 1955 I came first in the long jump and third in the boot race, while my brother once came second in the wheelbarrow race with Dion Shirer—together with evidence of achievements long forgotten, like my certificate for Perfect Attendance during one primary-school term. Here too are Grandpa's First World War medals— proofs of attendance in France, 1916–17, a time he would never talk about.

This shallow drawer is also big enough to contain the family's photographic archive. Packets labelled 'Us', 'The Boys' and 'Antiques' in my father's handwriting. Here is Dad in schoolmaster's gown and RAF uniform, black tie, hiking shorts and cricket whites, usually with cigarette in hand or pipe in mouth. Here is Mum in chic home-tailored clothes, unrevealing two-piece swimsuit, and swanky outfit for a Masonic dinner dance. Here is the French *assistant* who probably photographed *Maxim: le chien* and the later *assistant* who helped scatter my parents' ashes on the west coast of France. Here are my brother and me in younger, blonder days, modelling a range of home knitwear, attended by dog, beach ball and junior wheelbarrow; here we are athwart the same tricycle; here we are in multiple, scattershot polyphoto, and later cardboard-framed as Souvenirs of Nestlé's Playland, Olympia 1950.

Here too is Grandpa's photographic record, a

red cloth-bound album titled 'Scenes from Highways & Byways', bought in Colwyn Bay in August 1913. It covers the period 1912 to 1917, after which, it seems, he laid down his camera. Here are Bert and his brother Percy, Bert and his fiancée Nell, then the two of them on their wedding day: 4th August 1914, the day the First World War broke out. Here, among the faded sepia prints of unidentifiable relations and chums, is a sudden defacement: the photograph of a woman in a white blouse, sitting in a deckchair, dated 'Sept 1915'. Next to this date, a pencil marking—a name? a place?—has been more or less erased. The woman's face has been venomously ripped and gouged until only her chin and her wiry, Weetabixy hair remain visible. I wonder who did that, and why, and to whom.

In my teens, I had my own photographic period, which included modest home processing: the plastic developing tank, orange darkroom light, and contact printing frame. At some point during this enthusiasm, I answered an advertisement in a magazine for an inexpensive yet magical product which promised to turn my humble black-and-white prints into rich and living colour. I can't remember if I consulted my parents before sending away, or if I was disappointed when the promised kit turned out to consist of a small brush and some coloured oblongs of a paint which would adhere to photographic paper. But I set to work, and made the pictorial record of my family more vivid, if not more true. Here is Dad in bright yellow cords and green sweater against a monochrome garden; Grandpa in trousers of exactly the same green, Grandma in a watered-down green blouse. All

34

three of them have hands and faces of a preternaturally hot-flush pink.

My brother distrusts the essential truth of memories; I distrust the way we colour them in. We each have our own cheap mail-order paintbox, and our favourite hues. Thus, I remembered Grandma a few pages ago as 'petite and unopinionated'. My brother, when consulted, takes out his paintbrush and counterproposes 'short and bossy'. His mental album also contains more snaps than mine of a rare three-generational family outing to Lundy Island in the early 1950s. For Grandma it was almost certainly the only time she left the British landmass; for Grandpa, his first since returning from France in 1917. The sea was choppy that day, Grandma wretchedly sick, and when we reached Lundy we were told it was too rough for us to disembark. My memories of all this are faded sepia, my brother's still lurid. He describes how Grandma spent the whole trip below deck, vomiting into a succession of plastic beakers, while Grandpa, flat cap pulled down over his eyebrows, doggedly received each filled receptacle. Instead of disposing of them, he lined all the beakers up on a shelf, as if to embarrass her. This is, I think, my brother's favourite childhood memory.

Petite or merely short, unopinionated or bossy? Our differing adjectives reflect scrappy memories of half-forgotten feelings. I have no way of working out why I preferred Grandma, or she me. Did I fear Grandpa's authoritarianism (though he never beat me), and find his example of masculinity more coarse-grained than Dad's? Was I simply drawn to Grandma as a female presence, of which there were few enough in our family? Though my brother and I knew her for twenty years, we can barely remember anything she said. The two examples he can provide are both of occasions when she enraged our mother; so her words may have adhered more for their delighting effect than their intrinsic content. The first was on a winter's evening, with our mother warming herself by the fire. Grandma advised: 'Don't sit so close, you'll spoil your legs.' The second took place almost a whole generation later. My brother's daughter C., then aged about two, was offered a piece of cake, and accepted it without acknowledgement. 'Say Ta, dear,' her great-grandmother suggested—at which 'our mother blew her top that such a vulgarism should have been uttered'.

Do such scraps say more about Grandma, our mother, or my brother? Are they indicators of bossiness? My own evidence for her 'unopinionatedness' is, I realize, actually non-existent; but then perhaps it might be, by definition. And though I search my memory, I cannot find a single direct quote from this woman whom I think I loved when a child; only an indirect one. Long after Grandma was dead, Ma passed on to me a piece of her received wisdom. 'She used to say, "There would be no bad men in the world if there were no bad women."' Grandma's endorsement of the sin of Eve was retailed to me with considerable scorn.

*   *   *

When I was clearing out my parents' bungalow, I found a small stack of postcards dating from the

1930s to the 1980s. All had been sent from abroad; clearly those posted from within Britain, however flavourful the message, had at some point been culled. Here is my father writing to his mother in the thirties ('Warm greetings from cold Brussels'; 'Austria calling!'); my father in Germany to my mother—then his girlfriend? fiancée?—in France ('I'm wondering whether you got all the letters I wrote from England. Did you?'); my father to his small sons at home ('I hope you are doing your duty and listening to the Test Match'), announcing his acquisition of stamps for me and matchboxes for my brother. (I had forgotten the matchboxes, remembering only that he collected orange papers.) Then there are cards from my brother and me, full of adolescent jocosity. Me to him from France: 'Holiday began with a superb burst of 5 cathedrals. Tomorrow a quick burn-up of the chateaux of the Loire.' He to me from Champéry, where Dad had taken him on a school outing: 'We arrived here safely, and, except for the ham sandwiches, we were satisfied with the journey.'

I can't date the earliest postcards, the stamps having been steamed off—doubtless for my collection—and with them the postmarks. But I note the varying ways my father signs off to his mother: 'Leonard', 'Yours as ever, Leonard', up to 'Love, Leonard' and even 'Love and kisses, Leonard'. On cards to my mother he is 'Pip', 'Your Pip', 'As ever, Pip', 'Lots of love, Pip' and 'All my love, Pip': rising gradations from the unreachable days of the courtship which led to my existence. I follow my father through his trail of changing names. He was christened Albert Leonard, and known to his parents and siblings as Leonard.

When he became a schoolmaster the Albert took over, and in common rooms he was known for forty years as 'Albie' or 'Albie boy'—though this might have been derived from his initials, A.L.B.—and occasionally, in satirical mode, as 'Wally', after the Arsenal fullback Wally Barnes. My mother disliked both given names (doubtless Wally too), and decided to call him Pip. After *Great Expectations*? But he was hardly Philip Pirrip, any more than she was Estella. During the war, when he was in India with the RAF, he changed again. I have two of his dip pens, hand-decorated along the shaft by a local artisan. A blood-red sun sets over a minaretted temple, and also over my father's name: 'Rickie Barnes 1944 Allahabad'. Where did that Rickie spring from, and go to? The following year, my father came back to England, and back to being Pip. It's true he had a certain boyishness to him, but the name suited him decreasingly as he turned sixty, seventy, eighty . . .

He brought home various artefacts from India: the brass tray, the inlaid cigarette box, the ivory letter-knife with the elephant on top, and the pair of collapsible side tables which often collapsed. Then there was an item which in my childhood seemed as desirable as it was exotic: the circular leather pouffe. Who else in Acton had an Indian leather pouffe? I used to take running dives at it; later, when we moved from inner to outer suburbia and I was beyond childish gestures, I used to drop my full adolescent weight down onto it, with a kind of aggressive affection. This also elicited a vaguely farty noise as the air was squeezed out through the joins in the leather. Eventually, the seams began to give way under my maltreatment, and I made the sort of discovery psychoanalysts might relish. For what Rickie Barnes had brought back from Allahabad or Madras was not, of course, a full, fat pouffe, but rather a decorated leather casing which he—now Pip again—and his wife had to stuff.

They stuffed it with the letters of their courtship and early married years. I was an idealistic adolescent, who swerved easily into cynicism when confronted with life's realities; this was one such moment. How could they have taken their love letters (doubtless kept in ribboned bundles), torn them into tiny pieces, and then watched other people's fat arses hunker down on top? 'They': I meant, of course, my mother, since such practical recycling fitted my reading of her, rather than what I judged to be my father's more sentimental nature. How to imagine that decision, and that scene? Did they tear the letters up together, or did she do it while he was at work? Did they argue, did they agree, did one of them secretly resent it? And even supposing they agreed, how did they then go about it? Here's a haunting would-you-rather. Would you rather tear up your own expressions of love, or the ones you had received?

In company, I would now lower myself gently onto the pouffe; alone, I would drop heavily, so that its exhalation might jet out a scrap of blue airmail paper bearing one or other of my parents' youthful hands. If this were a novel, I would have discovered some family secret—*but no one will know the child isn't yours*, or *they will never find the knife now*, or *I always wanted J. to be a girl*—and my life would have been changed for ever. (Actually, my mother did want me to be a girl, and had the name Josephine waiting, so that would have been no secret.) Or—on the other hand—I might have discovered only the best words my parents' hearts could find for one another, their tenderest expressions of devotion and truth. And no mystery.

The collapsing pouffe was at some point chucked out. But instead of being put in the dustbin, it was dumped at the bottom of the garden, where it became heavy, rain-sodden and increasingly discoloured. I would kick it occasionally as I passed, my wellington ejecting a few more blue scraps, the ink now running, the likelihood of legible secrets being divulged even less. My kicks were those of a disheartened Romantic. So this is what it all comes to?

*   *   *

Thirty-five years later, I was faced with the final leavings of my parents' lives. My brother and I each wanted a few things; my nieces had their pick; then the house-clearer came in. He was a decent, knowledgeable fellow, who talked to the items as he handled them. I presume the habit must have started as a way of gently preparing the customer for disappointment, but it had turned into a kind of conversation between himself and the object in his hand. He also recognized that what would soon be haggled over coldly in his shop was now, here, for the last time, something which had once been chosen, then lived with, wiped, dusted, polished, repaired, loved. So he found praise where he could: 'This is nice—not valuable, but nice'; or 'Victorian moulded glass—this is getting rarer—it's not valuable, but it's getting rarer.' Scrupulously polite to these now ownerless things, he avoided criticism or dislike, preferring either regret or long-term hope. Of some 1920s Melba glasses (*horrible*, I thought): 'Ten years ago these were very fashionable; now no one wants them.' Of a basic Heal's green-and-white checkerboard plant holder: 'We need to wait another forty years for this.'

He took what was saleable and departed in a peel of fifty-pound notes. Then it was a matter of filling the back of the car and making several trips to the local recycling centre. Being my mother's son, I had bought a number of heavy green plastic sacks for the job. I carried the first of them to the rim of the big yellow skip and realized—now even more my mother's son—that they were far too useful to throw away. And so, instead of leaving the final remnants of my parents' lives confidentially bagged, I poured the house-clearer's rejects into the skip and kept the sacks. (Is this what my mother would have wanted?) One of the last items was a stupid metal cowbell that Dad had bought in Champéry, on that trip from which my brother reported a disappointing ham sandwich; it ding-donged clonkily down into the skip. I looked at the spread of stuff below me and, though there was nothing incriminating or even indiscreet, felt slightly cheap: as if I had buried my parents in a paper bag rather than a proper coffin.

*   *   *

This is not, by the way, 'my autobiography'. Nor am I 'in search of my parents'. I know that being someone's child involves both a sense of nauseated familiarity and large no-go areas of ignorance—at

41

least, if my family is anything to judge by. And though I still wouldn't mind a transcript of that pouffe's contents, I don't think my parents had any rare secrets. Part of what I'm doing—which may seem unnecessary—is trying to work out how dead they are. My father died in 1992, my mother in 1997. Genetically, they survive in two sons, two granddaughters and two great-granddaughters: an almost indecent demographic orderliness. Narratively, they survive in the memory, which some trust more than others. My brother first expressed his suspicion of this faculty when I asked him about the food we ate at home. After confirming porridge, bacon and suchlike, he went on:

At least, that's how things stand in my memory. But you no doubt remember them differently, and I don't think much of memory as a guide to the past. I first met my colleague and chum Jacques Brunschwig in 1977. It was at a conference in Chantilly. I missed my stop and got off the train at Créteil, thence taking a (very expensive) taxi and arriving late at the conference place, where Jacques greeted me. All that is wonderfully clear in my memory. In an interview, published in his Festschrift, Jacques talks a bit about some of his friends. He describes how he first met me, in 1977, at a conference in Chantilly: he met me at the station and recognized me as I stepped off the train. All that is wonderfully clear in his memory.

Well, you might think, that's professional philosophers for you: too busy theorizing in the abstract to notice what station they're at, let alone what's going on in the non-abstract world the rest of us inhabit. The French writer Jules Renard once speculated that 'Perhaps people with a very good memory cannot have general ideas.' If so, my brother might get the untrustworthy memory and the general ideas; while I get the reliable memory and the particular ideas.

I also have the family documentation in the shallow drawer to back me up. Here, for instance, are the results of my O level exams, taken when I was fifteen. Memory would certainly not have told me that my best marks were for mathematics, and my worst, embarrassingly, for English. 77 out of 100 for the language paper, and a humiliating 25 out of 50 for the English essay.

My second-worst marks were, unsurprisingly, for General Science. The biology section of that exam included such tasks as drawing the transverse section of a tomato, and describing the process of fertilization as enjoyed by stamens and pistils. That was about as far as we got at home, too: parental *pudeur* redoubled the silence of the syllabus. As a result, I grew up with little knowledge of how the body worked; my grasp of sexual matters had all the vivid imbalance of a sisterless autodidact at a boys-only school; and though the calibrated academic progress I made through school and university was thanks to my brain, I hadn't the slightest idea how this organ worked. I emerged into adulthood with the unthinking assumption that you no more needed to understand human biology in order to live than you did car mechanics in order to drive. There were always hospitals and garages for when things went wrong.

I remember being surprised to learn that the cells of my body would not last a lifetime, but would replace themselves at intervals (still, you could rebuild a car from spare parts, couldn't you?). I wasn't sure how often these makeovers occurred, but the awareness of cellular renewal mainly authorized jokes along the lines of 'She was no longer the woman he had fallen in love with'. I hardly thought it a matter for panic: after all, my parents and grandparents must have gone through one if not two such refreshings, and they seemed to have suffered no seismic fracture; indeed, they remained all too unswervingly themselves. I don't remember considering that the brain was part of the body, and therefore the same principles must apply up there as well. I might have been a little more inclined to panic had I discovered that the basic molecular structure of the brain, far from thoughtfully renewing itself as and when the need arises, is in fact incredibly unstable; that *fats and proteins are falling apart almost as soon as they are made*; that every molecule around a synapse is replaced by the hour, and some molecules by the minute. Indeed, that *the brain you had even last year will have been rebuilt many times over by now*.

Memory in childhood—at least, as I remember it—is rarely a problem. Not just because of the briefer time span between the event and its evocation, but because of the nature of memories then: they appear to the young brain as exact simulacra, rather than processed and coloured-in versions, of what has happened. Adulthood brings approximation, fluidity and doubt; and we keep the

44

doubt at bay by retelling that familiar story, with pauses and periods of a calculated effect, pretending that the solidity of narrative is a proof of truth. But the child or adolescent rarely doubts the veracity and precision of the bright, lucid chunks of the past it possesses and celebrates. So at that age it seems logical to think of our memories as stored in some left-luggage office, available for retrieval when we produce the necessary ticket; or (if that seems an antique comparison, suggesting steam trains and ladies-only compartments), as goods left in one of those self-storage units now a feature of arterial roads. We know to expect the seeming paradox of old age, when we shall start to recall lost segments of our early years, which then become more vivid than our middle ones. But this only seems to confirm that it's all really up there, in some orderly cerebral storage unit, whether we can access it or not.

My brother doesn't remember that more than half a century ago he came second in a wheelbarrow race with Dion Shirer, and is therefore unable to confirm which of them was the barrow and which the trundler. Nor does he remember the unacceptable ham sandwiches on the journey to Switzerland. Instead he remembers matters he failed to mention on his postcard: that it was the first time he saw an artichoke, and the first time he was 'sexually approached by another chap'. He also admits that over the years he has transposed the whole action to France: a confusion, perhaps, between the lesser-known Champéry in Switzerland (source of cowbells) and the more familiar Chambéry in France (source of the aperitif). We talk about our memories, but should perhaps talk more about our forgettings, even if that is a more difficult—or logically impossible—feat.

Perhaps I should warn you (especially if you are a philosopher, theologian or biologist) that some of this book will strike you as amateur, do-it-yourself stuff. But then we are all amateurs in and of our own lives. When we veer into other people's professionalisms, we hope that the graph of our approximate understanding roughly shadows the graph of their knowledge; but we cannot count on it. I should also warn you that there are going to be a lot of writers in this book. Most of them dead, and quite a few of them French. One is Jules Renard, who said: 'It is when faced with death that we turn most bookish.' There will also be some composers. One of them is Stravinsky, who said: 'Music is the best way we have of digesting time.' Such artists—such dead artists—are my daily companions, but also my ancestors. They are my true bloodline (I expect my brother feels the same about Plato and Aristotle). The descent may not be direct, or provable—wrong side of the blanket, and all that—but I claim it nonetheless.

My brother forgets the ham sandwich, remembers the artichoke and the sexual approach, and has suppressed Switzerland. Can you feel a theory coming on? Perhaps the thistly rebarbativeness of the artichoke attached itself to the memory of the sexual approach. In which case, the connection might have put him off artichokes (and Switzerland) thereafter. Except that my brother eats artichokes and worked in Geneva for several years. Aha—so perhaps he welcomed the approach? Idle, interesting questions, answered at the touch of an e-mail. 'As far as I recall, I neither welcomed it nor found it repugnant—merely bizarre. After that on the Metropolitan [line] I used to adopt the geometry homework strategy.'

He certainly sounds more sanguine and practical than I was, when, in the crush of the morning Tube, some brute in a suit jammed his thigh between my legs as if there really was nowhere else to put it. Or when Edwards (as he was not called), an older boy with a pustular complexion, attempted what was more an assault than a seduction in a Southern Region compartment on the way back from rugby. I found it unwelcome and, if not repugnant, certainly alarming, and have always been able to remember the exact words I used when rebuffing his attention. 'Don't get sexy, Edwards,' I said (though it was not Edwards). The words worked, but I remembered them not so much for their effectiveness as because even so they felt not quite right. What he had done—a quick finger-slash at my trousered balls—was not remotely what I considered sexy (which involved breasts, for a start), and I felt my answer had suggested something not really the case.

*   *   *

At Oxford, I read Montaigne for the first time. He is where our modern thinking about death begins; he is the link between the wise exemplars of the Ancient World and our attempt to find a modern, grown-up, non-religious acceptance of our inevitable end. *Philosopher, c'est apprendre à mourir*. To be a philosopher is to learn how to die.

47

Montaigne is quoting Cicero, who is in turn referring to Socrates. His learned and famous pages on death are stoical, bookish, anecdotal, epigrammatic and consoling (in purpose, anyway); they are also urgent. As my mother pointed out, people didn't live half so long in the old days. Forty was doing very well, given pestilence and war, with the doctor as likely to kill as cure. To die from 'a draining away of one's strength caused by extreme old age' was in Montaigne's day a 'rare, singular and extraordinary death'. Nowadays we assume it as our right.

Philippe Ariès observed that when death really began to be feared, it ceased to be talked about. Increased longevity has compounded this: since the matter seems less immediately pressing, it has become morbidly bad manners to raise it. The way we strenuously put off thinking about death reminds me of a long-running advertisement for Pearl Insurance which my brother and I liked to quote to one another. Pensions, like false teeth and chiropodists, were something so far distant as to be largely comical. This was somehow confirmed by the naive line drawings of a man with an increasingly anxious face. At age twenty-five, the face is cheerily complacent: 'They tell me the job is not pensionable.' By thirty-five, a little doubt has begun to set in: 'Unfortunately, my work does not bear a pension.' And so on—with the word 'pension' set each time amid an admonitory oblong of grey—until age sixty-five: 'Without a pension I really don't know what I shall do.' Yes, Montaigne would say, you certainly should have started thinking about death a little earlier.

In his day, the question was constantly in front

of you—unless you took the remedy of the common people who, according to Montaigne, pretended that it did not exist. But philosophers, and the mentally curious, looked to history, and to the Ancients, in search of how best to die. Nowadays, our ambitions have grown more puny. 'Courage,' Larkin wrote in 'Aubade', his great death-poem, 'means not scaring others.' Not back then it didn't. It meant a great deal more: showing others how to die honourably, wisely and with constancy.

One of Montaigne's key instances is the story of Pomponius Atticus, a correspondent of Cicero's. When Atticus fell ill, and medical attempts to prolong his existence merely prolonged his pain, he decided that the best solution was to starve himself to death. No need to petition a court in those days, citing the terminal deterioration in your 'quality of life': Atticus, being a Free Ancient, merely informed his friends and family of his intention, then refused food and waited for the end. In this, he was much confounded. Miraculously, abstinence turned out to be the best cure for his (unnamed) condition; and soon, the sick man was undeniably on the mend. There was much rejoicing and feasting; perhaps the doctors even withdrew their bills. But Atticus interrupted the merriment. Since we all must die one day, he announced, and since I have already made such fine strides in that direction, I have no desire to turn around now, only to start again another time. And so, to the admiring dismay of those around him, Atticus continued to refuse food and went to his exemplary death.

Montaigne believed that, since we cannot defeat

49

death, the best form of counter-attack is to have it constantly in mind: to think of death whenever your horse stumbles or a tile falls from a roof. You should have the taste of death in your mouth and its name on your tongue. To anticipate death in this way is to release yourself from its servitude: further, if you teach someone how to die, then you teach them how to live. Such constant death-awareness does not make Montaigne melancholy; rather, it renders him prone to fanciful dreaming, to reverie. He hopes that death, his companion, his familiar, will make its final house-call when he is in the middle of doing something ordinary—like planting his cabbages.

Montaigne tells the instructive story of a Roman Caesar approached by an ancient and decrepit soldier. The man had once served under him, and is now seeking permission to rid himself of his burdensome life. Caesar looks the fellow up and down, then asks, with the rough wit generalship seems to inspire, 'What makes you think the thing you have at the moment is life?' For Montaigne, the death of youth, which often takes place unnoticed, is the harder death; what we habitually refer to as 'death' is no more than the death of old age (forty or so in his time, seventy and more in ours). The leap from the attenuated survival of senescence into non-existence is much easier than the sly transition from heedless youth to crabbed and regretful age.

But Montaigne is a compendious writer, and if this argument fails to convince, he has many others. For instance: if you have lived well, used life to the full, then you will be happy to let it go; whereas if you have misused life and found it miserable, then you will not regret its passing. (A proposition which seems to me entirely reversible: those in the first category might want their happy lives to continue indefinitely, those in the second might hope for a change of luck.) Or: if you've truly lived for a single day, in the fullest sense, then you've seen everything. (No!) Well then, if you've lived like that for a whole year, you've seen everything. (Still no.) Anyway, you should make room on earth for others, just as others have made room for you. (Yes, but I didn't ask them to.) And why complain of being taken, when all are taken? Think of how many others will die on the same day as you. (True, and some of them will be as pissed off as I am about it.) Further, and finally, what exactly are you asking for when you complain against death? Do you want an immortality spent on this earth, given the terms and conditions currently applicable? (I see the argument, but how about a bit of immortality? Half? OK, I'll settle for a quarter.)

*   *   *

My brother points out that the first joke about cellular renewal was made in the 5th century BC, and involved 'a chap refusing to repay a debt on the grounds that he was no longer the chap who had been lent the money'. He further points out that I have misinterpreted Montaigne's tag line *philosopher, c'est apprendre à mourir*. What Cicero meant was not that thinking regularly about death makes you fear it less, but rather that the philosopher, when philosophizing, is practising for death—in the sense that he is spending time with

51

his mind and ignoring the body which death will obliterate. For Platonists, after death you became a pure soul, liberated from corporeal impediment, and thus better able to think freely and clearly. So while alive, the philosopher had to prepare for this post-mortal state, by techniques such as fasting and self-flagellation. Platonists believed that, after death, things started looking up. Epicureans, on the other hand, believed that, after death, there was nothing. Cicero, apparently (I use 'apparently' in the sense of 'my brother also told me'), combined the two traditions into a cheery Antique either/or: 'After death, either we feel better or we feel nothing.'

I ask what is supposed to happen to the very large population of non-philosophers in the Platonic afterworld. Apparently, all ensouled creatures, including animals and birds—and perhaps even plants—are judged on their behaviour in the life they've just finished. Those who don't make the grade return to earth for another corporeal round, perhaps going up or down a species (becoming, say, a fox or a goose) or just up or down within a species (being promoted, for instance from female to male). Philosophers, my brother explains, don't automatically win disembodiment: you have to be a good chap as well for that. But if they do win, they then have a head start on the multitudes of non-philosophers—not to mention water lilies and dandelions. They also, of course, have a better go of things in this life, by their advance closeness to that ultimate ideal condition. 'Yes,' he continues. 'There are some questions you might want to raise (e.g. what's the point of getting a head start in a race that goes on for ever?). But it's not really worth the time thinking about the matter—it is (in technical philosophical jargon) a complete load of bollocks.'

I ask him to elaborate on his dismissal of the line 'I don't believe in God, but I miss Him' as 'soppy'. He admits that he isn't really sure how to take my statement: 'I suppose as a way of saying "I don't believe there are any gods, but I wish there were (or perhaps: but I wish I did)". I can see how someone might say something like that (try putting "dodos" or "yetis" for "gods"), tho' for my part I'm quite content with the way things are.' You can tell he teaches philosophy, can't you? I ask him about a specific matter, he breaks down the proposition logically, and supplies alternative nouns to display its absurdity, or weakness, or soppiness. But his answer seems just as strange to me as my question did to him. I hadn't asked him what he thought about someone missing dodos or yetis (or even gods in the lower case plural), but God.

I check whether he has ever had any religious feelings or yearnings. NO and NO is his reply— 'Unless you count being moved by the *Messiah*, or Donne's sacred sonnets.' I wonder if this certainty has been passed on to his two daughters, now in their thirties. Any religious sentiments/faith/ supernatural longings, I ask. 'No, never, not at all,' replies the younger. 'Unless you count not walking on the lines on the pavement as a supernatural longing.' We agree that we don't. Her sister admits to 'a brief yearning to be religious when I was about eleven. But this was because my friends were, because I wanted to pray as a way of getting things, and because the Girl Guides pressured you to be Christian. This went away fairly quickly when

53

my prayers went unanswered. I suppose I am agnostic or even atheist.'

I am glad she has maintained the family tradition of giving up religion on trivial grounds. My brother because he suspected George VI had not gone to heaven; me in order not to be distracted from masturbation; my niece because the stuff she prayed for wasn't immediately delivered. But I suspect such breezy illogic is quite normal. Here, for instance, is the biologist Lewis Wolpert: 'I was quite a religious child, saying my prayers each night and asking God for help on various occasions. It did not seem to help and I gave it all up around sixteen and have been an atheist ever since.' No subsequent reflection from any of us that perhaps God's main business, were He to exist, might not be as an adolescent helpline, goods-provider or masturbation-scourge. No, out with Him once and for all.

A common response in surveys of religious attitudes is to say something like, 'I don't go to church, but I have my own personal idea of God.' This kind of statement makes me in turn react like a philosopher. Soppy, I cry. You may have your own personal idea of God, but does God have His own personal idea of you? Because that's what matters. Whether He's an old man with a white beard sitting in the sky, or a life force, or a disinterested prime mover, or a clockmaker, or a woman, or a nebulous moral force, or Nothing At All, what counts is what He, She, It or Nothing thinks of you rather than you of them. The notion of redefining the deity into something that works for you is grotesque. It also doesn't matter whether God is just or benevolent or even observant—of which there seems startlingly little proof—only that He exists.

The only old man with a white beard that I knew when growing up was my great-grandfather, my mother's father's father: Alfred Scoltock, a Yorkshireman and (inevitably) schoolmaster. There is a photo of my brother and me standing on either side of him in some now unidentifiable back garden. My brother is perhaps seven or eight, I am four or five, and Great-Grandpa is as old as the hills. His beard is not long and flowing as in cartoons of God, but short cut and bristly. (I don't know if the scrape of it against my infant cheek actually happened, or is merely the memory of an apprehension.) My brother and I are smart and smiling—I more smiling than him—in short-sleeved shirts beautifully ironed by our mother; my shorts still have decent creases in them, though his are rather shockingly rumpled. Great-Grandpa is unsmiling, and to my eye looks faintly pained, as if aware that he is being recorded for a posterity he is on the very verge of. A friend, looking at this photo, dubbed him my 'Chinese ancestor', and there is something slightly Confucian about him.

Quite how wise he was, I have no idea. According to my mother, who favoured the males in her family, he was a highly intelligent autodidact. Two examples of this were ritually given: that he had taught himself chess, and was able to play to a high standard; and that when my mother, reading modern languages at Birmingham University, went on an exchange visit to Nancy, Great-Grandpa had taught himself French from a book so that he could converse with her pen pal when the two young women returned.

My brother met him several times, but his memories are less flattering, and perhaps explain why his smile in the photograph is more restrained than mine. The family's Confucian 'stank something horrible', and was accompanied by 'his daughter (Auntie Edie) who was unmarried, slightly soft in the head, and covered in eczema'. My brother recalls no chess playing or French speaking. In his memory, there is only an ability to do the *Daily Mail* crossword without filling in a single square. 'He would doze after lunch, occasionally muttering *aardvark* or *zebu*.'

*　　　*　　　*

'I don't know if God exists, but it would be better for His reputation if He didn't.' 'God does not believe in our God.' 'Yes, God exists, but He knows no more about it than we do.' The varying suppositions of Jules Renard, one of my dead, French, non-blood relatives. Born in 1864, he grew up in the Nièvre, a rustic and little-visited part of northern Burgundy. His father François was a builder who rose to be mayor of their village, Chitry-les-Mines. He was taciturn, anti-clerical and rigidly truthful. His mother, Anne-Rosa, was garrulous, bigoted and mendacious. The death of their first-born child so embittered François that he barely concerned himself with the next three: Amélie, Maurice and Jules. After the birth of the youngest, François stopped speaking to Anne-Rosa, and didn't address her again for the remaining thirty years of his life. In this silent war Jules—whose sympathies lay with his father—was often used as go-between and porte parole: an unenviable role for a child, if an instructive one for a future writer.

Much of this upbringing finds its way into Renard's best-known work, *Poil de Carotte*. In Chitry, many disliked this *roman-à-clef*: Jules, the red-headed village boy, had gone to Paris, become sophisticated, and written a book about a red-headed village boy which denounced his own mother. More importantly, Renard was denouncing, and helping put an end to, the whole sentimental, Hugolian image of childhood. Routine injustice and instinctive cruelty are the norms here; moments of pastoral sweetness the exception. Renard never indulges his child alter ego with retrospective self-pity, that emotion (normally arising in adolescence, though it may last for ever) which renders many reworkings of childhood fake. For Renard, a child was 'a small, necessary animal, less human than a cat'. This remark comes from his masterpiece, the *Journal* he kept from 1887 until his death in 1910.

Despite metropolitan fame, he was rooted in the Nièvre. In Chitry, and the neighbouring village of Chaumot, where he lived as an adult, Renard knew peasants still living as they had done for centuries: 'The peasant is the only species of human being who doesn't like the country and never looks at it.' There he studied birds, animals, insects, trees, and witnessed the arrival of the train and motor car which between them would change everything. In 1904, he was in turn elected Mayor of Chitry. He enjoyed his civic functions—handing out school prizes, performing marriages. 'My speech made the women cry. The bride gave me her cheeks to kiss, and even her mouth; it cost me 20 francs.' His

57

politics were socialist, Dreyfusard, anti-clerical. He wrote: 'As a mayor, I am responsible for the upkeep of rural roads. As a poet, I would prefer to see them neglected.'

In Paris, he knew Rodin and Sarah Bernhardt, Edmond Rostand and Gide. Both Bonnard and Toulouse-Lautrec illustrated his *Histoires naturelles*, while Ravel set some of them to music. Once, he stood as second in a duel in which the opposing second was Gauguin. Yet he could be a sombre presence in such company, unforgiving and bearish. He once said to Daudet, who had been kind to him, 'I don't know whether I love you or loathe you, *mon cher maître.*' '*Odi et amo*,' replied Daudet, unfazed. Parisian society sometimes found him unfathomable. One sophisticate described him as a 'rustic cryptogram'—like one of those secret marks tramps used to chalk on outbuildings, decipherable only by other tramps.

Renard came to writing prose at a time when it seemed the novel might be finished, when the great descriptive and analytical project of Flaubert, Maupassant, Goncourt and Zola had used the world up and left nothing for fiction to do. The only way forward, Renard concluded, was through compression, annotation, pointillism. Sartre, in a grand and rather grudging tribute to the *Journal*, acclaimed Renard's dilemma more than his solution to it: 'He is at the origin of many more modern attempts to seize the essence of the single thing'; and 'If he is where modern literature begins, it is because he had the vague sense of a domain which he forbade himself to enter.' Gide, whose own *Journal* overlaps for many years with Renard's, complained (perhaps rivalrously) that the latter's was 'not a river but a distillery'; though he subsequently admitted reading it 'with rapture'.

Do you want a distillery or a river? Life rendered as a few drops of the hard stuff, or as a litre of Normandy cider? These are choices for the reader. The writer has little control over personal temperament, none over the historical moment, and is only partly in charge of his or her own aesthetic. Distillation was both Renard's response to the literature that had gone before, and an expression of his unexpansive nature. In 1898, he noted: 'It may be said of almost all works of literature that they are too long.' This remark occurs on page 400 of the thousand-page *Journal*, a work which would have been half as long again had Renard's widow not burnt those pages she did not wish outsiders to see.

In the *Journal*, he attends to the natural world with intense precision, describing it with an unsentimental admiration. He attends to the human world with the same precision, describing it with scepticism and irony. But he also understood, as many do not, the nature and function of irony. On 26 December 1899, just as the century which would most need it was about to begin, he wrote: 'Irony does not dry up the grass. It just burns off the weeds.'

*   *   *

Renard's friend Tristan Bernard, playwright and wit, once flagged down a hearse as if it were a taxi. When the vehicle stopped, he airily enquired, 'Are you free?' Renard had been within hailing distance of death several times before his own came at the age of forty-six. Here are the occasions when he attended to it most carefully:

1) In May 1897, his brother Maurice removes their father's revolver from his bedside table on the pretext of cleaning it. A family row ensues. François Renard is unimpressed both by his son's action and his excuse: 'He's lying. He's afraid I'll kill myself. But if I wanted to, I wouldn't use an instrument like that. It'd probably just leave me crippled.' Jules's wife is shocked: 'Stop talking like that,' she protests. But the Mayor of Chitry is unrelenting: 'No, I wouldn't mess around. I'd take my shotgun.' Jules suggests sardonically, 'You'd do far better to take an enema.'

François Renard, however, knows or believes himself to be incurably ill. Four weeks later, he locks the bedroom door, takes his shotgun, and uses a walking stick to press the trigger. He succeeds in firing both barrels, just to make sure. Jules is summoned; he breaks down the door; there is smoke and the smell of powder. At first he thinks his father must be joking; then he is obliged to believe in the sprawled figure, the unseeing eyes, and the 'dark place above the waist, like a small extinguished fire'. He takes his father's hands; they are still warm, still pliant.

François Renard, both an anti-clerical and a suicide, is the first person to be buried in the cemetery at Chitry without benefit of clergy. Jules judges that his father has died heroically, showing Roman virtues. He notes: 'On the whole, this death has added to my sense of pride.' Six weeks after the funeral, he concludes: 'The death of my father makes me feel as if I had written a beautiful book.'

2) In January 1900, Maurice Renard, a seemingly healthy thirty-seven-year-old clerk of works in the Highways Department, collapses in his Paris office. He has always complained about the steam-driven heating system in the building. One of its main pipes runs just behind his desk, and the temperature often rises to 20 degrees. 'They'll kill me with their central heating,' the country boy would predict; but angina proved the greater threat. Maurice is about to leave his office at the end of the day when he faints at his desk. He is carried from his chair to a couch, has trouble breathing, doesn't utter a word, and is dead in a couple of minutes.

Jules, in Paris at the time, is again summoned. He sees his brother lying athwart the couch with one knee flexed; the exhausted pose reminds him of their father in death. The writer cannot help noticing the improvised cushion on which his dead brother's head is resting: a Paris telephone directory. Jules sits down and weeps. His wife embraces him, and he senses in her the fear that it will be his turn next. His eye is caught by an advertisement printed in black along the edge of the telephone directory; from a distance, he tries to read it.

Jules and his wife watch over the body that night. Every so often, Jules lifts the handkerchief covering his brother's face and looks at the half-open mouth, expecting it to start breathing again. As the hours pass, the nose seems to become fleshier, while the ears turn as hard as seashells. Maurice becomes quite stiff and cold. 'His life has now passed into the furniture, and each time it gives the slightest creak, we shiver.'

Three days later, Maurice is buried at Chitry. The priest waits to be called but is denied. Jules walks behind the hearse, watches the wreaths jiggling, thinks the horse looks as if it has been given a special coat of dirty black paint that morning. When they lower the coffin into the deep family pit, he notices a fat worm seeming to rejoice on the grave's edge. 'If a worm could strut, this one would be strutting.'

Jules concludes: 'All I feel is a kind of anger at death and its imbecile tricks.'

3) In August 1909, a small boy perched on a waggon in the middle of Chitry sees a woman sitting on the stonework of the village well, and then, suddenly, falling backwards. It is Renard's mother, who over the last years has been losing her mind. Jules is summoned for a third time. He comes running, throws down his hat and cane and peers into the well: he sees some floating skirts and 'the soft eddy familiar to those who have drowned an animal'. He tries to get down using the bucket; when he steps in, he notices that his boots seem ridiculously long and are bending up at the ends like fish in a pail. Then someone arrives with a ladder; Jules gets out of the bucket, descends the rungs, succeeds only in getting his feet wet. Two efficient villagers go down and retrieve the body; there is not a scratch on it.

Renard cannot determine whether it was an accident or another suicide; he calls his mother's death 'impenetrable'. He argues: 'Perhaps the fact that God is incomprehensible is the strongest argument for His existence.' He concludes: 'Death is not an artist.'

While living among the priests in Brittany, I discovered the work of the great Belgian singer-songwriter Jacques Brel. In his early years, he was known as 'Abbé Brel' for his preachiness; and in 1958 recorded a track called *'Dites, si c'était vrai'* ('And what if it were true?'). It is less a song than a prayer-poem tremulously intoned against the background growl of an organ. Brel asks us to imagine what things would be like 'if it were true'. If Christ really had been born in that stable in Bethlehem . . . If what the Evangelists wrote were true . . . If that *coup de théâtre* at the wedding in Cana had really happened . . . or that other coup, the stuff with Lazarus . . . If all of it were true, Brel concludes, then we would say Yes, because it is all so beautiful when one believes that it is true.

I now find this one of the worst tracks Brel ever recorded; and the mature singer was to become as mockingly irreligious as his younger self was God-bothering. But this early song, wincingly sincere, makes the point. If it were true, it would be beautiful; and because it was beautiful, it would be the more true; and the more true, the more beautiful; and so on. YES BUT IT'S NOT TRUE YOU IDIOT, I hear my brother interject. Such rambling is even worse that those hypothetical desires you attribute to our dead mother.

No doubt; but the Christian religion didn't last so long merely because everyone else believed it, because it was imposed by ruler and priesthood, because it was a means of social control, because it was the only story in town, and because if you didn't believe it—or disbelieved it too vociferously—you might have a quickly truncated life. It lasted also because it was a beautiful lie, because the characters, the plot, the various *coups de théâtre*, the overarching struggle between Good and Evil, made up a great novel. The story of Jesus—high-minded mission, facing-down of the oppressor, persecution, betrayal, execution, resurrection—is the perfect example of that formula Hollywood famously and furiously seeks: a tragedy with a happy ending. Reading the Bible as 'literature' as that puckish old schoolmaster was trying to point out to us, is not a patch on reading the Bible as truth, the truth endorsed by beauty.

I went to a concert in London with my friend J. The sacred choral work we heard has gone from my memory, but not his question afterwards: 'How many times in the course of that did you think of our Risen Lord?' 'None,' I replied. I wondered if J. had himself been thinking of our Risen Lord; after all, he is the son of a clergyman, and has the habit—unique among those I know—of saying 'God bless' as a farewell. Might this be indicative of some residual belief? Or is it just a linguistic remnant, like saying *'Grüss Gott'* in parts of Germany?

Missing God is focused for me by missing the underlying sense of purpose and belief when confronted with religious art. It is one of the haunting hypotheticals for the non-believer: what would it be like 'if it were true' . . . Imagine hearing the Mozart *Requiem* in a great cathedral—or, for that matter, Poulenc's fishermen's mass in a clifftop chapel damp from salt spray—and taking the text as gospel; imagine reading Giotto's holy strip-cartoon in the chapel at Padua as non-fiction;

64

imagine looking on a Donatello as the actual face of the suffering Christ or the weeping Magdalene. It would—to put it mildly—add a bit of extra oomph, wouldn't it?

This may seem an irrelevant and vulgar wish—for more gas in the tank, more alcohol in the wine; for a better (or somehow bigger) aesthetic experience. But it's more than that. Edith Wharton understood the feeling—and the disadvantage—of admiring churches and cathedrals when you no longer believe in what those buildings represent; and she described the process of trying to imagine yourself back through the centuries in order to understand it and feel it. Yet even the best imaginer-back cannot end up with exactly what a Christian would have felt gazing up at the newly installed stained glass of Bourges Cathedral, or listening to a Bach cantata in St Thomas's, Leipzig, or rereading a long-told Biblical story in a Rembrandt etching. That Christian would, presumably, have been concerned more with truth than aesthetics; or at least, their estimation of an artist's greatness would have been guided by the effectiveness and originality (or, for that matter, familiarity) with which the tenets of religion were expounded.

Does it matter if we take the religion out of religious art, if we aestheticize it into mere colours, structures, sounds, their essential meaning as distant as a childhood memory? Or is that a pointless question, as we don't have the choice? Pretending to beliefs we don't have during Mozart's *Requiem* is like pretending to find Shakespeare's horn jokes funny (though some theatre goers still relentlessly laugh). A few years ago I was at the Birmingham City Art Gallery. In one glassed-in corner, there is a small, intense painting by Petrus Christus of Christ displaying his wounds: with outstretched forefinger and thumb he indicates where the spear went in—even invites us to measure the gash. His crown of thorns has sprouted into a gilt, spun-sugar halo of glory. Two saints, one with a lily and the other with a sword, attend him, drawing back the green velvet drapes of a strangely domestic proscenium. As I was stepping away from my inspection, I became aware of a track-suited father and small son travelling towards me at a lively art-hating clip. The father, equipped with better trainers and more stamina, held a yard or two's advantage as they turned this corner. The boy glanced into the exhibition case and asked, in a strong Brummy accent, 'Why's that man holding his chest, Dad?' The father, without breaking stride, managed a quick look back and an instant answer: 'Dunno.'

However much pleasure and truth we draw from the non-religious art created especially for us, however fully it engages our aesthetic selves, it would be a pity if our reaction to what has preceded it was finally diminished to a Dunno. But of course this is happening. Wall captions in galleries increasingly explain such events as the Annunciation, or the Assumption of the Virgin— though rarely the identity of all those squadrons of symbol-bearing saints. I would have needed my own iconographical dictionary if someone had asked me to name the two attendants in the Petrus Christus.

What will it be like when Christianity joins the list of dead religions, and is taught in universities as part of the folklore syllabus; when blasphemy becomes not legal or illegal but simply impossible? It will be a bit like this. Recently, I was in Athens, and found myself looking for the first time at Cycladic marble figurines. These were made around 3000–2000 BC, are predominantly female, and come in two main types: semi-abstract violin shapes, and more naturalistic representations of a stylistically elongated body. The latter typically propose: a long nose on a shield-like head devoid of other features; a stretched neck; arms folded across the stomach, left arm invariably above the right; a sketched pubic triangle; a chiselled division between the legs; feet in a tiptoe position.

They are images of singular purity, gravity and beauty, which come at you like a quiet, sustained note heard across a hushed concert hall. From the moment you see one of these forms, most no higher than a handspan, rising before you, you seem to understand them aesthetically; and they appear to collude in this, urging you to bypass any historico-archaeological wall information. This is partly because they evoke so clearly their modernist descendants: Picasso, Modigliani, Brancusi. Both evoke, and surpass: it is good to see those admirable tyrants of modernism being made to look less original by a community of unknown Cycladic carvers; good also to be reminded that the history of art is circular as well as linear. When this brief moment of vaguely pugilistic self-congratulation has passed, you settle into, and open yourself up to, the tranquillity and symbolic withholdingness of the figures. Now, different comparisons come to mind: Piero or Vermeer. You are in the presence of a stately simplicity, and a transcendent calm which seems to contain all the depths of the Aegean, and offer a rebuke to our frantic modern world. A world which has increasingly admired these items, and so desired more of them than can possibly exist. Forgery, like hypocrisy, is the homage vice pays to virtue, and in this case much homage has been paid.

But what exactly have you, or rather I—yes, I'd better take the blame for this one—been looking at? And were my reactions, however pantingly authentic, relevant to the objects in front of me? (Or do aesthetic objects, over time, become, or dwindle into, our reactions to them?) That all-over pale creaminess which lends such an air of serenity would not originally have existed: the heads, at least, would have been vibrantly painted. The minimalist—and proto-modernist—incising is at least in part a practical consequence of the marble being extremely hard to carve. The vertical presence—the way these small images rise to meet us on tiptoe, and thereby seem to calmly dominate us—is a curatorial invention, since most were intended to be lain down horizontally. As for the rebuking tranquillity they emanate, it is rather the stillness and rigidity of the tomb. We may look at Cycladic figurines aesthetically—we cannot do otherwise—but their function was as grave goods. We value them by displaying them in museums under carefully arranged light; their creators would have valued them by burying them in the ground, invisible to all except the spirits of the dead. And what exactly—or even roughly—did they believe, the people who produced such objects? Dunno.

*　　　*　　　*

The art, of course, is only a beginning, only a metaphor, as it always is. Larkin, visiting an empty church, wonders what will happen when 'churches fall completely out of use'. Shall we 'keep / A few cathedrals chronically on show' (that 'chronically' always produces a burn of envy in this writer), or 'Shall we avoid them as unlucky places'? Larkin concludes that we shall still—always—be drawn towards such abandoned sites, because 'someone will forever be surprising / A hunger in himself to be more serious.'

Is this what underlies the sense of Missing? God is dead, and without Him human beings can at last get up off their knees and assume their full height; and yet this height turns out to be quite dwarfish. Emile Littré, lexicographer, atheist, materialist (and translator of Hippocrates), concluded that 'Man is a most unstable compound, and the Earth a decidedly inferior planet.' Religion used to offer consolation for the travails of life, and reward at the end of it for the faithful. But above and beyond these treats, it gave human life a sense of context, and therefore seriousness. Did it make people behave better? Sometimes; sometimes not; believers and unbelievers have been equally ingenious and vile in their criminality. But was it true? No. Then why miss it?

Because it was a supreme fiction, and it is normal to feel bereft on closing a great novel. In the Middle Ages, they used to put animals on trial—locusts that destroyed crops, death-watch beetles that munched church beams, pigs that dined off drunkards lying in ditches. Sometimes the animal would be brought before the court, sometimes (as with insects) necessarily tried *in absentia*. There would be a full judicial hearing, with prosecution, defence, and a robed judge, who could hand down a range of punishments—probation, banishment, even excommunication. Sometimes there was even judicial execution: a pig might be hanged by the neck until it was dead by a gloved and hooded officer of the court.

It all seems—to us, now—extravagantly daft, an expression of the inaccessible medieval mind. And yet it was perfectly rational, and perfectly civilized. The world was made by God, and therefore all that happened within it was either an expression of divine purpose, or a consequence of God granting free will to His creation. In some cases, God might employ the animal kingdom to rebuke His human creation: for instance, by sending a punitive plague of locusts, which the court was therefore legally bound to find innocent. But what if a stupefied drunkard fell into a ditch, had half his face eaten off by a pig, and the deed could not be interpreted as divinely intended? Another explanation must be found. Perhaps the pig had been possessed by a devil, which the court might instruct to depart. Or perhaps the pig, while lacking free will itself, might still be held causally responsible for what had happened.

To us, this might appear further proof of man's ingenious beastliness. Yet there is another way of looking at it: as raising the status of the animals. They were part of God's creation and God's purpose, not merely put on earth for Man's pleasure and use. The medieval authorities brought animals to court and seriously weighed their delinquencies; we put animals in

70

concentration camps, stuff them with hormones, and cut them up so that they remind us as little as possible of something that once clucked or bleated or lowed. Which world is the more serious? Which the more morally advanced?

Bumper stickers and fridge magnets remind us that Life is Not a Rehearsal. We encourage one another towards the secular modern heaven of self-fulfilment: the development of the personality, the relationships which help define us, the status-giving job, the material goods, the ownership of property, the foreign holidays, the acquisition of savings, the accumulation of sexual exploits, the visits to the gym, the consumption of culture. It all adds up to happiness, doesn't it—doesn't it? This is our chosen myth, and almost as much of a delusion as the myth that insisted on fulfilment and rapture when the last trump sounded and the graves were flung open, when the healed and perfected souls joined in the community of saints and angels. But if life *is* viewed as a rehearsal, or a preparation, or an anteroom, or whichever metaphor we choose, but at any rate as something contingent, something dependent on a greater reality elsewhere, then it becomes at the same time less valuable and more serious. Those parts of the world where religion has drained away and there is a general acknowledgement that this short stretch of time is all we have, are not, on the whole, more serious places than those where heads are still jerked by the cathedral's bell or the minaret's muezzin. On the whole, they yield to a frenetic materialism; although the ingenious human animal is well capable of constructing civilizations where religion coexists with frenetic materialism (where the

71

former might even be an emetic consequence of the latter): witness America.

So what; you might reply. All that matters is what is true. Would you prefer to bow down before codswallop and pervert your life at the whim of a priesthood, all in the name of a supposed seriousness? Or would you prefer to grow to your full dwarfishness, and indulge all your trivial wants and desires, in the name of truth and freedom? Or is this a false opposition?

My friend J. remembers the work we heard at that concert some months ago: a Haydn Mass. When I allude to our conversation afterwards, he smiles gnomically. So I ask in my turn, 'How many times did you think of our Risen Lord during that piece?' 'I think of him constantly,' J. replies. Since I can't tell whether he is being entirely serious or entirely frivolous, I put a question I can't remember putting to any of my adult friends before. 'Are you—to what extent are you— religious?' Best to get this clear after thirty years of knowing him. A long, low chuckle: 'I am irreligious.' Then he corrects himself: 'No, I am *very* irreligious.'

*　　　*　　　*

Montaigne observed that 'religion's surest foundation is the contempt for life'. To have a low opinion of this rented world was logical, indeed essential, for a Christian: an over-attachment to the earth—let alone a desire for some form of terrestrial immortality—would have been an impertinence to God. Montaigne's nearest British equivalent, Sir Thomas Browne, wrote: 'For a pagan there might be some motives to be in love with life, but, for a Christian to be amazed at [i.e. terrified of] death, I cannot see how he can escape this dilemma—that he is too sensible of this life, or hopeless of the life to come.' Therefore Browne honours anyone who despises death: 'Nor can I highly love any that is afraid of it: this makes me naturally love a soldier, and honour those tattered regiments that will die at the command of a sergeant.'

Browne also notes that 'It is a symptom of melancholy to be afraid of death, yet sometimes to desire it.' Larkin again, a melancholic defining perfectly the fear of death: 'Not to be here, / Not to be anywhere, / And soon; nothing more terrible, nothing more true.' And elsewhere, as if in confirmation of Browne: 'Beneath it all, desire of oblivion runs.' This line perplexed me when I first read it. I am certainly melancholic myself, and sometimes find life an overrated way of passing the time; but have never wanted not to be myself any more, never desired oblivion. I am not so convinced of life's nullity that the promise of a new novel or a new friend (or an old novel or an old friend), or a football match on television (or even the repeat of an old match) will not excite my interest all over again. I am Browne's unsatisfactory Christian—'too sensible of this life, or hopeless of the life to come'—except that I am not a Christian.

*   *   *

Perhaps the important divide is less between the religious and the irreligious as between those who

73

fear death and those who don't. We fall thereby into four categories, and it's clear which two regard themselves as superior: those who do not fear death because they have faith, and those who do not fear death despite having no faith. These groups take the moral high ground. In third place come those who, despite having faith, cannot rid themselves of the old, visceral, rational fear. And then, out of the medals, below the salt, up shit creek, come those of us who fear death and have no faith.

I'm sure my father feared death, and fairly certain my mother didn't: she feared incapacity and dependence more. And if my father was a death-fearing agnostic and my mother a fearless atheist, this difference has been replicated in their two sons. My brother and I are now both over sixty, and I have only just asked him—a few pages ago— what he thinks of death. When he replied, 'I am quite content with the way things are,' did he mean that he is quite content with his own personal extinction? And has his immersion in philosophy reconciled him to the brevity of life, and its inevitable ending for him within, say, the next thirty years?

'Thirty years is pretty generous,' he replies (well, I had inflated it, for my comfort as much as his). 'I expect to be dead within the next fifteen. Am I reconciled to that fact? Am I reconciled to the fact that the splendid hornbeam which I can see through my window will fall and decay within the next fifty years? I'm not sure reconciliation is the *mot juste*: I know it's going to happen, and there's nothing I can do about it. I don't exactly welcome it, but it doesn't worry me either—and I can't

74

really imagine anything which would be more welcome (certainly not an eternal quasi-life in the company of saints—what could be less enticing?).'

How quickly he and I—children of the same flesh, products of the same school and university—part company. And though the manner in which my brother discusses mortality is (in both senses) philosophical, though he distances his own final dissolution by a comparison with a hornbeam, I don't think it is his life in and with philosophy that has wrought the difference. I suspect that he and I are as we are in such matters because we have been like this from the beginning. It doesn't feel like that, of course. You come into the world, look around, make certain deductions, free yourself from the old bullshit, learn, think, observe, conclude. You believe in your own powers and autonomy; you become your own achievement. So, over the decades, my fear of death has become an essential part of me, and I would attribute it to the exercise of the imagination; while my brother's detachment in death's face is an essential part of him, which he probably ascribes to the exercise of logical thought. Yet perhaps I am only this way because of our father, he that way because of our mother. Thanks for the gene, Dad.

'I can't really imagine anything that would be more welcome [than extinction,]' says my brother. Well, I can imagine all sorts of things more welcome than utter obliteration within fifteen years (his calculation) or thirty (my fraternal gift). How about living longer than that hornbeam, for a start? How about being given the option to die when you feel like it, when you've had enough: to go on for two hundred, three hundred years, and

75

then be allowed to utter your own euthanasiastic 'Oh, get on with it, then' at a time of your choosing? Why not imagine an eternal quasi-life spent talking to the great philosophers or the great novelists? Or some version of reincarnation—a mixture of Buddhism and *Groundhog Day*—in which you get to live your life again, conscious of how it went the first time, yet able to make adjustments from that rehearsal? The right to try again and do differently. Next time, I might resist my brother's assertion of philatelic primogeniture and collect something different from Rest of the World. I could become Jewish (or try, or bluff). I could leave home earlier, live abroad, have children, not write books, plant hornbeams, join a utopian community, sleep with all the wrong people (or at least, some different wrong people), become a drug addict, find God, do nothing. I could discover quite new sorts of disappointment.

My mother told me that Grandpa had once told her that the worst emotion in life was remorse. What, I asked, might he have been referring to? She said she had no idea, as her father had been a man of the utmost probity (no leaky pouffe there). And so the remark—an untypical one for my grandfather—hangs there unanswerably in time. I suffer from little remorse, though it may be on its way, and in the meantime am making do with its close chums: regret, guilt, memory of failure. But I do have a growing curiosity about the unled, the now unleadable lives, and perhaps remorse is currently hiding in their shadow.

*   *   *

76

Arthur Koestler, before committing suicide, left a note in which he expressed 'some timid hopes for a depersonalised afterlife'. Such a wish is unsurprising—Koestler had devoted many of his last years to parapsychology—but to me distinctly unalluring. Just as there seems little point in a religion which is merely a weekly social event (apart, of course, from the normal pleasures of a weekly social event), as opposed to one which tells you exactly how to live, which colours and stains everything, which is *serious*, so I would want my afterlife, if one's on offer, to be an improvement— preferably a substantial one—on its terrestrial predecessor. I can just about imagine slopping around half-unawares in some gooey molecular remix, but I can't see that this has any advantage over complete extinction. Why have hopes, even timid ones, for such a state? Ah, my boy, but it's not about what you'd prefer, it's about what turns out to be true. The key exchange on this subject happened between Isaac Bashevis Singer and Edmund Wilson. Singer told Wilson that he believed in some kind of survival after death. Wilson said that as far as he was concerned, he didn't want to survive, thank you very much. Singer replied, 'If survival has been arranged, you will have no choice in the matter.'

The fury of the resurrected atheist: that would be something worth seeing. And while we're on the subject, I think the company of saints might be distinctly interesting. Many of them led exciting lives—dodging assassins, confronting tyrants, preaching at medieval street corners, being tortured—and even the quieter ones could tell you about beekeeping, lavender-growing, Umbrian

77

ornithology, and so on. Dom Perignon was a monk, after all. You might have been hoping for a broader social mix, but if it 'has been arranged', then the saints would keep you going for longer than you might expect.

My brother does not fear extinction. 'I say that confidently, and not just because it would be irrational to have such a fear' (sorry—interruption—irrational? IRRATIONAL? It's the most rational thing in the world—how can reason not reasonably detest and fear the end of reason?). 'Three times in my life I've been convinced I was on the point of dying (the last time I came to in a reanimation ward); I did, on each occasion, have an emotional response (once a burning rage, at myself who had put myself into such a situation, once shame mixed with vexation at the thought that I was leaving my affairs in a mess) but never one of fear.' He has even had a dry run at the deathbed utterance. 'The last time I nearly died, my almost last words were, "Make sure that Ben gets my copy of Bekker's Aristotle".' He adds that his wife found this 'insufficiently affectionate'.

He admits that nowadays he thinks of death more than he used to, 'in part because old friends and colleagues are dying off'. He regards it calmly once a week; whereas I've put in the years and the slog, done the hard yards and the heavy lifting, without acquiring any mellowness or philosophy. I could try to scare up a few arguments in favour of death-awareness but I'm not sure they'd convince. I can't claim that confronting death (no, that sounds too active, too pretend-heroic—the passive mode is better: I can't claim that being confronted by death) has given me any greater

78

accommodation with it, let alone made me wiser, or more serious, or more . . . anything, really. I could try arguing that we cannot truly savour life without a regular awareness of extinction: it's the squeeze of lemon, the pinch of salt that intensifies the flavour. But do I really think that my death-denying (or religious) friends appreciate that bunch of flowers/work of art/glass of wine less than I do? No.

On the other hand, it's not just a visceral matter. Its manifestations—from skin-puncturing prod to mind-blanking terror, from the brute alarm bell in the unfamiliar hotel room to klaxons shrieking over the city—may be. But I repeat and insist that I suffer from rational (yes RATIONAL) fear. The earliest known Dance of Death, painted on a wall of the Cimetière des Innocents in Paris in 1425, had a text which began '*O créature roysonnable / Qui desires vie eternelle*' [O rational creature / Who wishes for eternal life]. Rational fear: my friend the novelist Brian Moore liked to quote the old Jesuit definition of man as '*un être sans raisonnable raison d'être*'. A being without a reasonable reason for being.

Is death-awareness connected to my being a writer? Perhaps. But if so, I don't want to know, or investigate. I remember the case of a comedian who, after years of psychotherapy, finally understood the reasons why he needed to be funny; and having understood, stopped. So I wouldn't want to risk it. Though I can imagine one of those would-you-rather choices. 'Mr Barnes, we've examined your condition, and we conclude that your fear of death is intimately connected to your literary habits, which are, as for many in your profession, merely a trivial response to mortality. You make up stories so that your name, and some indefinable percentage of your individuality, will continue after your physical death, and the anticipation of this brings you some kind of consolation. And although you have intellectually grasped that you might well be forgotten before you die, or if not, shortly afterwards, and that all writers will eventually be forgotten, as will the entire human race, even so it seems to you worth doing. Whether writing is for you a visceral response to the rational, or a rational response to the visceral, we cannot be sure. But here's something for you to consider. We have devised a new brain operation which takes away the fear of death. It's a straightforward procedure which doesn't require a general anaesthetic—indeed, you can watch its progress on-screen. Just keep an eye on this fiery orange locus and watch its colour gradually fade. Of course, you'll find that the operation will also take away your desire to write, but many of your colleagues have opted for this treatment and found it most beneficial. Nor has society at large complained about there being fewer writers.'

I'd have to think about it, of course. I might wonder how my backlist would stack up by itself, and whether that next idea is really as good as I imagine. But I hope I'd decline—or at least negotiate, get them to put more in the pot. 'How about eliminating not the fear of death but death itself? That would be seriously tempting. You get rid of death and I'll give up writing. How about *that* for a deal?'

My brother and I have inherited some things in common. Our four ears have sprouted three deaf aids between them. My deafness is on the left side. Jules Renard, *Journal*, 25 July 1892: 'He is deaf in his left ear: he does not hear on the side of the heart.' (Bastard!) When the ear-nose-and-throat specialist diagnosed my condition, I asked if there was anything I might have done to cause it. 'You can't give yourself Ménière's disease,' he replied. 'It's congenital.' 'Oh good,' I said. 'Something I can blame my parents for.' Not that I do. They were just doing their genetic duty, passing on what had been passed on to them, all the old stuff, from slime and swamp and cave, the evolution stuff— without which my complaining self would not have come into existence.

A few inches from these congenitally malfunctioning ears there lies, within my own skull, a fear of death, and within my brother's, its absence. Where, nearby, might religion or its absence lie? In 1987 an American neuroscientist claimed to have located exactly where in the brain a certain electrical instability triggers religious feelings: the so-called 'God spot'—a different, even more potent form of G spot. This researcher has also recently devised a 'God helmet' which stimulates the temporal lobes with a weak magnetic field and supposedly induces religious states. Valiantly—or foolhardily—he tried it on perhaps the least suggestible person on the planet, Richard Dawkins, who duly reported not a flicker of the Immanent Presence.

Other investigators believe that there is no

single God spot to be located. In one experiment, fifteen Carmelite nuns were asked to remember their most profound mystical experiences: scans showed electrical activity and blood oxygen levels surging in at least twelve separate regions of their brains. The neuromechanics of faith, though, will neither find, nor prove (or disprove) God, nor establish the underlying reason for our species' belief in deities. That may come when evolutionary psychology lays out religion's adaptive usefulness to the individual and group. Though will even this do for God, the great escapologist? Don't count on it. He will make a tactical retreat, as He has been doing for the last 150 or so years, into the next unscannable part of the universe. 'Perhaps the fact that God is incomprehensible is the strongest argument for His existence.'

Differences between brothers: when I was at the age of maximum teenage embarrassment, one of my parents' friends asked Dad, in front of me, which of his sons was the cleverer. My father had his eye—his gentle, liberal eye—on me as he carefully replied: 'Jonathan probably. Julian's more of an all-rounder, wouldn't you say so, Ju?' I was obliged to be complicit in the judgement (with which I probably agreed anyway). But I also recognized the euphemism. Rest of the World, Low Voice, All-Rounder: huh.

The differences my mother observed in her two sons pleased me more. 'When they were boys, if I was ill, Julian climbed into bed and snuggled up to me, while his brother brought me a cup of tea.' Another distinction she reported: my brother once cacked his pants and responded with the words, 'It will never happen again'—and it didn't; whereas,

82

when I failed to control my infant bowels, I was discovered merrily smearing my shit into the cracks between the floorboards. My favourite differentiation, however, was made much later in our mother's life. By this time both her sons were established in their separate fields. This is how she expressed her pride in them: 'One of my sons writes books I can read but can't understand, and the other writes books I can understand but can't read.'

Whenever I used to reflect on our divergent natures, I would often ascribe it to a puerperal detail. After my brother's birth, our mother had been ill with a streptococcal infection. Unable to breastfeed, she had raised him on whatever bottle-gruel was available in the wartime England of 1942. I knew that my birth, in 1946, had occurred without medical complication, and therefore I must have been breastfed. In moments of sibling competitiveness I would fall back on this essential fact. He was the clever one, all icy intellect and practical action, the shit-retaining tea-bearer; I was the all-rounder, the snuggler, the shit-smearer, the emotional one. He had the brain as he had the British Empire; I had the Rest of the World in all its rich diversity. This was pathetically reductivist, of course, and whenever critics and commentators applied similar reductivism to art (El Greco simplified into a case of astigmatism, Schumann's music the notation of approaching madness), I would be grossly irritated. But I hugged this explanation to myself at a time when I needed it— a time when observers of my emotional life might have concluded that I wasn't collecting Rest of the World so much as specializing in rare postmarks of

Norway and the Faroe Islands.

*   *   *

Fear of death replaces fear of God. But fear of
God—an entirely sane early principle, given the
hazard of life and our vulnerability to thunderbolts
of unknown origin—at least allowed for
negotiation. We talked God down from being the
Vengeful One and rebranded Him the Infinitely
Merciful; we changed Him from Old to New, like
the Testaments and the Labour Party. We levered
up His graven image, put it on runners, and
dragged it to a place where the weather was
sunnier. We can't do the same with death. Death
can't be talked down, or parlayed into anything; it
simply declines to come to the negotiating table.
It doesn't have to pretend to be Vengeful or
Merciful, or even Infinitely Merciless. It is
impervious to insult, complaint or condescension.
'Death is not an artist': no, and would never claim
to be one. Artists are unreliable; whereas death
never lets you down, remains on call seven days a
week, and is happy to work three consecutive
eight-hour shifts. You would buy shares in death, if
they were available; you would bet on it, however
poor the odds. When my brother and I were
growing up, there was a minor celebrity called Dr
Barbara Moore, a long-distance walker and
propagandizing vegetarian who thought she could
outface nature; she once told a newspaper, a little
ambitiously, that she would have a baby at 100 and
live to be 150. She didn't get even halfway there.
She died at seventy-three, and not at the hands of
an anxious bookmaker either. Oddly, she did

death's work for it, starving herself into extinction. That was a fine day on the exchange for death.

Atheists in morally superior Category One (no God, no fear of death) like to tell us that the lack of a deity should not in any way diminish our sense of wonder at the universe. It may have all seemed both miraculous and user-friendly when we imagined God had laid it on especially for us, from the harmony of the snowflake and the complex allusiveness of the passion flower to the spectacular showmanship of a solar eclipse. But if everything still moves without a Prime Mover, why should it be less wonderful and less beautiful? Why should we be children needing the teacher to show us things, as if God were some superior version of a TV wildlife expert? The Antarctic penguin, for instance, is just as regal and comic, just as graceful and awkward, whether pre- or post-Darwin. Grow up, and let's examine together the allure of the double helix, the darkling glimmer of deep space, the infinite adjustments of plumage which demonstrate the laws of evolution, and the packed, elusive mechanism of the human brain. Why do we need some God to help us marvel at such things?

We don't. Not really. And yet. If what is out there comes from nothing, if all is unrolling mechanically according to a programme laid down by nobody, and if our perceptions of it are mere micro-moments of biochemical activity, the mere snap and crackle of a few synapses, then what does this sense of wonder amount to? Should we not be a little more suspicious of it? A dung beetle might well have a primitive sense of awe at the size of the mighty dung ball it is rolling. Is this wonder of ours merely a posher version? Perhaps, the Category

One atheist might reply, but at least it is based on a knowledge of what is the case. Compare the soppy fantasies of that disciple of Rousseau, who claimed that the striations on the rind of a melon were God's handiwork—the Almighty nannyishly marking the fruit into fair and equal portions for His children. Do you want to go back to such preposterous thinking, to the gastronome's pathetic fallacy? Where is your sense of truth?

Still hanging in there, I hope. Though—just out of interest—it would be useful to know whether an atheist's sense of wonder at the universe is quantifiably as great as that of a believer. No reason why we can't measure such things (if not now, soon). We can compare the number of synapses that fire during the female and the male orgasm—very bad news for competitive blokes—so why not try a similar test? Find some anchorite who still believes that the passion flower illustrates Christ's suffering: that the leaf symbolizes the spear, the five anthers the five wounds, the tendrils the whips, the column of the ovary the pillar of the cross, the stamens the hammers, the three styles the three nails, the fleshy threads within the flower the crown of thorns, the calyx the nimbus, the white tint purity and the blue tint heaven. This monk would also believe that the flower stays open for precisely three days, one for each year of Christ's ministry. Wire him up alongside a TV botanist and let's see who fires the more synapses. And then let's take the wiring kit along to a concert hall and test my 'very irreligious' friend J. against a believer who will listen to that Haydn Mass as a full expression of eternal truth as well as—or instead of—a great piece of music. Then we

86

shall be able to see, and measure, what happens when you take the religion out of religious art, and God out of the universe.

This may seem like rather desperate stuff to those cool minds who thrill even more to the beauty of scientific law precisely because it is not God's handicraft. But if this sounds like nostalgia, it's nostalgia for something I've never known— which is, admittedly, the more toxic kind. Maybe another part of my condition is envy of those who lost faith—or gained truth—when losing faith was fresh and young and bold and dangerous. François Renard, suicide and anti-clerical, was the first person to be buried in the cemetery at Chitry without the aid and comfort of a priest. Imagine the shock of that in the remote Burgundy countryside in 1897; imagine the pride of unbelief. Maybe I'm suffering from—well, call it historical remorse, so that my grandfather can sympathize.

*   *   *

'A happy atheist.' The date I might have advanced to college chaplain and captain of boats as the key moment when aesthetic rapture began to replace religious awe, is January 1811; the place, Florence. It was a few days before Stendhal's twenty-eighth birthday—or rather, the twenty-eighth birthday of Henri Beyle, who had not yet transformed himself into his *nom de plume*. Beyle/Stendhal did not believe in God, and affected a logical ignorance of His existence: 'Waiting for God to reveal himself, I believe that his prime minister, Chance, governs this sad world just as well.' He continued: 'I feel I am an honest man, and that it would be impossible to be otherwise, not for the sake of pleasing a Supreme Being who does not exist, but for my own sake, who need to live in peace with my habits and prejudices and to give purpose to my life and nourishment to my thoughts.'

In 1811 Beyle was the impoverished author of plagiaristic musical biographies, and had begun a history of Italian painting he was never to complete. He had first come to Italy as a seventeen-year-old in the baggage-train of Napoleon's army. When the camp followers reached Ivrea, Beyle immediately went looking for the town's opera house. He found a third-rate theatre with a down-at-heel company playing Cimarosa's *Il Matrimonio segreto*, but it came as a revelation: *'un bonheur divin'*, he reported to his sister. From that moment, he became a profound and tremulous admirer of Italy, susceptible to all its aspects: once, returning to Milan after many years, he noted that 'the very particular odour of horse dung in the streets' moved him to tears.

And now he comes to Florence for the first time. He is arriving from Bologna; the coach crosses the Apennines and begins its descent towards the city. 'My heart was leaping wildly within me. What utterly childlike excitement!' As the road bends, the cathedral, with Brunelleschi's famous dome, comes into sight. At the city gate, he abandons the coach—and his luggage—to enter Florence on foot, like a pilgrim. He finds himself at the church of Santa Croce. Here are the tombs of Michelangelo and Galileo; nearby is Canova's bust of Alfieri. He thinks of the other great Tuscans: Dante, Boccaccio, Petrarch. 'The tide of emotion that overwhelmed me flowed so deep that

88

it was scarce to be distinguished from religious awe.' He asks a friar to unlock the Niccolini Chapel and let him look at the frescoes. He seats himself 'on the step of a faldstool, with my head thrown back to rest upon the desk, so that I might let my gaze dwell on the ceiling'. The city and the proximity of its famous children have already put Beyle in a state of near trance. Now he is 'absorbed in the contemplation of *sublime beauty*'; he attains 'the supreme degree of sensibility where the *divine intimations* of art merge with the impassioned sensuality of emotion'. The italics are his.

The physical consequence of all this is a fainting fit. 'As I emerged from the porch of Santa Croce, I was seized with a fierce palpitation of the heart . . . The wellspring of life dried up within me, and I walked in constant fear of falling to the ground.' Beyle (who was Stendhal by the time he published this account in *Rome, Naples and Florence*) could describe his symptoms but not name his condition. Posterity, however, can, since posterity always knows best. Beyle was suffering, we can now tell him, from Stendhal's Syndrome, a condition identified in 1979 by a Florentine psychiatrist who had noted almost a hundred cases of dizziness and nausea brought on by exposure to the city's art treasures. A recent issue of *Firenze Spettacolo* helpfully lists the prime sites to avoid if you might be susceptible to this syndrome—or, for that matter, to visit, should you want to tough it out aesthetically. The top three are 'Santa Croce's Cappella Niccolini, with Giotto's Frescoes', the Accademia for Michelangelo's *David*, and the Uffizi for Botticelli's *Primavera*.

The sceptical might wonder if those hundred or

so dizzy twentieth-century visitors were indeed suffering from a violent aesthetic reaction, or merely from the rigours of the modern tourist's life: city confusion, timetable stress, masterpiece anxiety, information overload, and too much hot sun mixed with chilly air conditioning. The very sceptical might wonder whether Stendhal himself was really suffering from Stendhal's Syndrome. What he describes might have been the cumulative effect of successive powerful impressions: the mountains, the dome, the arrival, the church, the mighty dead, the great art—and hence the final swoon. A medical, rather than psychiatric, opinion might also be useful: if you sit with your head back, staring for a long time at a painted wall, and then get to your feet and walk from the cool darkness of a church into the bright, dusty, frenetic swirl of a city, might you not expect to feel a little faint?

But still, the story remains. Beyle/Stendhal is the modern art-lover's progenitor and justification. He went to Florence and fainted at great art. He was in a church, but he was not a religious man, and his rapture was purely secular and aesthetic. And who would not understand and envy a man swooning at the Giottos in Santa Croce, the more so as he was seeing them with a mind and eye untrammelled by previous reproduction? The story is true, not least because we want it, we need it to be true.

Genuine pilgrims arriving at Santa Croce five centuries before Beyle would have seen in Giotto's newly painted fresco cycle of the life of St Francis an art that told them the absolute truth, and could save them, in this world and the next. It would have been the same for those who first read Dante, or first heard Palestrina. The more beautiful because true, the more true because beautiful, and these joyful multiplications continuing in an eternity of parallel mirrors. In a secular world, where we cross ourselves and genuflect before great works of art in a purely metaphorical way, we tend to believe that art tells us the truth—that's to say, in a relativist universe, more truth than anything else—and that in turn this truth can save us—up to a point—that's to say, enlighten us, move us, elevate us, even heal us—though only in this world. How much simpler it used to be, and not just grammatically.

Flaubert rebuked Louise Colet for having 'the love of art' but not 'the religion of art'. Some see art as a psychological replacement for religion, still supplying a sense of the world beyond themselves to those reduced creatures who now no longer dream of heaven. One modern critic, Professor S. of Cambridge, argues that art is essentially religious because the artist aims at immortality by avoiding 'the banal democracy of death'. This grand statement is rebutted by Professor C. of Oxford, who points out that even the greatest art lasts no more than an eye-blink in geological time. The two statements are, I suppose, compatible, since the artist's motivation might ignore the subsequent cosmic reality. But Professor C. has a grand statement of his own, namely that 'The religion of art makes people worse, because it encourages contempt for those considered inartistic.' There may be something in this, though the larger problem, in Britain at least, is that of contempt from the opposite direction: from the complacent philistine towards those who practise and value the arts. And do such feelings make *them* better people?

'The religion of art': when Flaubert used the expression, he was talking about the dedicated practice, not the snobbish worship, of art; the monkishness required, the hair shirt, and the silent, solitary meditation before the act. If art is to be compared to a religion, it's certainly not one in the traditional Catholic mode, with papal authoritarianism above and obedient servitude below. Rather, it is something like the early Church: fertile, chaotic and schismatic. For every bishop there is a blasphemer; for every dogma there is a heretic. In art now, as in religion then, false prophets and false gods abound. There are artistic priesthoods (disapproved of by Professor C.) which seek to exclude the unwashed, which disappear into hermetic intellectualism and inaccessible refinement. On the other side (and disapproved of by Professor S.) there is inauthenticity, mercantilism and an infantile populism; artists who flatter and compromise, who dodge for votes (and cash) like politicians. Pure or impure, high-minded or corrupt, all—like golden lads and girls and chimneysweepers—will come to dust, and their art not long afterwards, if not before. But art and religion will always shadow one another through the abstract nouns they both invoke: truth, seriousness, imagination, sympathy, morality, transcendence.

*   *   *

Missing God is for me rather like Being English: a feeling roused mainly by attack. When my country is abused, a dormant, not to say narcoleptic,

92

patriotism stirs. And when it comes to God, I find myself more provoked by atheistic absolutism than by, say, the often bland tentative hopefulness of the Church of England. The other month, I found myself at dinner with neighbours. A dozen of us around a kitchen table long enough to seat Christ and his disciples. Several conversations were proceeding simultaneously, when an argument suddenly spiked a few places away and a young man (the son of the house) shouted sarcastically, 'But why should God do that for His son and not for the rest of us?' I found myself uncivilly turning out of my own conversation and shouting back, 'Because He's *God*, for Christ's sake.' The exchange spread; my host C., an old friend and notorious rationalist, backed up his son: 'There's a book about how people survived crucifixion, how sometimes they weren't dead when they were taken down. The centurions could be bribed.' Me: 'What's that got to do with it?' He (exasperatedly rationalist): 'The point is, it couldn't have happened. *It couldn't have happened.*' Me (rationally exasperated with rationality): 'But that's *the whole point*—that it couldn't have happened. The point is, that if you're a Christian, it did.' I might have added that his argument was as old as . . . well, at least as old as *Madame Bovary*, where Homais, the bigoted materialist, declares the notion of the Resurrection to be not only 'absurd' but 'contrary to all the laws of physics'.

Such scientific objections and 'explanations'— Christ wasn't 'really' walking on the water, but on a thin sheet of ice, which, under certain meteorological conditions . . . would have convinced me in my youth. Now they seem quite irrelevant. As Stravinsky put it, reasoned proof (and hence disproof) is to religion no more than what counterpoint exercises are to music. Faith is about believing precisely what, according to all the known rules, 'could not have happened'. The Virgin Birth, the Resurrection, Mohammed leaping up to heaven leaving a footprint in the rock, life hereafter. It couldn't have happened by all we understand. But it did. Or it will. (Or, of course, it certainly didn't and assuredly won't.)

Writers need certain stock replies for certain stock questions. When asked What The Novel Does, I tend to answer, 'It tells beautiful, shapely lies which enclose hard, exact truths.' We talk of the suspension of disbelief as the mental prerequisite for enjoying fiction, theatre, film, representational painting. It's just words on a page, actors on a stage or screen, colours on a piece of canvas: these people don't exist, have never existed, or if they did, these are mere copies of them, briefly convincing simulacra. Yet while we read, while our eyes explore, we believe: that Emma lives and dies, that Hamlet kills Laertes, that this brooding fur-trimmed man and his brocaded wife might step out of their portrayals by Lotto and talk to us in the Italian of sixteenth-century Brescia. It never happened, it could never have happened, but we believe that it did and might. From such suspension of disbelief it is not far to the active acknowledgement of belief. Not that I am suggesting that fiction reading might soften you up for religion. On the contrary—very much the contrary: religions were the first great inventions of the fiction writers. A convincing representation and a plausible explanation of the world for understandably confused minds. A beautiful, shapely story containing hard, exact lies.

Another week, another meal: seven writers meet in the upstairs room of a Hungarian restaurant in Soho. Thirty or more years ago, this Friday lunch was instituted: a shouty, argumentative, smoky, boozy gathering attended by journalists, novelists, poets and cartoonists at the end of another working week. Over the years the venue has shifted many times, and the personnel been diminished by relocation and death. Now there are seven of us left, the eldest in his mid-seventies, the youngest in his late—very late—fifties.

It is the only all-male event I knowingly, or willingly, attend. From weekly it has slipped to being merely annual; at times it is almost like the memory of an event. Over the years, too, its tone has shifted. It is now less shouty and more listening; less boastful and competitive, more teasing and indulgent. Nowadays, no one smokes, or attends with the stern intention of getting drunk, which used to seem worth doing for its own sake. We need a room to ourselves, not out of self-importance, or fear that our best lines will be stolen by eavesdroppers, but because half of us are deaf—some openly so, thumbing in their deaf aids as they sit down, others as yet unadmittedly. We are losing hair, needing glasses; our prostates are swelling slowly, and the lavatory cistern at the turn of the stair is given a good workout. But we are cheerful on the whole, and all still working.

The talk follows familiar tracks: gossip, bookbiz, litcrit, music, films, politics (some have done the ritual shuffle to the Right). This is no lemon table, and I can't remember death, as a general topic,

95

ever being discussed. Or religion, for that matter, though one of our number, P., is a Roman Catholic. For years, he has been relied upon to put the awkward, insinuatingly moral question. When one of the more philandering lunchers was ruminating on how uxorious he had lately become, it was P. who broke in to ask, 'Is that love, do you think, or age?' (and received the answer that, alas, it was probably age).

This time, however, we have a matter of doctrine on which to quiz P. The new—German—pope has just announced the abolition of limbo. At first we require clarification: of what and where it was, who got sent there, and who, if anyone, was let out. There is a brief swerve into painting and Mantegna (though limbo has hardly been a popular subject, and is presumably not much of a loss to whatever Catholic painters are still out there). We note the mutability of these Final Places: even hell has been downgraded over the years in both probability and infernality. We agree, companionably, that Sartre's 'Hell is other people' is a nonsense. But what we really want to ask P. is whether, and how much, he believes in the reality of such destinations; and specifically, whether he believes in heaven. 'Yes,' he replies, 'I hope so. I hope there is heaven.' But for him such a belief is far from straightforwardly consoling. He explains that it is painful for him to consider that, if there is the eternity and heaven of his faith, it might involve separation from his four children, all of whom have abandoned the religion in which they were brought up.

And not just them: he must also consider being parted from his wife of more than forty years.

Though one must, he says, hope for divine grace. It is far from certain that overt believers will necessarily be saved, or that the good deeds of non-believers and apostates will not reunite them with their believing, if far from perfect, husbands and progenitors. P. then supplies a marital detail previously unknown to me. His wife E. had been brought up an Anglican, and as a thirteen-year-old schoolgirl was sent to lodge—Daniel-like—in the atheistic den of the philosopher A.J. Ayer. There she quickly lost her faith, and not even forty years of husbandly example could subsequently dent her agnosticism.

At this point a referendum is called on belief in an afterlife. Five and three-quarters of the remaining six give it no credence; the fractional party calls religion a 'cruel con' yet admits he 'wouldn't mind if it were true'. But whereas in previous decades this might have led to some affectionate mockery of our Catholic member, now there is a sense that the rest of us are much closer to the oblivion in which we believe, whereas he, at least, has a moderate, modest hope of salvation and heaven. It seems to me—though we do not have a referendum on this—that we quietly envy him. We do not believe, we have insistently not believed for decades, more than half a century in some cases; but we do not like what we see ahead of us, and our resources for dealing with it are not as good as they might be.

I don't know if P. would be consoled, or alarmed, if I were to quote him Jules Renard (*Journal*, 26 January 1906): 'I'm happy to believe anything you suggest, but the justice of this world doesn't exactly reassure me about the justice of the next. I fear that God will just carry on blundering: He'll welcome the wicked into heaven, and boot the good down into hell.' But my friend P.'s dilemma—I know of no one who does such precise and woe-filled calculations about their possible afterlife—makes me reconsider something I have always, too lightly, maintained (and was doing so only a few pages ago). Agnostics and atheists observing religion from the sideline tend to be unimpressed by milksop creeds. What's the point of faith unless you and it are serious—*seriously* serious—unless your religion fills, directs, stains and sustains your life? But 'serious' in most religions invariably means punitive. And so we are wishing on others what we would hardly wish upon ourselves.

Seriousness: I wouldn't, for instance, have fancied being born in the Papal States as recently as the 1840s. Education was so discouraged that only two per cent of the population could read; priests and the secret police ran everything; 'thinkers' of any kind were held a dangerous class; while 'a distrust of anything not medieval led Gregory XVI to prohibit the intrusion of railways and telegraphs into his dominions'. No, that all sounds 'serious' in quite the wrong way. Then there's the world as decreed in Pius IX's 1864 Syllabus of Errors, in which he claimed for the Church control over all science, culture and education, while rejecting freedom of worship for other faiths. No, I wouldn't fancy that either. First they go after schismatics and heretics, then other religions, then they come for people like me. And as for being a woman under most faiths . . .

Religion tends to authoritarianism as capitalism

tends to monopoly. And if you think popes seem a sitting—or enthroned—target, consider someone as unpopish as one of their notorious enemies: Robespierre. The Incorruptible One first came to national prominence in 1789 with an attack on the luxury and worldliness of the Catholic Church. In a speech to the Estates General, he urged the priesthood to reacquaint itself with the austerity and virtue of early Christendom by the obvious means of selling all its property and distributing the proceeds to the poor. The Revolution, he implied, would be happy to help if the Church proved reluctant.

Most of the Revolutionary leaders were atheists or serious agnostics; and the new state quickly disposed of the Catholic God and his local representatives. Robespierre, however, was the exception, a Deist who thought atheism in a public man little short of lunacy. His theological and political terminologies were intermingled. In a grand phrase, he declared that 'atheism is aristocratic'; whereas the concept of a Supreme Being who watches over human innocence and protects our virtue—and, presumably, smiles as unvirtuous heads are lopped—was 'democratic through and through'. Robespierre even quoted (seriously) Voltaire's (ironic) dictum that 'If God did not exist, it would be necessary to invent him.' From all this, you might imagine that when the Revolution introduced an up-to-date belief system, it might avoid the extremism of the one it replaced; might be rational, pragmatic, even liberal. But what did the invention of a shiny new Supreme Being lead to? At the start of the Revolution, Robespierre presided over the slaughter of priests;

99

by its end, he was presiding over the slaughter of atheists.

*　　　*　　　*

In my early twenties, I read a lot of Somerset Maugham. I admired the lucid pessimism and ranging geography of his stories and novels; also, his sane reflections on art and life in such books as *The Summing Up* and *A Writer's Notebook*. I enjoyed being prodded and startled by his truth-telling and sophisticated cynicism. I didn't envy the writer his money, his smoking jackets or his Riviera house (though I wouldn't have minded his art collection); but I did envy him his knowledge of the world. I knew so little about it myself, and was ashamed of my ignorance. In my second term at Oxford, I had decided to give up modern languages for the more 'serious' study of philosophy and psychology. My French tutor, a benign Mallarmé scholar, courteously asked my reasons. I gave him two. The first was prosaic (literally so—the weekly grind of turning chunks of English prose into French and vice versa), the second more overwhelming. How, I asked him, could I possibly be expected to have any understanding of, or sensible opinions about, a play like *Phèdre* when I had only the remotest experience of the volcanic emotions depicted in it? He gave me a wry, donnish smile: 'Well, which of us can ever say that we have?'

At this time, I kept a box of green index cards, onto which I copied epigrams, witticisms, scraps of dialogue and pieces of wisdom worth preserving. Some of them strike me now as the meretricious

100

generalizations that youth endorses (but then they would); though they do include this, from a French source: 'The advice of the old is like the winter sun: it sheds light but does not warm us.' Given that I have reached my advice-giving years, I think this may be profoundly true. And there were two pieces of Maugham's wisdom that echoed with me for years, probably because I kept arguing with them. The first was the claim that 'Beauty is a bore.' The second, from chapter 77 of *The Summing Up* (a green index card informs me), ran: 'The great tragedy of life is not that men perish, but that they cease to love.' I cannot remember my response to this at the time, though I suspect it might have been: Speak for yourself, old man.

Maugham was an agnostic who thought that the best frame of mind in which to conduct life was one of humorous resignation. In *The Summing Up* he runs through the various unpersuasive arguments—from prime cause, from design, from perfection—which have convinced others of God's reality. More plausible than these, to his mind, was the long unfashionable argument *e consensu gentium*, 'from general agreement'. Since the beginning of human time, the vast majority of people, including the greatest and wisest of them, from vastly divergent cultures, have all entertained some kind of belief in a God. How could such a widespread instinct exist without the possibility of its being satisfied?

For all his practical wisdom and knowledge of the world—and for all his fame and his money—Maugham failed to hold on to the spirit of humorous resignation. His old age contained little serenity: all was vindictiveness, monkey glands,

101

and hostile will-making. His body was kept going in vigour and lust while his heart grew harder and his mind began to slip; he declined into an empty rich man. Had he wished to write a codicil to his own (wintry, unwarming) advice, it might have been: the additional tragedy of life is that we do not perish at the right time.

While Maugham was still lucid, however, he arranged a meeting of which, alas, no detailed minutes, or even the sketchiest outline, survive. During the era of piety, princes and rich burghers used to summon priest and prelate to reassure them of the certainty of heaven and the rewards their prayers and monetary offerings had ensured. The agnostic Maugham now did the opposite: he summoned A.J. Ayer, the most intellectually and socially fashionable philosopher of the day, to reassure him that death was indeed final, and that nothing, and nothingness, followed it. The need for such reassurance might be explained by a passage in *The Summing Up*. There Maugham relates how, as a young man, he lost his belief in God, but nonetheless retained for a while an instinctive fear of hell, which it took him another metaphysical shrug to dislodge. Perhaps he was still looking over his shoulder.

Ayer and his wife, the novelist Dee Wells, arrived at the Villa Mauresque in April 1961 for this oddest, and most poignant, of freebies. If this were a short story or a play, the two principals might begin by sounding one another out, and seeking to establish the rules of the encounter; then the narrative would build towards a set piece in Maugham's study, probably after dinner on the second evening. Brandy glasses would be filled, swirled and sniffed; we might equip Maugham with a cigar, Ayer with a pack of French cigarettes rolled in yellow paper. The novelist would list the reasons why he long ago ceased to believe in God; the philosopher would endorse their correctness. The novelist might sentimentally raise the argument *e consensu gentium*; the philosopher would smilingly dismantle it. The novelist might wonder whether, even without God, there might not still, paradoxically, be hell; the philosopher—reflecting to himself that this fear might be a sign of vestigial homosexual guilt—would put him right. The brandy glasses would be refilled, and then, to make his presentation complete (and justify his air ticket) the philosopher would outline the latest and most logical proofs of the non-existence of God and the finiteness of life. The novelist would rise a little unsteadily, brush some ash off his smoking jacket, and suggest they rejoin the ladies. In company again, Maugham would pronounce himself profoundly satisfied, and become jolly, almost skittish, for the rest of the evening; the Ayers might exchange knowing glances.

(A professional philosopher, considering this imaginary scene, might protest at the writer's gross vulgarization of Ayer's actual position. The Wykeham Professor regarded all religious language as essentially unverifiable; so for him the statement 'There is no God' was as meaningless as the statement 'God exists'—neither being susceptible to philosophical proof. In reply, the writer might plead literary necessity; and also counter that since Ayer was here talking to a layman and benefactor, he might have held back on technicality.)

103

But since this is life, or rather the remnants of it that become available to biographers, we have no evidence of such a private audience. Perhaps there was just a brisk, convivial reassurance over the breakfast table. This might make for a better short story (though not play): the Great Matter dismissed in a few phrases during a clatter of knives, with perhaps the counterpoint of a parallel discussion about social arrangements for the day: who wanted to go shopping in Nice, and where exactly along the Grande Corniche Maugham's Rolls Royce should transport them for lunch. But in any event, the required exchange somehow took place, Ayer and his wife returned to London, while Maugham, after this rare secular shriving, proceeded towards his death.

*   *   *

A few years ago, I translated the notebook Alphonse Daudet began keeping when he realized his syphilis had reached its tertiary stage, and would inevitably bring his death. At one point in the text he starts bidding goodbye to those he loves: 'Farewell wife, children, family, the things of my heart . . .' And then he adds: 'Farewell me, cherished me, now so hazy, so indistinct.' I wonder if we can somehow farewell ourselves in advance. Can we lose, or at least thin, this resilient sense of specialness until there is less of it to disappear, less of it to miss? The paradox being, of course, that it is this very 'me' which is in charge of thinning itself. Just as the brain is the only instrument that we have to investigate the workings of the brain. Just as the theory of the Death of the Author was

104

inevitably pronounced by . . . an Author.

Lose, or at least thin, the 'me'. Two stratagems suggest themselves. First, to ask how much, in the scale of things, that 'me' is worth. Why should the universe possibly need its continuing existence? This 'me' has already been indulged with several decades of life, and in most cases will have reproduced itself; how can it be of sufficient importance to justify any more years? Further, consider how boring that 'me' would become, to both me and others, if it went on and on and on (see Bernard Shaw, author of *Back to Methuselah*; also see Bernard Shaw, old man, incorrigible poseur and tedious self-publicist). Second stratagem: see the death of 'me' through the eyes of others. Not those who will mourn and miss you, or those who might hear of your death and raise a momentary glass; or even those who might say 'Good!' or 'Never liked him anyway' or '*Terribly* overrated'. Rather, see the death of 'me' from the point of view of those who have never heard of you—which is, after all, almost everybody. Unknown person dies: not many mourn. That is our certain obituary in the eyes of the rest of the world. So who are we to indulge our egotism and make a fuss?

Such wintry wisdom may briefly convince. I almost persuaded myself for the time I was writing the paragraph above. Except that the indifference of the world has rarely reduced anyone's egotism. Except that the universe's judgement of our value rarely accords with our own. Except that we find it difficult to believe that, if we went on living, we would bore ourselves and others (there are so many foreign languages and musical instruments to learn, so many careers to try out and countries to live in and people to love, and after that we can always fall back on tango and *langlauf* and the art of watercolour . . .). And the other snag is that merely to consider your own individuality, which you are mourning in advance, is to reinforce the sense of that individuality; the process is one of digging yourself into an ever larger hole that will eventually become your grave. The very art I practise also runs counter to the idea of a calm farewell to a thinned self. Whatever the writer's aesthetic—from subjective and autobiographical to objective and author-concealing—the self must be strengthened and defined in order to produce the work. So you could say that by writing this sentence I am making it just a little harder for myself to die.

Or you could say: Oh, get on with it then—fuck off and die anyway, and take your noxious arty self with you. It is the last Christmas before my sixtieth birthday, and a few weeks ago the website belief.net ('Meet Christian singles in your area'; 'Health and Happiness Tips Daily in Your In-box') has asked Richard Dawkins—or, as the site's subscribers have nicknamed him, 'Mister Meaninglessness'—about the despair aroused in some by the implications of Darwinism. He replies: 'If it's true that it causes people to feel despair, that's tough. The universe doesn't owe us condolence or consolation; it doesn't owe us a nice warm feeling inside. If it's true, it's true, and you'd better live with it.' Fuck off and die, indeed. Of course, Dawkins is right in his argument. But Robespierre was also right: atheism is aristocratic. And the lordly tone recalls the punitive hardliners of old Christianity. The universe isn't arranged by God for your comfort. You don't like it? Tough. You—unbaptized soul—get off to limbo. You—blaspheming masturbator—straight to hell, do not pass Go, and no Get Out of Jail card for you, ever. You—Catholic husband—this way; you lot—apostate children and wife who lodged with the atheist Ayer—that way. Naught for your comfort. Jules Renard imagined just such a parade-ground God, who would keep reminding those who finally made it to heaven: 'You aren't here to have *fun*, you know.'

Grow up, says Dawkins. God is an imaginary friend. When you're dead, you're dead. If you want a sense of spiritual awe, get it from contemplating the Milky Way through a telescope. At the moment you're holding a child's kaleidoscope up to the light and pretending that those coloured lozenges were put there by God.

Grow up. On 17 July 1891, Daudet and Edmond de Goncourt went for a morning walk and discussed the minuscule chance of an afterlife. Much as he longed to see his dead, beloved brother Jules again, Edmond was sure that we are 'totally annihilated at death', being 'ephemeral creatures lasting only a few days longer than those which live a single day'. He then produced an original argument, one from number, like Maugham's *e consensu gentium*, yet with a contrary conclusion: even if there were a God, expecting the Deity to provide a second, post-death existence for each and every member of the human race is laying far too great a task of bookkeeping upon Him.

This is perhaps more witty than convincing. If we can conceive of a God in the first place, then the ability to bear in mind, tabulate, care for (and resurrect) every single one of us is, I'd have thought, pretty much the least we should expect as a job description. No, the more convincing argument springs not from God's incapacity, but ours. As Maugham puts it, in his first entry for the year 1902, in *A Writer's Notebook*: 'Men, commonplace and ordinary, do not seem to me fit for the tremendous fact of eternal life. With their little passions, their little virtues and their little vices, they are well enough suited in the workaday world; but the conception of immortality is much too vast for beings cast on so small a scale.' Before becoming a writer, Maugham had trained as a doctor, and witnessed patients die both peacefully and tragically: 'And never have I seen in their last moments anything to suggest that their spirit was everlasting. They die as a dog dies.'

Possible objections: 1. Dogs, too, are part of God's creation (as well as being His anagram). 2. Why should a doctor, concentrating on the body, notice where the spirit is? 3. Why should the inadequacy of man preclude the possibility of a spiritual afterlife? Who are we to decide that we are not worthy? Isn't the whole point the hope of improvement, of rescue through grace? Sure we're unimpressive, sure there's a long way to go, but isn't that the point—or what's a heaven for? 4. Fallback Singerian position: 'If survival has been arranged . . .'

But Maugham is right: we die as dogs die. Or rather—given medicine's advances since 1902—we die as well-groomed, well-tranquillized dogs with good health insurance policies might die. But still caninely.

*　　　*　　　*

During my inner-suburban childhood, we had a black-and-white Bakelite wireless, whose controls my brother and I were not allowed to touch. Dad would be in charge of turning the instrument on, tuning it, making sure it was properly warmed up in time. Then he might fiddle with his pipe, poking and tamping it before unleashing the scratchy flare of a Swan Vesta. Mum would get out her knitting or mending, and perhaps consult the *Radio Times* in its tooled-leather slip cover. Then the wireless would project the rounded opinions of the *Any Questions?* panel: glib MPs, worldly bishops, professional wise men like A.J. Ayer, and amateur, self-made sages. Mum would award them interjectory ticks—'Talks a lot of sense'—or crosses—anything from 'Stupid fool!' up to 'Ought to be shot.' On another day the wireless would disgorge *The Critics*, a band of suave aesthetic experts droning on about plays we would never see and books that never came into the house. My brother and I would listen with a kind of stunned boredom, which was not just of the present, but anticipatory: if such opinion-giving and -receiving was what adulthood contained, then it seemed not merely unattainable, but actively undesirable.

In my outer-suburban adolescence, the wireless acquired a rival: a vast television set, bought second-hand at auction. Swathed in walnut, with full-length double doors concealing its function, it was the size of a dwarf's armoire, and guzzled furniture polish. On top of it sat a family Bible, as outsize as the television, and just as deceptive. For

109

it was the family Bible of someone else's family, with their lineage not ours inscribed on the front endpaper. It too had been bought at auction, and was never opened except when Dad jovially consulted it for a crossword clue.

The chairs now pointed in a different direction, but the ritual was unchanged. The pipe would be lit and the sewing laid out, or perhaps the nail equipment: emery board, varnish remover, split-binding tape, undercoat, top coat. The smell of pear drops sometimes takes me back to making model aeroplanes, but more often to my mother doing her nails. And especially to an emblematic moment from my adolescence. My parents and I were watching an interview with John Gielgud—or rather, watching him effortlessly turn his interlocutor's questions into pretexts for elaborate, self-mocking anecdotes. My parents enjoyed the theatre, from amateur dramatics to the West End, and would certainly have seen Gielgud from the gods a few times. His voice was for half a century one of the most beautiful instruments on the London stage: one not of rough power but of refined mobility, the sort my mother would admire on social as well as critical grounds. As Gielgud unfolded another of his urbane and slightly giggly reminiscences, I became aware of a quiet yet insistent noise, as if Dad was discreetly trying to light a Swan Vesta, but constantly failing. Dry scrape succeeded dry scrape, aural graffiti scratching on Gielgud's voice. It was, of course, my mother filing her nails.

The dwarf's armoire was more fun than the wireless, as it contained Western serials: *The Lone Ranger*, naturally, but also *Wells Fargo* with Dale

Robertson. My parents preferred grown-up fighting, like *Field Marshal Montgomery On Command In Battle*, a six-parter in which the general explained how he had pursued the Germans from North Africa all across Europe until taking their surrender at Lüneberg Heath; or, as my brother recently remembered it, 'Ghastly little Monty poncing around in black and white'. There was also *The Brains Trust*, like a postgraduate—i.e. even more stultifying—version of *Any Questions?*, and also starring A.J. Ayer. More unitedly, the family watched wildlife programmes: Armand and Michaela Denis, with their frolicsome Belgian accents and multipocketed desert suits; Captain Cousteau with his frog-feet; David Attenborough panting through the undergrowth. Viewers had to keep their wits about them in those days, as monochrome creatures moved in camouflage across a monochrome veldt, seabed or jungle. Nowadays, we have it easy, pampered by colour and close-up, given a God's-eye-view of all the intricacy and beauty of a God-free universe.

Emperor penguins have been in fashion lately, with cinematic and TV voiceovers urging us to anthropomorphism. How can we resist their loveably incompetent bipedalism? See how they rest lovingly on one another's breasts, shuffle a precious egg between parental feet, share the food search just as we share supermarket duties. Watch how the whole group huddles together against the snowstorm, demonstrating social altruism. Aren't these egg-devoted, chore-dividing, co-parenting, seasonally monogamous Emperors of the Antarctic strangely reminiscent of us? Perhaps; but

111

only to the extent that we are unstrangely reminiscent of them. We are just as good as they are at passing for God-created while being smacked and wheedled by implacable evolutionary urges. And given that this is so, what—again—does this make of the proposal that wonder at the natural but empty universe is a full replacement for wonder at the works of an imaginary friend we have created for ourselves? Having come to evolutionary self-consciousness as a species, we cannot go back to being penguins, or anything else. Before, wonder was a sense of babbling gratitude for a creator's munificence, or squittering terror at his ability to deliver shock and awe. Now, alone, we must consider what our Godless wonder might be for. It cannot be just itself, only purer and truer. It must have some function, some biological usefulness, some practical, life-saving or life-prolonging purpose. Perhaps it is there to help us look for somewhere else to live against the day when we have irremediably trashed our own planet. But in any case, how can reductiveness not reduce?

A question, and a paradox. Our history has seen the gradual if bumpy rise of individualism: from the animal herd, from the slave society, from the mass of uneducated units bossed by priest and king, to looser groups in which the individual has greater rights and freedoms—the right to pursue happiness, private thought, self-fulfilment, self-indulgence. At the same time, as we throw off the rules of priest and king, as science helps us understand the truer terms and conditions on which we live, as our individualism expresses itself in grosser and more selfish ways (what is freedom for if not for that?), we also discover that this individuality, or illusion of individuality, is less than we imagined. We discover, to our surprise, that as Dawkins memorably puts it, we are 'survival machines—robot vehicles blindly programmed to preserve the selfish molecules known as genes'. The paradox is that individualism—the triumph of free-thinking artists and scientists—has led us to a state of self-awareness in which we can now view ourselves as units of genetic obedience. My adolescent notion of self-construction—that vaguely, Englishly, existentialist ego-hope of autonomy—could not have been further from the truth. I thought the burdensome process of growing up ended with a man standing by himself at last—*homo erectus* at full height, *sapiens* in full wisdom—a fellow now cracking the whip on his own account. This image (and I melodramatize it a little—such realizations and self-projections were always insecure and provisional) must be replaced by the sense that, far from having a whip to crack, I am the very tip of the whip itself, and that what is cracking me is a long and inevitable plait of genetic material which cannot be shrugged or fought off. My 'individuality' may still be felt, and genetically provable; but it may be the very opposite of the achievement I once took it for.

That is the paradox; here is the question. We grow up; we trade in our old sense of wonder for a new one—wonder at the blind and fortuitous process which has blindly and fortuitously produced us; we don't feel depressed by this, as some might, but 'elated' as Dawkins himself is; we enjoy the things which Dawkins lists as making life worth living—music, poetry, sex, love (and

113

science)—while also perhaps practising the humorous resignation advocated by Somerset Maugham. We do all this, and do we get any better at dying? Will you die better, shall I die better, will Richard Dawkins die better than our genetic ancestors hundreds or thousands of years ago? Dawkins has expressed the hope that 'When I am dying, I should like my life taken out under general anaesthetic, exactly as if it were a diseased appendix.' Clear enough, if illegal; yet death has an obstinate way of denying us the solutions we imagine for ourselves.

From a medical point of view—and depending where we live on the planet—we may well die better, and less caninely. Factor that out. Also factor out those things we might confuse with dying well: for instance, having no regret or remorse. If we have enjoyed our time, made provision for our dependants, and have little to feel sadness over, then looking back on life will be more bearable. But that's a different matter from looking forwards to what is immediately ahead: total extinction. Are we going to get any better at that?

I don't see why we should. I don't see why our cleverness or self-awareness should make things better rather than worse. Why should those genes in whose silent servitude we dwell spare us any terror? Why would it be in their interest? We presumably fear death not just for its own sake but because it is useful to us—or useful to our selfish genes, which will not get passed on if we fail to fear death enough, if we fall for that camouflaged-tiger trick as others used to, or eat that bitter plant which our taste buds have taught us (or rather, been taught themselves, by mortal trial and error) to avoid. What conceivable use or advantage might our deathbed comfort be to these new masters?

* * *

'One must be equal to one's destiny, that's to say, impassive like it. By dint of saying "That is so! That is so!" and of gazing down into the black pit at one's feet, one remains calm.' Flaubert's experience of pit-gazing began early. His father was a hospital surgeon; the family lived above the shop; Achille Flaubert would often come straight from his operating table to his dining table. The boy Gustave would climb a trellis and peer in at his father instructing medical students how to dissect corpses. He saw bodies covered in flies, and students casually resting their lit cigars on the limbs and trunks they were hacking away at. Achille would glance up, spot his son's face at the window, and wave him away with his scalpel. A late-Romantic morbidity infected the adolescent Gustave; but he never lost the realist's need, and demand, to look where others averted their gaze. It was a human duty as well as a writerly one.

In April 1848, when Flaubert was twenty-six, the literary friend of his youth, Alfred Le Poittevin, died. In a private memorandum which has only just come to light, Flaubert recorded how he looked at this death, and looked at himself looking at it. He kept a vigil over his dead friend for two consecutive nights; he cut a lock of hair for Le Poittevin's young widow; he helped wrap the body in its shroud; he smelt the stink of decomposition. When the undertakers arrived with the coffin, he kissed his friend on the temple. A decade later, he still remembered that moment: 'Once you have kissed a corpse on the forehead there always remains something on your lips, a distant bitterness, an aftertaste of the void that nothing will efface.'

This was not my experience after kissing my mother's forehead; but I was by then twice Flaubert's age, and perhaps the taste of bitterness was on my lips already. Twenty-one years after Le Poittevin's death, Louis Bouilhet, the literary friend of Flaubert's maturity, died; again, he composed a private memorandum describing his actions and reactions. He was in Paris when he heard the news; he returned to Rouen; he went to Bouilhet's house and embraced the dead poet's common-law wife. You might think—if pit-gazing worked—that the previous experience would make this one more bearable. But Flaubert found that he could not bear to see, watch over, embrace, wrap or kiss the friend who had been so close that he once called him 'my left testicle'. He spent the night in the garden, sleeping a couple of hours on the ground; and he shunned his friend's presence until the closed coffin was brought out of the house. In the memorandum, he specifically compared his ability to confront the two deaths: 'I did not dare see him! I feel weaker than I did twenty years ago . . . I lack any internal toughness. I feel *worn out*.' Pit-gazing for Flaubert induced not calm, but nervous exhaustion.

*   *   *

When I was translating Daudet's notes on dying,

116

two friends separately suggested that it must be depressing work. Not at all: I found this example of proper, adult pit-gazing—the exact glance, the exact word, the refusal either to aggrandize or to trivialize death—exhilarating. When, at the age of fifty-eight, I published a collection of short stories dealing with the less serene aspects of old age, I found myself being asked if I wasn't being premature in addressing such matters. When I showed the first fifty pages of this book to my close (and close-reading) friend H., she asked, concernedly, 'Does it help?'

Ah, the therapeuto-autobiographical fallacy. However well meant, it irritates me as much as a hypothetical want of the dead does my brother. Something bad happens in your life—or, in the case of death, is slated to happen; you write about it; and you feel better about that bad thing. In very small, local circumstances, I can imagine this applying. Jules Renard, *Journal*, 26 September 1903: 'The beauty of literature. I lose a cow. I write about its death, and this brings me in enough to buy another cow.' But does it work in any wider sense? Perhaps with certain kinds of autobiography: you have a painful childhood, nobody loves you, you write about it, the book is a success, you make lots of money, and people love you. A tragedy with a happy ending! (Though for every such Hollywood moment, there must be a few which go: you have a painful childhood, nobody loves you, you write about it, the book is unpublishable, and still nobody loves you.) But with fiction, or any other transformative art? I don't see why it should, or why the artist should want it to. Brahms described his late piano

117

intermezzi as 'the lullabies of all my tears'. But we don't believe they worked for him as a handkerchief. Nor does writing about death either diminish or increase my fear of it. Though when I am roared awake in the enveloping and predictive darkness, I try to fool myself that there is at least one temporary advantage. This isn't just another routine bout of *timor mortis*, I say to myself. This is research for your book.

Flaubert said: 'Everything must be learned, from speaking to dying.' But we don't get much practice at the latter. We have also become more sceptical about exemplary deaths of the kind Montaigne enumerated: scenes in which dignity, courage and concern for others are displayed, consoling last words uttered, and the sombre action unfolds without farcical interruption. Daudet, for instance, died at his own dinner table, surrounded by his family. He took a few spoonfuls of soup, and was chatting away happily about the play he was working on, when the death rattle was heard and he fell back in his chair. That was the official version, and it sounds close to his friend Zola's definition of *une belle mort*—to be crushed suddenly, like an insect beneath a giant finger. And it is true as far as it goes. But the obituarists did not record what happened immediately afterwards. Two doctors had been summoned, and for an hour and a half—*an hour and a half*—they attempted artificial respiration by the then fashionable method of rhythmical traction of the tongue. When this unsurprisingly failed to work, they switched, with no greater success, to a primitive form of electrical defibrillation.

I suppose there is some rough professional irony

118

here—the *langue* being what made Daudet's name, and the *langue* being what the doctors yanked on when attempting to save him. Perhaps he might (just) have appreciated it. I suppose that up to the moment he died, it was a good death—apart from having been preceded by the torments of tertiary syphilis, of course. George Sand died simply, lucidly, encouragingly, in the pastoral peace of her house at Nohant, while looking out over trees she had planted herself many years previously. That was a good death, too—apart from its being preceded by the pain of incurable cancer. I am more inclined to believe in the good death of Georges Braque, mainly because it sounds as his art looks (though this might be a sentimentalism). His dying was characterized by 'a calm achieved through self-mastery rather than apathy'. Towards the end, as he was slipping in and out of consciousness, he called for his palette; and he died 'without suffering, calmly, his gaze fixed until the last moment on the trees in his garden, the highest branches of which were visible from the great windows of his studio'.

I do not expect such luck, or such calmness. Looking out at trees you have planted yourself? I have only planted a fig and a gooseberry bush, neither of which is visible from the bedroom window. Calling for your palette? I trust that I shall be disobeyed if, in my last moments, I ask for my electric typewriter, an IBM 196c of such weight that I doubt my wife could lift it. I imagine I shall die rather as my father did, in hospital, in the middle of the night. I expect that a nurse or doctor will say that I just 'slipped away', and that someone was with me at the end, whether or not this will

119

have been the case. I expect my departure to have been preceded by severe pain, fear, and exasperation at the imprecise or euphemistic use of language around me. I hope that whoever is offered the binliner of my clothes does not discover in it a pair of unworn, brown, Velcro-fastened slippers. Perhaps my trousers will inhabit some park bench or grim hostel for a season or two after my death.

I find this in my diary, written twenty and more years ago:

> People say of death, 'There's nothing to be
> frightened of.' They say it quickly, casually.
> Now let's say it again, slowly, with
> re-emphasis. 'There's NOTHING to be
> frightened of.'

Jules Renard: 'The word that is most true, most exact, most filled with meaning, is the word "nothing".'

*   *   *

When we let the mind roam to the circumstances of our own death, there is usually a magnetic pull towards the worst case or the best case. My worst imaginings usually involve enclosure, water, and a period of time in which to endure the certainty of coming extinction. There is, for instance, the overturned-ferry scenario: the air pocket, darkness, slowly rising water, screaming fellow mortals, and the competition for breath. Then there is the solitary version of this: bundled into the boot of a car (perhaps your own) while your captors drive from one cashpoint to another, and then, when your credit card is finally refused, the giddying lurch from river bank or sea cliff, the splash, and the greedy glug of water coming for you. Or the analogous, if more improbable, wildlife version of this: being taken by a crocodile, dragged under water, losing consciousness and then regaining it on a shelf above the waterline in the croc's lair, and realizing that you have just become the waiting contents of the beast's larder. (And such things happen, in case you doubt.)

The best case, in my fantasizing, used to turn on a medical diagnosis which left me just enough time, and just enough lucidity, in which to write that last book—the one which would contain all my thoughts about death. Although I didn't know if it was going to be fiction or non-fiction, I had the first line planned and noted many years ago: 'Let's get this death thing straight.' But what kind of doctor is going to give you the diagnosis that suits your literary requirements? 'I'm afraid there's good news and bad news.' 'Tell me straight, Doc, I need to know. How long?' 'How long? I'd say about 200 pages. 250 if you're lucky, or work fast.'

No, it isn't going to happen like that, so it's best to get the book done before the diagnosis. Of course, there is a third possibility (which I have been entertaining since page one): you start the book, you are nearly halfway through—just about here, for instance—and then you get the diagnosis! Maybe the narrative is flagging a bit by this stage, so enter the chest pain, the fainting fit, the X-rays, the CAT scan . . . Would that, I wonder, look a little contrived? (The readers' group confers. 'Oh, I always thought he was going to die at the end—

well, after the end, didn't you?' 'No, I thought he might be bluffing. I wasn't sure he was even ill. I thought it might be, what do you call it, meta-fiction?')

It probably isn't going to happen this way either. When we imagine our own dying, whether best or worst case, we tend to imagine dying lucidly, dying while aware (all too aware) of what is going on, able to express ourselves and understand others. How successfully can we imagine dying—and the long lead-up to the event itself—in a state of incoherence and misunderstanding? With the same original pain and fear, of course, but now with an added layer of confusion. Not knowing quite who anybody is, not knowing who is alive or dead, not knowing where you are. (But just as shit-scared anyway.) I remember visiting an elderly and demented friend in hospital. She would turn to me, and in her soft, rather genteel voice which I had once much loved, would say things like, 'I do think you will be remembered as one of the worst criminals in history.' Then a nurse might walk past, and her mood change swiftly. 'Of course,' she would assure me, 'the maids here are frightfully good.' Sometimes I would let such remarks pass (for her sake, for my sake), sometimes (for her sake, for my sake) correct them. 'Actually, they're nurses.' My friend would give a cunning look expressing surprise at my naivety. 'Some of them are,' she conceded. 'But *most* of them are maids.'

My father had a series of strokes which reduced him, over the years, from an erect man of my height, first to a figure hunched over a Zimmer, his head cocked in that awkward angled lift the frame compels, and then to the half-humiliated occupant

122

of a wheelchair. When the social services came to assess his level of incapacity, they explained that he would need, and they would pay for, a handrail to help him from bed to door. My mother overrode the suggestion: 'Not having that ugly thing in the room.' She maintained that it would spoil the bungalow's decor; but her refusal was, I now suspect, an oblique way of denying what had happened—and what might await her too. One thing she did allow—to my surprise—was an alteration to Dad's armchair. This was the sturdy green high-backed Parker Knoll in which Grandpa used to read his *Daily Express*, and mistake Grandma's stomach for the telephone. Now, its legs were extended with metal sheaths, so that Dad could get in and out more easily.

This slow physical crumbling was paralleled by an erosion of my father's speech: of his articulation, and memory for words. (He had been a French teacher, and now his *langue* was going.) I see again the shuffle-and-push of his slow Zimmer progress from lounge to front door when he came to see me off: a stretch of time which felt endless, and where every conversational topic sounded utterly false. I would pretend to linger, look searchingly at a jug of flowers on the sideboard, or pause to observe again some knick-knack I had always disliked. Eventually, the three of us would make it to the front mat. On one occasion, my father's farewell words were, 'And next time, bring . . . bring . . .' Then he got stuck. I didn't know whether to wait, or, with a pretence of understanding, nod agreeingly. But my mother said firmly, 'Bring who?'—as if my father's mental fallibility were something correctible by the right

123

sort of questioning. 'Bring . . . bring . . .' His expression was now one of furious frustration at his own brain. 'Bring *who*?' my mother repeated. By now the answer was so obvious and unnecessary that I wanted to run out of the door, jump in the car and drive away. Suddenly, Dad found a way round his aphasia. 'Bring . . . Julian's wife.' Ah, relief. But not quite. My mother, to my ear not sounding all that sympathetic, said, 'Oh, you mean P.'—thus turning my schoolmaster father into some test-failing schoolboy.

He would stand at the front door, crouched over his frame with its stupid, empty metal basket clipped to the handlebars; his head would be tilted, as if he were trying to prevent the action of gravity on his lower jaw. I would say goodbye and set off the dozen yards or so to my car, whereupon—inevitably—my mother would 'remember' something, come at a trot down the little curve of tarmac (her hurried gait emphasizing my father's immobility) and tap on the window. I would lower it reluctantly, guessing what she was going to say. 'What do you think? He's deteriorated, hasn't he?' I would look past my mother to my father, who knew we were talking about him, and knew that I knew that he knew. 'No,' I would usually reply, out of loyalty to Dad, because the only alternative would have been to bellow, 'He's had a fucking stroke, Ma, what do you expect—volleyball?' But she would judge my diplomatic reply proof of inattention, and as I slowly let out the clutch and inched my way down the tarmac, would hold on to the window and give examples of the deterioration I had failed to observe.

I do not mean that she was unkind to him; but

124

her way of dealing with my father's condition was to stress her own inconvenience and suffering, while implying that his suffering was a little more his own fault than people realized. 'Of course, when he falls down, he panics,' she would complain. 'Well, I can't lift him, so I have to get someone from the village to help. But he panics because he can't get up.' Black mark. Then there was the matter of my father's pedalling machine, which the hospital physiotherapist had provided. He was supposed to sit in his Parker Knoll and pump away at this shiny little bicycle remnant. Whether mock-cycling in an armchair struck my father as absurd, or whether he simply decided that it wouldn't make the slightest difference to his condition, I don't know. 'He's so stubborn,' my mother would complain.

Of course, when it came to her turn, she was just as stubborn. Her initial stroke was far more immobilizing than Dad's first one: she was largely paralysed down her right side, and her speech was more damaged than his. She showed herself most coherent when in greatest rage at what had happened. With her good hand she would reach across and pick up her stricken arm. 'And of course,' she said, sounding for a moment exactly like her old self, 'this thing's *completely useless*.' This thing had let her down, rather as my father had. And then, exactly like Dad, she treated the physiotherapists with scepticism. 'They're pushing and pulling at me,' she would complain. When I told her they were pushing and pulling at her to help her recover, she replied, satirically, 'Yes, sir.' Yet she was admirably unflinching, and dismissive of what she saw as false morale-boosting. 'They tell

125

you to do something, and then they say, "Very good." It's so stupid, I *know* it isn't very good.' So she stopped cooperating. Her way of remaining herself was to mock professional optimism and decline the hypothetical recovery.

My niece C. went to visit her. I called to ask how it had gone, and how Ma was. 'Completely bonkers when I got there, but once we started talking about make-up, completely sane.' Suspecting the harshness of youth in my niece's assessment, I asked—perhaps a little stiffly—what form being 'bonkers' had taken. 'Oh, she was very angry with you. She said you'd stood her up three days running for tennis, and left her there on court.' OK, bonkers.

Not that my niece escaped censure. On one occasion she and I sat through twenty mysterious minutes of furious silence and stubborn avoidance of eye contact. Eventually, Ma turned to C. and said, 'You're a *proper monkey*, you are. But you do understand why I had to tear a strip off you, don't you?' Perhaps such dishing-out of fantastical blame gave her the illusion of control over her life. Blame which extended also to my brother, whose absence in France did not excuse or protect him. About two weeks after her first stroke, with her speech largely incomprehensible, we were discussing—or rather, I was telling her—how I would manage things while she was in hospital. I listed the people I could consult, adding that if there was any problem, I could always fall back on my brother's 'fine brain'. With struggling pauses between each word, our mother succeeded in putting together the flawless sentence: 'His fine brain doesn't think about anything but work.'

Despite months of stubborn non-cooperation in hospital, she recovered some of her speech, though none of her movement. Not being one to fool herself, she announced that she was incapable of returning to live in her bungalow. A staff nurse called Sally came to assess her ability to function in the nursing home C. and I were hoping to get her into. Ma claimed to have already inspected the place and found it 'pukka'; though I suspect that her 'visit' had been fabulated from reading a brochure. She told Staff Nurse Sally that she had decided to take her meals alone in her room: she couldn't eat with the other residents because she lacked the use of her right arm. 'Oh, don't be silly,' said the nurse. 'It doesn't matter.' My mother's reply was commanding: 'When I say it matters, *it matters*.' 'Have you ever been a teacher?' was Sally's canny riposte.

*   *   *

As a young man, I was terrified of flying. The book I would choose to read on a plane would be something I felt appropriate to have found on my corpse. I remember taking *Bouvard et Pécuchet* on a flight from Paris to London, deluding myself that after the inevitable crash a) there would be an identifiable body on which it might be found; b) that Flaubert in French paperback would survive impact and flames; c) that when recovered, it would still be grasped in my miraculously surviving (if perhaps severed) hand, a stiffened forefinger bookmarking a particularly admired passage, of which posterity would therefore take note. A likely story—and I was naturally too scared

127

during the flight to concentrate on a novel whose ironic truths in any case tend to be withheld from younger readers.

I was largely cured of my fear at Athens airport. I was in my mid-twenties, and had arrived in good time for my flight home—such good time (so eager to leave) that instead of being several hours early, I was a whole day and several hours early. My ticket could not be changed; I had no money to go back into the city and find a hotel; so I camped out at the airport. Again, I can remember the book—the crash companion—I had with me: a volume of Durrell's Alexandria Quartet. To kill time, I went up on to the viewing roof of the terminal building. From there, I watched plane after plane take off, plane after plane land. Some of them probably belonged to dodgy airlines and were crewed by drunks; but none of them crashed. I watched scores of planes not crash. And this visual, rather than statistical, demonstration of the safety of flying convinced me.

Could I try this trick again? If I looked on death more closely and more frequently—took a job as an undertaker's assistant or mortuary clerk—might I again, by the evidence of familiarity, lose my fear? Possibly. But there's a fallacy here, which my brother, as a philosopher, would quickly point out. (Although he would probably delete that descriptive phrase. When I showed him the opening pages of this book, he declined my assumption that it was 'as a philosopher' that he distrusted memory. 'Is it "as a philosopher" that I think all that? No more than it is "as a philosopher" that I think no second-hand car salesmen are reliable.' Perhaps; though even his

128

denial sounds to me like a philosopher's denial.) The fallacy is this: at Athens airport, I was watching thousands and thousands of passengers *not* die. At an undertaker's or mortuary, I would be confirming my worst suspicion: that the death rate for the human race is not a jot lower than one hundred per cent.

*　　*　　*

There's another flaw in that 'best-case' death scenario I was describing. Let's assume the doctor says you will live long enough and lucidly enough to complete your final book. Who wouldn't drag the work out as long as possible? Scheherazade never ran out of stories. 'Morphine drip?' 'Oh no, still quite a few chapters to go. The fact is, there's a lot more to say about death than I'd imagined . . .' And so your selfish wish to survive would act to the structural detriment of the book.

Some years ago, a British journalist, John Diamond, was diagnosed with cancer, and turned his condition into a weekly column. Rightly, he maintained the same perky tone that characterized the rest of his work; rightly, he admitted cowardice and panic alongside curiosity and occasional courage. His account sounded completely authentic: this was what living with cancer entailed; nor did being ill make you a different person, or stop you having rows with your wife. Like many other readers, I used to quietly urge him on from week to week. But after a year and more . . . well, a certain narrative expectation inevitably built up. Hey, miracle cure! Hey, I was just having you on! No, neither of those would

129

work as endings. Diamond had to die; and he duly, correctly (in narrative terms) did. Though—how can I put this?—a stern literary critic might complain that his story lacked compactness towards the end.

I may be dead by the time you are reading this sentence. In which case, any complaints about the book will not be answered. On the other hand, we may both be alive now (you by definition so), but you could die before me. Had you thought of that? Sorry to bring it up, but it is a possibility, at least for a few more years. In which case, my condolences to your nearest and dearest. And as the Friday lunchers were saying—or rather, never saying, though perhaps occasionally thinking—in that Hungarian restaurant: either I'll be going to your funeral, or you'll be coming to mine. Such has always been the case, of course; but this grimly unshiftable either/or takes on sharper definition in later years. In the matter of you and me—assuming I'm not already, definitively dead by the time you're reading this—you're more likely, actuarially, to see me out than the other way round. And there's still that other possibility—that I might die in the middle of writing this book. Which would be unsatisfactory for both of us— unless you were about to give up anyway, at exactly the point where the narrative breaks off. I might die in the middle of a sentence, even. Perhaps right in the middle of a wo

Just kidding. Though not entirely so. I've never written a book, except my first, without at some point considering that I might die before it was completed. This is all part of the superstition, the folklore, the mania of the business, the fetishistic

130

fuss. The right pencils, felt-tips, biros, notebooks, paper, typewriter: necessities which are also objective correlatives for the proper state of mind. This is created by putting aside all that might harmfully impinge, narrowing the focus until only what's important remains: me, you, the world and the book—and how to make it as good as it can possibly be. Reminding myself of mortality (or, more truthfully, mortality reminding me of itself) is a useful and necessary prod.

So is advice from those who have been there before. Instructions, epigrams, dicta pinned up either literally or metaphorically. Both William Styron and Philip Roth have worked beneath the Flaubertian self-reminder: 'Be regular and ordinary in your life, like a bourgeois, so that you may be violent and original in your work.' Perhaps you need to free your mind from the distraction of future critical response? Sibelius would be a help here—'Always remember that there is no city in Europe which contains a statue to a critic'— though my favourite comes from Ford Madox Ford: 'It is an easy job to say that an elephant, however good, is not a good warthog; for most criticism comes to that.' Many writers could benefit from that line of Jules Renard's: 'One could say of almost all works of literature that they are too long.' Further, and finally, they should expect to be misunderstood. On this, Sibelius again, with the gnomic and ironic instruction: 'Misunderstand me correctly.'

When I first began to write, I laid down for myself the rule—as part of the head-clearing, the focusing, the psychological primping and tamping—that I should write as if my parents were dead. This was not because I specifically wanted either to use or abuse them; rather, I didn't want to catch myself thinking of what might possibly offend or please them. (And in this, they were not just themselves, they were also standing for friends, colleagues, lovers, let alone warthog-describers.) The strange thing is, that though my parents are many years dead, I now need this rule more than ever.

Dying in the middle of a wo , or three-fifths of the way through a nov . My friend the nov ist Brian Moore used to fear this as well, though for an extra reason: 'Because some bastard will come along and finish it for you.' Here is a novelist's would-you-rather. Would you rather die in the middle of a book, and have some bastard finish it for you, or leave behind a work in progress that not a single bastard in the whole world was remotely interested in finishing? Moore died while at work on a novel about Rimbaud. An irony there: Rimbaud was one writer who made sure he wouldn't die in the middle of a stanza, two-thirds of the way through a *mo* , by abandoning literature half a lifetime before he died.

*   *   *

My mother, an only child who became the only woman in a household whose male members had little instinct for dominance, developed a solipsism which did not decrease with age. In widowhood, she became even more of a monologuist than in the days when some polite, loving and occasionally wry response could be elicited from the Parker Knoll. Inevitably, she became more of a repetitionist too. I was sitting with her one afternoon, my mind half elsewhere, when she took me aback with a new thought. She had been reflecting, she said, on the various forms of decrepitude that might await her, and wondering if she would rather go deaf or go blind. For a moment—naively—I imagined that she was asking my opinion, but she needed no extra input: deafness, she told me, would be her choice. An expression of solidarity with her father and her two sons? Not a bit of it. This was how she had argued the matter to herself: 'If I were blind, how would I do my nails?'

Death and dying generate a whole questionnaire of such would-you-rathers. For a start, would you rather know you were dying, or not know? Would you rather watch, or not watch? Aged thirty-eight, Jules Renard noted: 'Please, God, don't make me die too quickly! I shouldn't mind seeing how I die.' He wrote this on 24 January 1902, the second anniversary of the day he had travelled from Paris to Chitry to bury his brother Maurice—a brother transformed in a few silent minutes from a clerk of works complaining about the central heating system to a corpse with his head on a Paris telephone directory. A century later, the medical historian Roy Porter was asked to reflect on death: 'You know, I think it will be interesting to be conscious as one dies, because one must undergo the most extraordinary changes. Thinking, I'm dying now . . . I think I'd like to be fully conscious of it all. Because, you know, you'd just be missing out on something otherwise.' Such terminal curiosity is in a fine tradition. In 1777, the Swiss physiologist Albrecht von Haller was attended on his deathbed by a brother physician. Haller monitored his own pulse as it weakened, and died in character with the last words: 'My friend, the artery ceases to beat.' The following year, Voltaire similarly clung to his own pulse until the moment he slowly shook his head and, a few minutes later, died. An admirable death—with not a priest in sight—worthy of Montaigne's catalogue. Not that it impressed everyone. Mozart, then in Paris, wrote to his father, 'You probably already know that that godless arch-rogue Voltaire has died like a dog, like a beast—that's his reward!' Like a dog, indeed.

Would you rather fear death or not fear it? That sounds an easy one. But how about this: what if you never gave death a thought, lived your life as if there were no tomorrow (there isn't, by the way), took your pleasure, did your work, loved your family, and then, as you were finally obliged to admit your own mortality, discovered that this new awareness of the full stop at the end of the sentence meant that the whole preceding story now made no sense at all? That if you'd fully realized to begin with that you were going to die, and what that meant, you would have lived according to quite different principles?

And then there is the other way round, perhaps my own: what if you lived to sixty or seventy with half an eye on the ever-filling pit, and then, as death approached, you found that there was, after all, *nothing to be frightened of* ? What if you began to feel contentedly part of the great cycle of nature (please, take my carbon atoms)? What if those easeful metaphors suddenly, or even gradually, began to convince? The Anglo-Saxon poet compared human life to a bird flying from

134

darkness into a brightly lit banqueting hall, and then flying out into the dark on the farther side: perhaps this image will calm one's pang at being human and being mortal. I can't say it works for me yet. It's pretty enough, but the pedantic side of me keeps wanting to point out that any right-thinking bird flying into a warm banqueting hall would perch on the rafters as long as it bloody well could, rather than head straight out again. Moreover, the bird, in its pre- and post-existence on either side of the carousing hall, is at least still *flying*, which is more than can or will be said for us.

When I first came to mortal awareness, it was simple: you were alive, then you were dead, and bid the Deity farewell: Godbye. But who can tell how age will affect us? When I was a young journalist, I interviewed the novelist William Gerhardie. He was then in his eighties, frail and bed-bound; death was not far away. At one point he picked up from his bedside table an anthology about immortality, and showed me a heavily underlined account of an out-of-body experience. This, he explained, was identical to one he had himself undergone as a soldier in the First World War. 'I believe in resurrection,' he said simply. 'I believe in immortality. Do you believe in immortality?' I was awkwardly silent (and failed to remember my own out-of-body experience as a schoolboy). 'No, well, nor did I at your age,' he went on sympathetically. 'But I do now.'

So perhaps I shall change my mind (though I doubt it). What's more likely is that the choice ahead will blur. Life versus Death becomes, as Montaigne pointed out, Old Age versus Death. What you—I—will be clinging on to is not a few

135

more minutes in a warm baronial hall with the smell of roast chicken and the cheery noise of fife and drum, not a few more days and hours of real living, but a few more days and hours of breathing decrepitude, mind gone, muscles wasted, bladder leaking. 'What makes you think the thing you have at the moment is life?' as the hard-hearted Caesar said to his former legionary. And yet—and worse—imagine this failing body now even more fearful of oblivion than when it was healthy and strong and could divert itself from contemplation of that oblivion by physical and mental activity, by social usefulness and the company of friends. A body, the compartments of whose mind now begin shutting down one by one, lucidity gone, speech gone, recognition of friends gone, memory gone, replaced by a fantasy world of proper monkeys and unreliable tennis partners. All that is left—the last bit of the engine still with stoking power—is the compartment that makes us fear death. Yes, that little bit of brain activity will keep going strong, puffing out the panic, sending the chill and the terror coursing through the system. They will give you morphine for your pain—and then, perhaps, a little more than you actually need, and then the necessary excess—but there is nothing they can give you to stop this grim cluster of brain cells scaring you shitless (or, perhaps, the opposite) until the very end. Then we might find ourselves regretting that we ever thought, with Renard, 'Please, God, don't make me die too quickly.'

The writer and director Jonathan Miller trained as a doctor. Despite having dissected the rigid and handled the waxily pliable from whom the breath of life had only just departed, he was in his forties before, as he put it, 'I began to think, well, hang on—this is something which I'm going to be doing some time.' Interviewed in his mid-fifties, he professed himself still unalarmed by the long-term consequences: 'The fear of just not existing—no, I don't have that at all.' What he admitted to instead was a fear of the deathbed, and what goes with it: agony, delirium, torturing hallucinations, and the lamenting family preparing for his departure. That seems a pretty fair line-up to me, though not as an alternative, merely as an add-on to the proper, grown-up fear of 'just not existing'.

Miller follows Freud in that he 'cannot actually conceive, can't make sense of the notion of total annihilation'. And so, it seems, his capacity for terror is transferred first on to the process and humiliations of dying, and secondly on to various possible states of semi-being or almost-being which might occur around or after death. He fears 'this residual consciousness which is not quite snuffed out', and imagines an out-of-body experience in which he is watching his own funeral: 'or, in fact, not watching it, but being immobilized inside the coffin'. I can picture this new tweak on that old fear of being buried alive, but fail to find it especially sinister. If there were a residual consciousness watching our own funeral and rippling around inside our coffin, why should it necessarily be one that fears enclosure?

Most of us have thought, or said, of death, 'Well, we shall find out'—while recognizing the near certainty that we shall never 'find out' the negative we expect. A lingering consciousness might be there to give us the answer. It might be a gentle way of saying No. It might hoveringly watch the

137

burial or cremation, farewell this pesky body of ours and the life that has been in it, and (assuming that it is still somehow attached to or representative of the self) allow 'us' to feel that what is happening is appropriate. It might produce a calming sensation, a laying-to-rest, a consolation, a sweet goodnight, an ontological nightcap.

I have a Swedish friend, K., who once, very gently and considerately, whispered to a mutual friend who had been too long dying of cancer, 'It's time to let go.' I have always teased her that I shall know things are really bad for me when I hear this lightly inflected voice in my ear, and those much-rehearsed words of advice. Perhaps the residual consciousness that Miller fears will turn out to be something useful and benevolent, a settling of accounts delivered in a soft Swedish accent.

*   *   *

That medieval bird flies from darkness into a lighted hall and back out again. One of the oh-so-sensible arguments against death-anxiety goes like this: if we don't fear and hate the eternity of time leading up to our brief moment of illuminated life, why therefore should we feel differently about the second spell of darkness? *Because*, of course, during that first spell of darkness, the universe—or at least, a very, very insignificant part of it—was leading up to the creation of something of decided interest, plaiting its genes appropriately and working its way through a succession of apelike, growling, tool-handling ancestors until such time as it gathered itself and spat out the three generations of schoolteachers who then made . . .

138

me. So that darkness had some purpose—at least, from my solipsistic point of view; whereas the second darkness has absolutely nothing to be said for it.

It could, I suppose, be worse. It almost always can—which is some mild consolation. We might fear the prenatal abyss as well as the post-mortal one. Odd, but not impossible. Nabokov in his autobiography describes a 'chronophobiac' who experienced panic on being shown home movies of the world in the months before he was born: the house he would inhabit, his mother-to-be leaning out of a window, an empty pram awaiting its occupant. Most of us would be unalarmed, indeed cheered, by all this; the chronophobiac saw only a world in which he did not exist, an acreage of himlessness. Nor was it any consolation that such an absence was mobilizing itself irresistibly to produce his future presence. Whether this phobia reduced his level of post-mortal anxiety, or on the other hand doubled it, Nabokov does not relate.

A more sophisticated version of the bird-in-hall argument comes from Richard Dawkins. We are indeed all going to die, and death is absolute and God a delusion, but even so, that makes us the lucky ones. Most 'people'—the vast majority of potential people—don't even get born, and their numbers are greater than all the grains of sand in all the deserts of Araby. 'The set of possible people allowed by our DNA . . . massively exceeds the set of actual people. In the teeth of these stupefying odds it is you and I, in our ordinariness, that are here.' Why do I find this such thin consolation? No, worse than that, such a disconsolation? Because look at all the evolutionary work, all the unrecorded pieces of cosmic luck, all the decision-making, all the generations of family care, all the thissing-and-thatting which have ended up producing me and my uniqueness. My ordinariness, too, and yours, and that of Richard Dawkins, yet a unique ordinariness, a staggeringly against-the-odds ordinariness. This makes it harder, not easier, to give a shrug and say philosophically, Oh well, might never have been here anyway, so may as well get on enjoying this little window of opportunity not granted to others. But then it's also hard, unless you're a biologist, to think of those trillions of unborn, genetically hypothetical others as 'potential people'. I have no difficulty imagining a stillborn or aborted baby as a potential person, but all those possible combinations that never came to pass? My human sympathy can only go so far, I'm afraid—the sands of Araby are beyond me.

So I cannot be philosophical. Are philosophers philosophical? Were the Laconians truly laconic, the Spartans really spartan? Just in comparative terms, I expect. Apart from my brother, the only philosopher I know well is my death-haunted friend G., who as a four-year-old beat me to mortal awareness by a decade. He and I once had a long exchange about free will. Like everyone, I have always—an amateur in and of my own life—assumed that I had free will, and always, to my own mind, behaved as if I did. Professionally, G. explained to me my delusion. He pointed out that though we might think we are free in acting as we want, we cannot determine what it is that we want (and if we deliberately decide to 'want to want' something, there is the usual problem of regression to a primal 'want'). At some point your wants must just be givens: the result of inheritance and upbringing. Therefore, the idea of anyone having true and ultimate responsibility for their acts is untenable; at most we can have a temporary, surface responsibility—and even that, with time, will be shown to be mistaken. G. might well have quoted to me Einstein's conclusion that 'a Being endowed with higher insight and more perfect intelligence, watching man and his doings, would smile about man's illusion that he was acting according to his own free will'.

At a certain point, I admitted that I had lost the argument, though carried on behaving in exactly the same way (which, on reflection, might have been a useful proof of G.'s point). G. consoled me by remarking that though, in his philosophical opinion, we cannot possibly have free will, such knowledge doesn't make the slightest practical difference to how we do, or even should, behave. And so I have continued to rely on this delusionary mental construct to help me along the mortal path to that place where no will of mine, free or fettered, will ever operate again.

There is What We Know (or think we know) To Be The Case, there is What We Believe To Be The Case (on the assurance of others whom we trust), and then there is How We Behave. Christian morality still loosely governs Britain, though congregations dwindle and church buildings make their inexorable transition to historic monuments—setting off in some 'a hunger to be serious'—and loft apartments. That sway extends to me too: my sense of morality is influenced by Christian teaching (or, more exactly, pre-Christian

141

tribal behaviour codified by the religion); and the God I don't believe in yet miss is naturally the Christian God of Western Europe and non-fundamentalist America. I don't miss Allah or Buddha, any more than I miss Odin or Zeus. And I miss the New Testament God rather than the Old Testament one. I miss the God that inspired Italian painting and French stained glass, German music and English chapter houses, and those tumbledown heaps of stone on Celtic headlands which were once symbolic beacons in the darkness and the storm. I also realize that this God I am missing, this inspirer of artworks, will seem to some just as much an irrelevant self-indulgence as the much-claimed 'own personal idea of God' I was deriding a while ago. Further, if any God did exist, He might very well find such decorative celebration of His existence both trivial and vainglorious, a matter for divine indifference if not retribution. He might think Fra Angelico cutesy, and Gothic cathedrals blustering attempts to impress Him by a creation which had quite failed to guess how He preferred to be worshipped.

*   *   *

My agnostic and atheistic friends are indistinguishable from my professedly religious ones in honesty, generosity, integrity and fidelity—or their opposites. Is this a victory for them, I wonder, or for us? When we are young, we think we are inventing the world as we are inventing ourselves; later, we discover how much the past holds us, and always did. I escaped what seemed to me the decent dullness of my family, only to find,

142

as I grow older, that my resemblance to my dead father strikes me more and more. There is the angle I sit at a table, the hang of my jaw, the incipient baldness pattern, and a particular kind of polite laugh I emit when not really amused: these (and doubtless much else that I fail to pick up) are genetic replicas and definitely not expressions of free will. My brother finds the same: he talks more and more like our father, using the same slang and half-finished sentences—he catches himself 'sounding just like him, and even shuffling in my slippers the way he used to'. He has also started to dream about Dad—after sixty years in which neither parent intruded upon his sleep.

Grandma, in her dementia, believed my mother was a sister of hers who had been dead for fifty years. My mother, in turn, welcomed back all the relatives she had known in childhood, come to express concern for her. In time, our family will come for my brother and for me (only please don't send my mother). But did the past ever really relax its grasp? We live broadly according to the tenets of a religion we no longer believe in. We live as if we are creatures of pure free will when philosophers and evolutionary biologists tell us this is largely a fiction. We live as if the memory were a well-built and efficiently staffed left-luggage office. We live as if the soul—or spirit, or individuality, or personality—were an identifiable and locatable entity rather than a story the brain tells itself. We live as if nature and nurture were equal parents when the evidence suggests that nature has both the whip hand and the whip.

Will such knowledge sink in? How long will it take? Some scientists think we shall never entirely

143

decipher the mysteries of consciousness because all we can use to understand the brain is the brain itself. Perhaps we shall never abandon the illusion of free will because it would take an act of the free will we don't have to abandon our belief in it. We shall go on living as if we are the full arbiters of our every decision. (The various adjustments of grammar and sense that I made to that last sentence, both immediately in the writing and after subsequent time and thought—how can 'I' not believe that 'I' made them? How can I believe that those words, and this parenthesis which follows them, and every elaboration I make within it, and the occasional misytpings, and the next word, whether completed or abandoned-halfway-through-as-I-have-second-thoughts-about-it and left as a wo , are not emanations of a coherent self making literary decisions by a process of free will? I cannot get my head round this not being the case.)

Perhaps it will be easier for you, or if not you, the generations born after you are dead. Perhaps I—and you—will seem to them like the 'old-type *natural* fouled-up guys' (and gals) of Larkin's poem. Perhaps they will regard as quaint and complacent the half-assumed, half-worked-out morality by which you and I seem to think we live. When religion first began to collapse in Europe— when 'godless arch-rogues' like Voltaire were at work—there was a natural apprehension about where morality was to come from. In a dangerously ungoverned world, every village might produce its Casanova, its Marquis de Sade, its Bluebeard. There were philosophers who, while refuting Christianity to their own satisfaction and that

144

of their intellectual circle, believed that the knowledge should be kept from peasant and potboy, lest the social structure collapse and the servant problem get completely out of hand.

But Europe stumbled on nonetheless. And if the dilemma now seems to pose itself in an even sharper form—what is the meaning of my actions in an empty universe where even more certainties have been undermined? why behave well? why not be selfish and greedy and blame it all on DNA?— the anthropologists and evolutionary biologists are able to offer comfort (if not to the faithful). Whatever religions may claim, we are set up— genetically programmed—to operate as social beings. Altruism is evolutionarily useful (ah!— there's your virtue—another illusion—gone); so whether or not there is a preacher with a promise of heaven and a threat of hellfire, individuals living in societies generally act in much the same way. Religion no more makes people behave better than it makes them behave worse—which might be a disappointment to the aristocratic atheist as much as to the believer.

*　　　*　　　*

When I was first studying French literature, I was puzzled by the concept of the *acte gratuit*. As I understood it, the notion went like this: in order to assert that we are now in charge of the universe, we must perform a spontaneous action for which there is no apparent motive or justification, and which lies outside conventional morality. The example that I recall, from Gide's *Les Caves du Vatican*, consisted of the gratuitous actor pushing a

145

complete stranger out of a moving train. Pure act, you see (and also, I now realize, a supposed proof of free will). I didn't see—or not enough. I found myself thinking about the unfortunate fellow dashed to death in the middle of the French countryside. Murder—or, perhaps, what bourgeois minds still mired in Christianity chose to call murder—as a means of demonstrating a philosophical point seemed too . . . too theoretical, too French, too repellent. Though my friend G. would say that the gratuitous actor would have been fooling himself (merely 'wanting to want' something). And I suppose that if his assertion of pure free will was a delusion, then so too was my reaction.

Are we like those Antarctic penguins, or are they like us? We go to the supermarket, they slither and wobble across miles of ice to the open sea in search of food. But here is one detail the wildlife programmes omit. When the penguins approach the water's edge, they begin to dawdle and loiter. They have reached food, but also danger; the sea contains fish, but also seals. Their long journey might result not in eating but getting eaten—in which case their offspring back in the penguin-huddle will starve to death and their own gene pool be terminated. So this is what the penguins do: they wait until one of their number, either more hungry or more anxious, gets to where the ice runs out, and is gazing down into the nutritious yet deadly ocean, and then, like a gang of commuters on a station platform, they nudge the imprudent bird into the sea. Hey, just testing! This is what those loveable, anthropomorphizable penguins are 'really like'. And if we are shocked, they are at least behaving more rationally—more usefully, even more altruistically—than the gratuitous actor of our own species pushing a man from a train.

That penguin doesn't have a would-you-rather. It is plunge or die—sometimes plunge and die. And some of our own would-you-rathers turn out to be equally hypothetical: ways of simplifying the unthinkable, pretending to control the uncontrollable. My mother considered quite seriously whether she would rather go deaf or go blind. Preferring one incapacity in advance seemed a superstitious method of ruling out the other. Except that, as it turned out, the 'choice' never arose. Her stroke affected neither her hearing nor her sight—and yet she never did her nails again in what was left of her life.

My brother hopes for Grandpa's death: felled by a stroke while gardening. (It was too early for Montaignean cabbage planting: he was trying to start his recalcitrant rotovator.) He fears the other family examples: Grandma's long-drawn-out senility, Dad's slow confinement and humiliation, Ma's half-self-aware delusions. But there are so many other possibilities to choose from—or to have chosen for us; so many different doors, even if they are all marked Exit. In this respect, death is multiple-choice not would-you-rather, and prodigally democratic in its options.

Stravinsky said: 'Gogol died screaming and Diaghilev died laughing, but Ravel died gradually. That is the worst.' He was right. There have been more violent artistic deaths, ones involving madness, terror, and banal absurdity (Webern shot dead by a GI after politely stepping on to the

147

porch to light a cigar), but few as cruel as that of Ravel. Worse, it had a strange prefiguration—a musical pre-echo—in the death of a French composer of the previous generation. Emmanuel Chabrier had succumbed to tertiary syphilis in 1894, the year after the Paris premiere of his only attempt at serious opera, *Gwendoline*. This piece— perhaps the only opera to be set in eighth-century Britain—had taken ten years to be staged; by which time Chabrier's disease was in its final phase, and his mind in never-never land. He sat in his box at the premiere, acknowledging the applause and smiling 'almost without knowing why'. Sometimes, he would forget the opera was his, and murmur to a neighbour, 'It's good, it's really very good.'

This story was well-known among the next generation of French composers. 'Horrible, isn't it?' Ravel used to say. 'To go to a performance of *Gwendoline* and not recognize your own music!' I remember my friend Dodie Smith, in great age, being asked the tender, encouraging question, 'Now, Dodie, you do remember that you used to be a famous playwright?' To which she replied, 'Yes, I *think* so'—in rather the tone I imagine my father using when he said to my mother, 'I think you're my wife.' A milliner might not recognize her own hat, a labourer his own speed bump, a writer her words, a painter his canvas; this is poignant enough. But there is extra pain, for those who witness it, when a composer fails to recognize his own notes.

Ravel died gradually—it took five years—and it was the worst. At first his decline from Pick's disease (a form of cerebral atrophy), though alarming, was non-specific. Words evaded him; motor skills went awry. He would grasp a fork by the wrong end; he became unable to sign his name; he forgot how to swim. When he went out to dinner, the housekeeper used to pin his address inside his coat as a precaution. But then the disease turned malignly particular and targeted Ravel the composer. He went to a recording of his string quartet, sat in the control room, offered various corrections and suggestions. After each movement had been recorded, he was asked if he wanted to listen through again, but declined. So the session went quickly, and the studio was pleased to have it all wrapped up in an afternoon. At the end, Ravel turned to the producer (and our guessing what he is going to say cannot lessen its impact): 'That was really very good. Remind me of the composer's name.' Another day, he went to a concert of his piano music. He sat through it with evident pleasure, but when the hall turned to acclaim him, he thought they were addressing the Italian colleague at his side, and so joined in their applause.

Ravel was taken to two leading French neurosurgeons. Another would-you-rather. The first judged his condition inoperable, and said that nature should be allowed to take its course. The second would have agreed had the patient been anyone but Ravel. However, if there were the slightest chance—for him a few more years, for us a little more music (which is 'the best way of digesting time') . . . And so the composer's skull was opened up, and the damage seen to be extensive and irreparable. Ten days later, his head still turbanned with hospital windings, Ravel died.

                    *   *   *

About twenty years ago I was asked if I would be
interviewed for a book about death. I declined on
writerly grounds: I didn't want to talk away stuff
which I might later need myself. I never read the
book when it came out: perhaps from a
superstitious—or rational—fear that one of its
contributors might have better expressed what I
was slowly working my way towards. Not long ago,
I began cautiously browsing the first chapter, an
interview with a certain 'Thomas'. Except that it
became instantly clear, after scarcely a page, that
this 'Thomas' was none other than my old death-
friend and free-will eradicator G.

   The primal would-you-rather about death
(though again one in which we don't have the
choice) is: ignorance or knowledge? Would you
prefer to receive *le réveil mortel* or to slumber on in
quilted blindness? This might seem an easy one:
if in doubt, opt for knowledge. But it's the
knowledge that causes the damage. As
'Thomas'/G. puts it: 'People who aren't afraid, I
think most of them just don't know what death
means . . . The standard theory of moral
philosophy is that it's a great evil for a person to be
suddenly cut off [in the flower of life]; but it seems
to me that the evil is knowing it's going to happen.
If it happened without your knowing, it wouldn't
matter.' Or at least, it would make us more akin to
those penguins: the dupe who toddles to the
water's edge and is shouldered in by a non-
gratuitous nudge may fear the seal but cannot
conceptualize the eternal consequences of the seal.

G. has no difficulty understanding, or believing, that human beings, in all their complexity, simply disappear for ever. It is all part of 'the profligacy of nature', like the micro-engineering of a mosquito. 'I think of it as nature sort of wildly over-shooting, splurging her gifts around; with human beings it's just more of the same kind of profligacy. These extraordinary brains and sensibilities, produced in millions, and then just thrown away, disappearing into eternity. I don't think man's a special case, I think the theory of evolution explains it all. It's a very beautiful theory, come to think of it, a marvellous and inspiring theory, though it has grim consequences for us.'

That's my man! And perhaps a sense of death is like a sense of humour. We all think the one we've got—or haven't got—is just about right, and appropriate to the proper understanding of life. It's everyone else who's out of step. I think my sense of death—which appears exaggerated to some of my friends—is quite proportionate. For me, death is the one appalling fact which defines life; unless you are constantly aware of it, you cannot begin to understand what life is about; unless you know and feel that the days of wine and roses are limited, that the wine will madeirize and the roses turn brown in their stinking water before all are thrown out for ever—including the jug— there is no context to such pleasures and interests as come your way on the road to the grave. But then I would say that, wouldn't I? My friend G. has a worse case of death, so I find his hauntedness excessive, not to say unhealthy (ah, the 'healthy' attitude to it all—where is that to be found?).

For G. our only defence against death—or

151

rather, against the danger of not being able to think about anything else—lies in 'the acquisition of worthwhile short-term worries'. He also consolingly quotes a study showing that fear of death drops off after the age of sixty. Well, I have got there before him, and can report that I am still waiting for the benefit. Only a couple of nights ago, there came again that alarmed and alarming moment, of being pitchforked back into consciousness, awake, alone, utterly alone, beating pillow with fist and shouting 'Oh no Oh No OH NO' in an endless wail, the horror of the moment—the minutes—overwhelming what might, to an objective witness, appear a shocking display of exhibitionist self-pity. An inarticulate one, too: for what sometimes shames me is the extraordinary lack of descriptive, or responsive, words that come out of my mouth. For God's sake, you're a *writer*, I say to myself. You do *words*. Can't you improve on that? Can't you face down death— well, you won't ever face it down, but can't you at least protest against it—more interestingly than this? We know that extreme physical pain drives out language; it's dispiriting to learn that mental pain does the same.

I once read that Zola was similarly startled from his bed like a projectile, launched from sleep into mortal terror. In my unpublished twenties, I used to think of him fraternally—and also with apprehension: if this stuff is still happening to a world-famous writer in his fifties, then there's not much chance of it getting better for me with the years. The novelist Elizabeth Jane Howard once told me that the three most death-haunted people she had ever known were her ex-husband Kingsley

Amis, Philip Larkin and John Betjeman. Tempting to conclude that it might be a writer thing, even a male writer thing. Amis used to maintain—comically, given his biography—that men were more sensitive than women.

I very much doubt it—both the male thing, and the writer thing. I used to believe, when I was 'just' a reader, that writers, because they wrote books where truth was found, because they described the world, because they saw into the human heart, because they grasped both the particular and the general and were able to re-create both in free yet structured forms, because they *understood*, must therefore be more sensitive—also less vain, less selfish—than other people. Then I became a writer, and started meeting other writers, and studied them, and concluded that the only difference between them and other people, the only, single way in which they were better, was that they were better writers. They might indeed be sensitive, perceptive, wise, generalizing and particularizing—but only at their desks and in their books. When they venture out into the world, they regularly behave as if they have left all their comprehension of human behaviour stuck in their typescripts. It's not just writers either. How wise are philosophers in their private lives?

'Not a whit wiser for being philosophers,' replies my brother. 'Worse, in their semi-public lives, far less wise than many other species of academics.' I remember once laying down Bertrand Russell's autobiography in a moment, not of disbelief, more a kind of appalled belief. This is how he describes the beginning of the end of his first marriage: 'I went out bicycling one afternoon, and suddenly, as

153

I was riding along a country road, I realized that I no longer loved Alys. I had no idea until this moment that my love for her was even lessening.' The only logical response to this, to its implications and manner of expression, would be: keep philosophers off bicycles. Or perhaps, keep philosophers out of marriage. Save them for discussing truth with God. I would want Russell on my side for that.

*   *   *

On my sixtieth birthday, I have lunch with T., one of my few religious friends. Or do I just mean faith-professing? Anyway, he is Catholic, wears a cross around his neck and, to the alarm of some past girlfriends, has a crucifix on the wall above his bed. Yes, that does sound more like religious than faith-professing, I know. T. is soon to marry R., who may or may not have the power to remove the crucifix. This being my birthday, I allow myself more interrogatory latitude, so ask why—apart from having been brought up as a Catholic—he believes in his God and his religion. He thinks for a while and replies, 'I believe because I want to believe.' Sounding perhaps a little like my brother, I counter with, 'If you said to me, "I love R. because I want to love R.", I wouldn't be too impressed, and nor would she.' As it is my birthday, T. refrains from throwing his drink over me.

When I return home, I find a small package pushed through the door. My first response is one of mild irritation, as I have specifically requested No Presents, and this particular friend, known for her giftliness, has been warned more than once on the subject. The package contains a lapel badge, battery driven, which flashes '60 TODAY' in blue and red points. What makes it not just acceptable, but the perfect present, turning my irritation into immediate good humour, are the manufacturer's words printed on the cardboard backing: 'WARNING: May Cause Interference With Pacemakers'.

One of the (possibly) 'worthwhile short-term worries' that follows my birthday is an American book tour. The arrival into New York—the transit from airport to city—involves passing one of the vastest cemeteries I have ever seen. I always half-enjoy this ritual memento mori, probably because I have never come to love New York. All the bustle in that most ever-bustling and narcissistic of cities will come to this; Manhattan mocked by the packed verticality of the headstones. In the past, I have merely noted the extent of the graveyards and the arithmetic of mortality (a job for the Accountancy God in whom Edmond de Goncourt couldn't believe). Now, for the first time, something else strikes me: that there is no one in them. These cemeteries are like the modern countryside: hectares of emptiness extending in every direction. And while you hardly expect a yokel with a scythe, a hedger-and-ditcher or a drystone-waller, the utter absence of human activity that agribusiness has brought to the former meadows and pastureland and hedgerowed fields is another kind of death: as if the pesticides have killed off all the farm workers as well. Similarly, in these Queens cemeteries, not a body—not a soul— stirs. Of course, it makes sense: the dead exbustlers are unvisited because the city's new replacement bustlers are much too busy bustling. But if there is anything more melancholy than a graveyard, it is an unvisited graveyard.

A few days later, on the train down to Washington, somewhere south of Trenton, I pass another cemetery. Though equally empty of the living, this one seems less grim: it straggles companionably alongside the tracks, and doesn't have the same feel of stained finality, of dead-and-doneness. Here, it seems, the dead are not so dead that they are forgotten, not so dead that they will not welcome new neighbours. And there, at the southern end of this unmenacing strip, is a cheery American moment: a sign proclaiming BRISTOL CEMETERY—LOTS AVAILABLE. It reads as if the pun on 'lots' is intended: come and join us, we have much more space than our rivals.

Lots available. Advertise, even in death—it's the American way. Whereas in Western Europe the old religion is in terminal decline, America remains a Christian country, and it makes sense that the creed still flourishes there. Christianity, which cleared up the old Jewish doctrinal dispute about whether or not there was life after death, which centralized personal immortality as a theological selling-point, is well suited to this can-do, reward-driven society. And since in America all tendencies are taken to the extreme, they have currently installed Extreme Christianity. Old Europe took a more leisurely approach to the final arrival of the Kingdom of Heaven—a long mouldering in the grave before resurrection and judgement, all in God's good time. America, and Extreme Christianity, likes to hurry things along.

Why shouldn't product delivery follow promised order sooner rather than later? Hence such fantasies as The Rapture, in which the righteous, while going about their daily business, are instantly taken up into Heaven, there to watch Jesus and the Antichrist duke it out down below on the battleground of planet Earth. The action-man, X-rated, disaster-movie version of the world's end.

Death followed by resurrection: the ultimate 'tragedy with a happy ending'. That phrase is routinely credited to one of those Hollywood directors who are assumed to be the source of all witticism; though I first came across it in Edith Wharton's autobiography *A Backward Glance*. There she ascribes the quip to her friend the novelist William Dean Howells, who offered it her as consolation after a first-night audience had failed to appreciate a theatrical adaptation of *The House of Mirth*. This would take the phrase back to 1906, before all those movie directors had started making wisecracks.

Wharton's success as a novelist is the more surprising—and the more admirable—given how little her view of life accorded with American hopefulness. She saw small evidence of redemption. She thought life a tragedy—or at best a grim comedy—with a tragic ending. Or, sometimes, just a drama with a dramatic ending. (Her friend Henry James defined life as 'a predicament before death'. And *his* friend Turgenev believed that 'the most interesting part of life is death'.)

Nor was Wharton seduced by the notion that life, whether tragic, comic or dramatic, is necessarily original. Our lack of originality is

157

something we usefully forget as we hunch over our—to us—ever-fascinating lives. My friend M., leaving his wife for a younger woman, used to complain, 'People tell me it's a cliché. But it doesn't feel like a cliché to me.' Yet it was, and is. As all our lives would prove, if we could see them from a greater distance—from the viewpoint, say, of that higher creature imagined by Einstein.

A biographer friend once suggested she take the slightly longer view and write my life. Her husband argued satirically that this would make a very short work as all my days were the same. 'Got up,' his version went. 'Wrote book. Went out, bought bottle of wine. Came home, cooked dinner. Drank wine.' I immediately endorsed this Brief Life. That will do as well as any other; as true, or as untrue as anything longer. Faulkner said that a writer's obituary should read: 'He wrote books, then he died.'

*　　　*　　　*

Shostakovich knew that making art from and about death was 'tantamount to wiping your sleeve on your nose'. When the sculptor Ilya Slonim did a portrait bust of him, the result failed to please the chairman of the Soviet Committee for the Arts. 'What we need,' the apparatchik told the sculptor (and by extension the composer) 'is an optimistic Shostakovich.' The composer loved repeating this oxymoron.

Apart from being a great brooder on death, he was also—in private, necessarily—a mocker of false hopes, state propaganda and artistic dross. One favourite target was a hit play of the 1930s by the long-forgotten regime creep Vsevolod Vishnevsky, of whom a Russian theatre scholar recently wrote: 'Even by the standards of our literary herbarium, this author was a very poisonous specimen.' Vishnevsky's play was set on board ship during the Bolshevik Revolution, and admirably portrayed the world as the authorities pretended it was. A young female commissar arrives to explain, and impose, the party line on a crew of anarchist sailors and old-school Russian officers. She is met with indifference, scepticism, and even assault: one of the sailors tries to rape her, whereupon she shoots him dead. Such an example of communist vigour and instant justice helps win over the sailors, who are soon moulded into an effective fighting unit. Deployed against the warmongering, God-worshipping, capitalistic Germans, they are somehow taken prisoner; but rise up heroically against their captors. During the struggle the inspirational commissar is killed, and dies urging the now fully Sovietized sailors, 'Always uphold . . . the high traditions . . . of the Red Fleet.' Curtain.

It wasn't the cartoonishly obedient plot of Vishnevsky's play that appealed to Shostakovich's sense of humour, but its title: *An Optimistic Tragedy*. Soviet Communism, Hollywood and organized religion were all closer than they knew, dream factories cranking out the same fantasy. 'Tragedy is tragedy', Shostakovich liked to repeat, 'and optimism has nothing to do with it.'

*   *   *

I have seen two dead people, and touched one of

them; but I've never seen anyone die, and may never do so, unless and until I see myself die. If death ceased to be talked about when it first really began to be feared, and then more so when we started to live longer, it has also gone off the agenda because it has ceased to be there, with us, in the house. Nowadays we make death as invisible as possible, and part of a process—from doctor to hospital to undertaker to crematorium—in which professionals and bureaucrats tell us what to do, up to the point where we are left to ourselves, survivors standing with a glass in our hands, amateurs learning how to mourn. But not so long ago the dying would have spent their final illness at home, expired among family, been washed and laid out by local women, watched over companionably for a night or two, then coffined up by the local undertaker. Like Jules Renard, we would have set off on foot behind a swaying, horse-drawn hearse for the cemetery, there to watch the coffin being lowered and a fat worm strutting at the grave's edge. We would have been more attending and more attentive. Better for them (though my brother will refer me to hypothetical wants of the dead), and probably better for us. The old system made for a statelier progressing from being alive to being dead—and from being dead to being lost from sight. The modern, rushing way is doubtless truer to how we see death nowadays—one minute you're alive, the next you're dead, and truly dead, so let's jump in the car and get it over with. (Whose car shall we take? Not the one she would have wanted.)

Stravinsky went to see Ravel's body before it was placed in the coffin. It was lying on a table

160

draped in black. Everything was black and white: black suit, white gloves, white hospital turban still encircling the head, black wrinkles on a very pale face, which had 'an expression of great majesty'. And there the grandeur of death ended. 'I went to the interment,' Stravinsky recorded. 'A lugubrious experience, these civil burials where everything is banned except protocol.' That was Paris, 1937. When Stravinsky's turn came, thirty-four years later, his body was flown from New York to Rome, then driven to Venice, where black and purple proclamations were posted up everywhere: THE CITY OF VENICE DOES HOMAGE TO THE REMAINS OF THE GREAT MUSICIAN IGOR STRAVINSKY, WHO IN A GESTURE OF EXQUISITE FRIENDSHIP ASKED TO BE BURIED IN THE CITY WHICH HE LOVED ABOVE ALL OTHERS. The Archimandrite of Venice conducted the Greek Orthodox service in the church of SS Giovanni et Paolo, then the coffin was carried past the Colleoni statue, and rowed by four gondoliers in a water-hearse out to the cemetery island of San Michele. There the Archimandrite and Stravinsky's widow dropped earth from their hands on to the coffin as it was lowered into the vault. Francis Steegmuller, the great Flaubert scholar, followed the day's events. He said that as the cortège processed from church to canal, with Venetians hanging from every window, the scene resembled 'one of Carpaccio's pageants'. More, much more than protocol.

Unless and until I see myself die. Would you rather be conscious of your dying, or unconscious of it? (There is a third—and highly popular—option: being deluded into the belief that you are

161

on the way to recovery.) But be careful what you wish for. Roy Porter wanted to be fully conscious: 'Because, you know, you'd just be missing out on something otherwise.' He went on: 'Clearly, one doesn't want excruciating pain and all the rest of it. But I think one would want to be with the people who mattered to one.' That is what Porter hoped for, and this is what he got. He was fifty-five, had recently taken early retirement, moved to Sussex with his fifth wife, and begun a life of freelance writing. He was bicycling home from his allotment (hard not to imagine the kind of country lane where Bertrand Russell had his marital aperçu) when he was suddenly blasted out by a heart attack, and died alone on the verge. Did he have any time to watch himself die? Did he know he was dying? Was his last thought an expectation that he would wake up in hospital? His final morning had been spent planting peas (perhaps the nearest we shall get to those French cabbages). And he was taking home a bunch of flowers, which were in a moment transformed into his own roadside tribute.

*   *   *

My grandfather said that remorse was the worst emotion life could contain. My mother did not understand the remark, and I do not know what events to attach it to.

Death and Remorse 1. When François Renard, ignoring his son's advice to take an enema, took a shotgun instead, and used a walking stick to fire both barrels and produce a 'dark place above the waist, like a small extinguished fire', Jules wrote: 'I do not reproach myself for not having loved him

162

enough. I reproach myself for not having understood him.'

Death and Remorse 2. Ever since I first read it, I have remained haunted by a line from Edmund Wilson's journals. Wilson died in 1972; the events referred to happened in 1932; I read about them in 1980, the year *The Thirties* was published.

At the beginning of that decade, Wilson had married, as his second wife, one Margaret Canby. She was a stocky, humorous-faced, upper-class woman with 'champagne tastes': Wilson was the first man she had known who had worked for a living. In the previous volume of his journals, *The Twenties*, Wilson had called her 'the best woman drinking companion I had ever known'. There he noted his first intention of marrying her, and also his sensible hesitation: 'Well though we got along, we did not have enough in common.' But marry they did, into an alcoholic companionship marked from the first by infidelity and temporary separations. If Wilson had his doubts about Canby, she had even stronger reservations about him. 'You're a cold fishy leprous person, Bunny Wilson,' she once told him—a remark which Wilson, with typical unsparingness, confided to his diary.

In September 1932 the couple, then married two years, were having one of their separations. Margaret Canby was in California, Wilson in New York. She went to a party in Santa Barbara wearing high heels. As she left, she tripped, fell down a flight of stone steps, broke her skull and died. The event produced, in Wilson's journal, forty-five pages of the most honest and self-flagellant mourning ever written. Wilson starts taking notes as his plane slowly hedge-hops west, as if the enforced literary act will help block off emotion. Over the next days, these jottings open out into an extraordinary monologue of homage, erotic remembrance, remorse and despair. 'A horrible night but even that seemed sweet in recollection,' he notes at one point. In California, Canby's mother urges him: 'You must believe in immortality, Bunny, you must!' But he doesn't and can't: Margaret is dead and unreturning.

Wilson spares himself, and his putative reader, nothing. He preserves every impaling rebuke Canby delivered. She once told her critical, complaining husband that the epitaph on his tombstone should read: 'You'd better go and fix yourself up.' He also celebrates her: in bed, in drink, in tears, in confusion. He remembers fighting off the flies when they made love on a beach, and iconizes her 'cunning' body with its small limbs. ('Don't say that!' she would protest. 'It makes me sound like a turtle.') He calls to mind the ignorances that charmed him—'I've found out what that thing over the door is—it's a lentil'—and places them alongside her running complaints: 'I'll crash someday! Why don't you do something about me?' She accused him of treating her as just another luxury item, like Guerlain scent: 'You'd be charmed if I were dead, you know you would.'

The fact that Wilson treated his wife badly, both before and after marriage, and that his grief was contaminated by justified guilt, is what gives this stream of mourning consciousness its power. The animating paradox of Wilson's condition is that he has been released into feeling by the death of the person who accused him of lack of feeling. And the line that has never left my memory is this: 'After

164

she was dead, I loved her.'

It doesn't matter that Bunny Wilson was a cold, fishy, leprous person. It doesn't matter that their relationship was a mistake and their marriage a disaster. It only matters that Wilson was telling the truth, and that the authentic voice of remorse is sounded in those words: 'After she was dead, I loved her.'

*   *   *

We may always choose knowledge over ignorance; we may wish to be conscious of our dying; we may hope for a best-case scenario in which a calm mind observes a gradual decline, perhaps with a Voltairean finger on the ebbing pulse. We may get all this; but even so, we should consider the evidence of Arthur Koestler. In *Dialogue with Death* he recorded his experiences in the Francoist prisons of Malaga and Seville during the Spanish Civil War. Admittedly, there is a difference between young men facing immediate execution by political opponents, and older men and women, most of their lives behind them, contemplating quieter extinctions. But Koestler observed many of those about to die—including, as he was assured, himself—and came to the following conclusions. First, that no one, even in the condemned cell, even hearing the sound of their friends and comrades being shot, can ever truly believe in his own death; indeed, Koestler thought this fact could be expressed quasi-mathematically—'One's disbelief in death grows in proportion to its approach.' Secondly, the mind has recourse to various tricks when it finds itself in the presence of

165

death: it produces 'merciful narcotics or ecstatic stimulants' to deceive us. In particular, Koestler thought, it is capable of splitting consciousness in two, so that one half is examining coolly what the other half is experiencing. In this way, 'the consciousness sees to it that its complete annihilation is never experienced'. Two decades previously, in 'Thoughts for the Times on War and Death', Freud had written: 'It is indeed impossible to imagine our own death; and whenever we attempt to do so, we can perceive that we are in fact still present as spectators.'

Koestler also casts doubt on the authenticity of deathbed self-observation, however apparently lucid and rational the mind. 'I don't believe that since the world began a human being has ever died *consciously*. When Socrates, sitting in the midst of his pupils, reached out for the goblet of hemlock, he must have been at least half convinced that he was merely showing off . . . Of course he knew that theoretically the draining of the goblet would prove fatal; but he must have had a feeling that the whole thing was quite different from what his perfervid, humourless pupils imagined it; that there was some clever dodge behind it all known only to himself.'

Koestler ends *Dialogue with Death* with a scene so cinematic, so neat and so implausible that he cannot possibly have made it up. He has been released from prison in exchange for the wife of a Francoist fighter ace, who is given the job of flying Koestler to the rendezvous. As their plane hovers over a vast white plateau, the black-shirted pilot takes his hand off the joystick and engages his political enemy in a shouted conversation about life and death, Left and Right, courage and cowardice. 'Before we were alive,' the writer bellows at the aviator at one point, 'we were all dead.' The pilot agrees, and asks, 'But why, then, is one afraid of death?' 'I have never been afraid of death,' Koestler replies, 'but only of dying.' 'With me, it's exactly the opposite,' shouts back the man in the black shirt.

Except that they were, presumably, shouting in Spanish. Fear of death or fear of dying, would you rather? Are you with the Communist or the Fascist, the writer or the flyer? Almost everyone fears one to the exclusion of the other; it's as if there isn't enough room for the mind to contain both. If you fear death, you don't fear dying; if you fear dying, you don't fear death. But there's no logical reason why one should block out the other; no reason why the mind, with a little training, cannot stretch to encompass both. As one who wouldn't mind dying as long as I didn't end up dead afterwards, I can certainly make a start on elaborating what my fears about dying might be. I fear being my father as he sat in a chair by his hospital bed and with quite uncharacteristic irateness rebuked me—'You said you were coming *yesterday'*—before working out from my embarrassment that it was he who had got things confused. I fear being my mother imagining that she still played tennis. I fear being the friend who, longing for death, would repeatedly confide that he had managed to acquire and swallow enough pills to kill himself, but was now seethingly anxious that his actions might get a nurse into trouble. I fear being the innately courteous literary man I knew who, as senility took hold, began spouting at

167

his wife the most extreme sexual fantasies, as if they were what he had always secretly wanted to do to her. I fear being the octogenarian Somerset Maugham, dropping his trousers behind the sofa and shitting on the rug (even if the moment might happily recall my childhood). I fear being the elderly friend, a man of both refinement and squeamishness, whose eyes showed animal panic when the nurse in the residential home announced in front of visitors that it was time to change his nappy. I fear the nervous laugh I shall give when I don't quite get an allusion or have forgotten a shared memory, or a familiar face, and then begin to mistrust much of what I think I know, and finally mistrust all of it. I fear the catheter and the stairlift, the oozing body and the wasting brain. I fear the Chabrier/Ravel fate of not knowing who I have been and what I have made. Perhaps Stravinsky, in extreme old age, had their endings in mind when he used to call out from his room for his wife or a member of the household. 'What is it you need?' they would ask. 'To be reassured of my own existence,' he would reply. And the confirmation might come in the form of a handclasp, a kiss, or the playing of a favourite record.

Arthur Koestler, in old age, was proud of a conundrum he had formulated: 'Is it better for a writer to be forgotten before he dies, or to die before he is forgotten?' (Jules Renard knew his answer: 'Poil de Carotte and I live together, and I hope that I die before him.') But it is a would-you-rather porous enough to allow a third possibility to sneak in: the writer, before dying, may have lost all memory of having been a writer.

When Dodie Smith was asked if she remembered having been a famous playwright, and replied, 'Yes, I *think* so', she said it in exactly the same way—with a kind of frowning concentration, morally conscious that truth was required—as I had seen her answer dozens of questions over the years. In other words, she at least remained in character. Beyond those nearer fears of mental and physical slippage, this is what we hope and hold to for ourselves. We want people to say, 'He was himself right to the end, you know, even if he couldn't speak/see/hear.' Though science and self-knowledge have led us to doubt what our individuality consists of, we still want to remain in that character which we have perhaps deceived ourselves into believing is ours, and ours alone.

Memory is identity. I have believed this since—oh, since I can remember. You are what you have done; what you have done is in your memory; what you remember defines who you are; when you forget your life you cease to be, even before your death. I once spent many years failing to save a friend from a long alcoholic decline. I watched her, from close at hand, lose her short-term memory, and then her long-term, and with them most of everything in between. It was a terrifying example of what Lawrence Durrell in a poem called 'the slow disgracing of the mind': the mind's fall from grace. And with that fall—the loss of specific and general memories being patched over by absurd feats of fabulation, as the mind reassured itself and her but no one else—there was a comparable fall for those who knew and loved her. We were trying to hold on to our memories of her—and thus, quite simply, to her—telling ourselves that 'she' was still there, clouded over but occasionally visible in sudden moments of truth and clarity. Protestingly, I would repeat, in an attempt to convince myself as much as those I was addressing, 'She's just the same underneath.' Later I realized that I had always been fooling myself, and the 'underneath' was being—had been—destroyed at the same rate as the visible surface. She had gone, was off in a world that convinced only herself—except that, from her panic, it was clear that such conviction was only occasional. Identity is memory, I told myself; memory is identity.

*   *   *

Dying in character: an instructive case. Eugene O'Kelly was a fifty-three-year-old chairman and CEO of a top American accountancy firm. By his own description, he was a paradigmatic success story: a 'type A' personality with 20,000 employees under him, a frenetic schedule, children he didn't see enough of, and a devoted wife he referred to as 'my own personal Sherpa'. Here is O'Kelly's account of what he termed 'My Perfect Day':

> I have a couple of face-to-face client meetings, my favourite thing of all. I'd meet with at least one member of my inner team. I'd speak on the phone with partners, in New York and in offices around the country, to see how I could help them. I'd put out some fires. Sometimes I'd have a discussion with one of our competitors about how we could work together towards one of our professional common goals. I'd complete lots of items

170

listed in my electronic calendar. And I'd
move ahead in at least one of three areas I'd
resolved to improve when I was elected to the
top spot by the partners of the firm three
years earlier: growing our business . . .
enhancing quality and reducing risk; and,
most vital to me and the long-term health of
the firm, making our firm an even better
place to work, indeed a great place to work,
one that allowed our people to live more
balanced lives.

In the spring of 2005, O'Kelly was 'one of
50 CEOs invited to participate at a White House
business roundtable with President Bush. Was
anyone luckier in his job than I?'

But just at that moment, O'Kelly's luck ran out.
What he thought was temporary tiredness after an
especially tough schedule turned into a slightly
drooping cheek muscle, then into a suspicion of
Bell's palsy, and then—suddenly, irreversibly—into
a diagnosis of inoperable brain cancer. This was
one fire that could not be put out. All the most
expensive experts could not divert the onrushing
truth: three months and barely a day longer.

O'Kelly responds to this news like the 'goal-
driven person' and ultimate corporate competitor
that he is. 'Just as a successful executive is driven to
be as strategic and prepared as possible to "win" at
everything, so I was now driven to be as methodical
as possible during my last hundred days.' He plans
to apply 'the skill set of a CEO' to his predicament.
He realizes that he must 'come up with new goals.
Fast.' He tries to 'figure out how I as an individual
needed to reposition swiftly to adjust to the new

171

circumstances of my life'. He draws up 'the final and most important to-do list of my life'.

Priorities, methods, targets. He gets his business and financial affairs in order. He decides how he is going to 'unwind' his relationships by creating 'perfect moments' and 'perfect days'. He begins 'transition to the next state'. He plans his own funeral. Ever competitive, he wants to make his death 'the best death possible', and after completing his to-do list, concludes: 'Now, I was motivated to "succeed" at death.'

For those who think that any Hundred Days inevitably leads to Waterloo, the notion of 'succeeding at death' may seem grotesque, even comic. But then everyone's death will be comic to someone. (Do you know what O'Kelly did shortly after learning that he had only three months to live? He wrote a *short story*! As if the world needed another one . . .) And then, with the help of what must inevitably be called a ghost, he put together the book you decide to write—the one about dying—when faced with your final delivery date.

O'Kelly lists and categorizes the friendships he needs to unwind. Even before he gets to his inner circle there are, astonishingly, a thousand names in his book. But with the speed and attack of one used to closing deals, he completes the job in three weeks flat: sometimes with a note or phone call, occasionally with a brief meeting which might perhaps contain a 'perfect moment'. When it comes to unwinding closer friendships there is some sporadic human resistance. One or two friends don't want to be fobbed off with a single farewell, a stroll round the park while shared memories are evoked. But like a true CEO,

O'Kelly overrides such clinging sentimentalists. He says firmly. 'I'd like this to be it. I set this up specifically so we could unwind. And we made a perfect moment out of this. Let's take that and go forward. Let's not schedule another one. Trying to improve on a perfect moment never works.'

No, I don't think I'd put it like that either. But then, I doubt I've met anyone quite like O'Kelly. The 'unwinding' he plans for his teenage daughter involves a trip to Prague, Rome and Venice. 'We would fly by private jet, which would require us to refuel somewhere in the far, far north, and that would give Gina an opportunity to meet and trade with the Inuits.' This is not so much dying in character as dying in caricature. You say goodbye to your daughter, but you also build in for her *an opportunity to trade with the Inuits*? And do you inform the Inuits what their privileged function is to be on this occasion?

Such moments may provoke a satirical and disbelieving gawp. But O'Kelly was surely dying as he had lived, and we should all be so lucky. Whether or not he cheated a little is another matter. The CEO had not previously had much truck with God, because of the tightness of his schedule; though he did use Him as a kind of emergency breakdown service. Some years previously, the prospective Inuit-trader had been diagnosed with juvenile arthritis, and her father remembered that 'You could find me in church often that year.' Now, with his own final deal shortly to be closed, O'Kelly again refers things upwards, to the transnational HQ in the sky. He prays, and learns to meditate. He feels supported from 'the other side' and reports that 'there is no

173

pain between this side and the other side'. His wife explains that 'If you conquer fear, you conquer death'—though you don't, of course, end up *not dead*. When O'Kelly expires it is, according to his own personal Sherpa, 'in a state of tranquil acceptance and genuine hope'.

Psychoanalysts tell us that those who are most attached to their own personalities have the most difficulty in dying. Given O'Kelly's A-typeness, his age, and the swiftness of his end, his behaviour is highly impressive. And perhaps God doesn't mind being addressed only in emergency. It may seem to bystanders that any sensible deity ought to be offended by such spotty, self-interested attention. But He might view things differently. He might, modestly, not want to be a daily, occluding presence in our lives. He might enjoy being a breakdown specialist, an insurance company, a longstop.

O'Kelly didn't want organ music at his funeral; he specified flute and harp. I gave my mother Mozart; she gave my father Bach. We spend time thinking about our funeral music; less about what music we wish to do our dying with. I remember the literary editor Terence Kilmartin, one of my early encouragers, lying on a bed downstairs when he was too weak to climb a stair, listening to late Beethoven string quartets on a portable boom box. Dying popes and emperors could summon their own choirs and instrumentalists to help them sample the glory to come. But modern technology has made popes and emperors of us all; and though you may reject the Christian heaven, you can have the Bach *Magnificat*, Mozart's *Requiem* or Pergolesi's *Stabat Mater* lighting up the inside of

174

your skull as your body fades. Sydney Smith thought of heaven as eating foie gras to the sound of trumpets—which has always felt to me like a clash rather than a concord. Still, you could have the rousing massed brass of Gounod's *St Cecilia Mass* thundering in your ears while a tube bubbles sugary feed into your arm.

I suspect that if I get any sort of decent dying time, I shall want music rather than books. Will there be space—head-space—for the wonderful trudgery of fiction, the work involved: plot, characters, situation . . . ? No, I think I'm going to need music, fittingly intravenous: straight to the bloodstream, straight to the heart. 'The best means we have of digesting time' will perhaps help us digest the beginnings of death. Music is also associated for me with optimism. I had an instant sense of fellow-feeling when I read that one of the pleasures of Isaiah Berlin's old age was booking concert tickets for months ahead (I often used to spot him, up in the same box at the Festival Hall). Getting the tickets somehow guarantees that you will hear the music, prolongs your life at least until the last echo of the final chords you have paid to hear dies away. Somehow, this wouldn't work with the theatre.

It would, however, depend upon successfully remaining in character. When first considering my best-case death scenario (*x* months, time for 200–250 pages), I took this matter for granted. I assumed that I would remain myself to the end, also instinctively insist on being a writer, keen to describe and define the world even as I was leaving it. But the character may be subjected to sudden jolts, magnifications and distortions in its final stages. A friend of Bruce Chatwin's first realized that the writer must be seriously ill when he paid for lunch, an action hitherto quite untypical of him. Who can predict the mind's response to its own short-dated termination?

*   *   *

Montaigne didn't die, as he had dreamed, while planting out his cabbage patch. Death came for the sceptic and epicurean, the tolerant deist, the writer of boundless curiosity and learning, while mass was being celebrated in his bedroom: at the exact moment (or so they said) of the elevation of the host. An exemplary death for the Catholic Church—which nevertheless put Montaigne's works on the Index within a century.

Twenty years ago, I visited his house—or rather, his writer's tower—outside Bordeaux. Chapel on the ground floor, bedroom on the first, study at the top. Four centuries on, both facts and furnishings were as unverifiable as any philosopher would know them to be. There was a broken chair on which the great essayist may possibly have sat—or if not, on something similar. The bedroom, in the silkily evasive French of the guidebook, was where 'nothing forbids us from thinking that this is where he might have died'. The study still had Greek and Latin tags painted on the beams, though they had been many times refreshed; while the thousand-volume library that had been Montaigne's universe was long dispersed. Even the shelves had gone: all that remained were a couple of D-shaped pieces of metal to which they might have been attached. This seemed properly philosophical.

Just off the bedroom where Montaigne might have expired while perhaps gazing at the elevated host (though nothing forbids us from thinking that his mind was on his cabbages), there was a small platform. From there, the philosopher would have been able to follow mass in the chapel below without interrupting his thoughts. A narrow, angled tunnel, made up of seven steps, offered a fine acoustic and a decent view of the priest. After the guide and the other tourists had moved on, some homage-paying instinct induced me stand on the platform, and then start creeping down this pseudo-staircase. Two steps later, I slipped, and in an instant found myself splayed and sprung against the side walls, trying to prevent myself being shot down this stone funnel into the chapel below. Clamped there, I felt the claustrophobia of a familiar dream—the one where you are lost underground, in some narrowing pipe or tube, in ever-increasing darkness, in panic and in terror. The dream which, even without waking from it, you know is straightforwardly about death.

I have always been suspicious of dreams; or rather, of excessive interest in them. I knew a couple, long and manifestly in love with one another, whose day always began with the wife recounting to her husband the dreams she had entertained that night. They were still doing it, devotedly, in their seventies. I prefer—indeed, treasure—my wife's extremely laconic approach to dream-narration. She wakes, and delivers her report, either as gnomic summary—'a bit of a desert'—or pithy critical assessment, such as 'Rather confusing', or 'Glad to get out of *that*.' Sometimes description and critique are combined:

'Indian dreams, like a long and rambling novel.' Then she goes back to sleep and forgets all about it.

This seems to put dreams into their proper perspective. When I first started writing fiction, I laid down two rules for myself: no dreams, and no weather. As a reader, I had long been irritated by 'significant' meteorology—storm clouds, rainbows, distant thunder—just as I was bored by 'significant' dreams, premonitions, visitations, and so on. I was even planning to call my first novel *No Weather*. But the book was so long in the writing that eventually the title came to seem coy.

I have death-dreams about as often as you might expect: some burial-oriented, involving subterranean enclosure and narrowing tunnels; others deploying a more active war-movie scenario—of being chased, surrounded, out-numbered, outgunned, of finding myself bulletless, held hostage, wrongly condemned to the firing squad, informed that there is even less time than I imagined. The usual stuff. I was relieved when, a few years back, a thematic variation finally came along: the dream in which I am registering at a suicide hostel in some country tolerant of death-seekers. I have signed the forms, and my wife has agreed—either to join me in the venture, or, more usually, to accompany and help me. However, when I get there, I find the place infinitely depressing—cheap furniture, a shabby bed reeking of past and future occupants, bored apparatchiks treating you as just another item of bureaucratic business. I realize I have made the wrong decision. I don't want to check out (or even check in), I have made a mistake, life is still full of interest and some small future; yet even as I think this, I am aware that once the process to which I have lent my signature has begun, I cannot back out, and yes, I shall be dead within hours, or even minutes, for now there is absolutely no escape, no possible Koestlerian 'clever trick' to help me out.

If not exactly proud of this new dream, I was at least pleased that my unconscious was getting updated, was still keeping pace with developments in the world. I was a little less pleased to discover from the poet D.J. Enright's last book, *Injury Time*, that he had been visited by almost exactly the same dream. The establishment he was booked into sounded a little smarter than mine, but, as is typical of the melancholic's dreamscape, something inevitably went wrong. In his case, the suicide hostel had run out of poison gas. So the new plan was for Enright and his wife to be transferred by van to the local post office, where he feared—all too plausibly—that the facilities would prove both less humane and less efficient.

I didn't, on reflection, mind the synchronicity too much (being proprietorial about dreams would be an odd vanity). I was more dismayed, elsewhere in Enright's book, to come across the following quotation: 'I should not really object to dying were it not followed by death.' But *I* said that first, I thought—I've been saying it for years, and written it too. Look, here it is in that first novel of mine, the one not called *No Weather*: 'I wouldn't mind Dying at all, as long as I didn't end up Dead at the end of it.' (Rereading that sentence, I wonder if I should be embarrassed by the repetition of *end*. Though if challenged, I would probably argue that it was a deliberate stressing of finality. Whether it

179

was or not, I can't remember.) So who is Enright quoting? One Thomas Nagel, in a book called *Mortal Questions*. I Google him: professor of philosophy and law at NYU; date of his book, 1979; date of mine, 1980. Damn. I could counter that I had started work on my novel some eight or nine years previously, but this would be about as convincing as a dream-protest in a suicide hostel. And doubtless someone got there before either of us. Probably one of those ancient Greeks my brother knows so well.

You may have noted—may even have pitied—the vehemence with which I wrote 'But *I* said that first.' *I*, the insistent, emphatic, italicized me. The *I* to which I am brutishly attached, the *I* that must be farewelled. And yet this *I*, or even its daily unitalicized shadow, is not what I think of it as. Around the time I was assuring the college chaplain that I was a happy atheist, there was a fashionable phrase: the integrity of the personality. This is what, amateurs of our own existence, we believe in, don't we? That the child is father, or mother, to the man, or woman; that slowly but inevitably we become ourselves, and that this self will have an outline, a clarity, an identifiability, an integrity. Through life we construct and achieve a unique character, one in which we hope to be allowed to die.

But the brain mappers who have penetrated our cerebral secrets, who lay it all out in vivid colours, who can follow the pulsings of thought and emotion, tell us that there is no one at home. There is no ghost in the machine. The brain, as one neuropsychologist puts it, is no more or less than 'a lump of meat' (not what I call meat—but then I am

180

unsound on offal). I, or even *I*, do not produce thoughts; thoughts produce me. The brain mappers, peer and pore as they may, can only conclude that 'there is no "self-stuff" to be located'. And so our notion of a persisting self or ego or I or *I*—let alone a locatable one—is another illusion we live by. Ego Theory—on which we have survived so long and so naturally—is better replaced by Bundle Theory. The notion of the cerebral submarine captain, the organizer in charge of the events of his or her life, must surrender to the notion that we are a mere sequence of brain events, bound together by certain causal connections. To put it in a final and disheartening (if literary) way: that 'I' of which we are so fond properly exists only in grammar.

At Oxford, after giving up modern languages, my old-fashioned I studied philosophy for a couple of terms, at the end of which it was told it lacked the appropriate brain for the job. Each week I would learn what one philosopher believed about the world, and the next week why those beliefs were false. This, at least, was how it appeared to me, and I wanted to cut to the chase: what's really true, then? But philosophy seemed more about the process of philosophizing rather than the purpose I had ascribed to it in advance: to tell us what the world consists of, and how best to live in that world. Doubtless these were naive expectations, and I should not have been so disappointed when moral philosophy, far from having any immediate applicability, began with a debate about whether 'goodness' was like 'yellowness'. And so, wisely no doubt, I left philosophy to my brother, and returned to literature, which did, and still does, tell

181

us best what the world consists of. It can also tell us how best to live in that world, though it does so most effectively when appearing not to do so.

One of the many correct-until-next-week versions of the world that I was taught was Berkeley's. He held that the world of 'houses, mountains, rivers and in a word all sensible objects' consists entirely of ideas, sensory experiences. What we like to think of as the real world, out there, corporeal, touchable, linear in time, is just private images—early cinema— unreeling in our heads. Such a world view was, by its very logic, irrefutable. Later, I remember rejoicing at Literature's reply to Philosophy: Dr Johnson kicking a stone and crying, 'I refute it thus!' You kick a stone, you feel its hardness, its solidity, its reality. Your foot hurts, and that is proof. The theorist is undone by the common sense of which we are so Britishly proud.

The stone that Dr Johnson kicked, we now know, wasn't solid at all. Most solid things consist mainly of empty space. The earth itself is far from solid, if by solid we mean impermeable: there are tiny particles called neutrinos, which can pass right through it, from one side to the other. Neutrinos can pass—were passing—through Dr Johnson's stone without any trouble; even diamonds, our epitome of hardness and impermeability, are in fact crumbly and full of holes. However, since human beings are not neutrinos, and it would be distinctly pointless for us to try passing through a rock, our brain informs us that the rock is solid. For our purposes, in our terms, it is solid. This is not what is true, but rather what it is useful for us to know. Common sense raises utility into factitious but practical truth. Common sense tells us we are individuals with (usually integrated) personalities, and those around us are as well. It is going to take a while before we start thinking of our parents, say, as bundles of genetic material lacking any 'self-stuff', rather than the dramatic or comic (or cruel or tedious) characters, all too riddled with self-stuff, in the narratives we turn our lives into.

*   *   *

My father was diagnosed with Hodgkin's disease in his early fifties. He didn't ask the doctors what was wrong with him, and therefore wasn't told. He went through the treatments, and the hospital recalls, and the gradually less frequent check-ups for twenty years without ever asking. My mother had asked, at the beginning, and so had been told. Whether or not she had also been warned that Hodgkin's was then invariably fatal, I have no means of knowing. I was aware that Dad had some illness, but his inherent tact, his lack of melodrama or self-pity, meant that I didn't worry about him, or imagine his condition serious. I think my mother told me—and swore me to secrecy—around the time I passed my driving test. Surprisingly, my father did not die. He carried on teaching until his retirement, at which point my parents moved from the outer London suburbs to a glorified crossroads in Oxfordshire, where they lived until their deaths. My mother would drive Dad into Oxford for his annual check-ups. After a few years, his specialist changed, and the new man, shuffling through the notes, assumed that since my father was clearly an intelligent man, and had survived what most died from, he must know about this. On the drive home Dad said to Mum, as a casual aside, 'Apparently this Hodgkin's thing can be a bit serious.' My mother, hearing on his tongue the word she had strenuously kept to her side of the marriage for twenty years, nearly put the car into a ditch.

My father, as he got older, rarely mentioned his health problems, unless there was an ironic gloss available: for instance, that warfarin, the anticoagulant he was taking, also served as rat poison. My mother was more robust and outspoken when it came to her turn, though it was also the case that her favourite topic of conversation had always been herself, and illness merely gave her an extra theme. Nor did she think it illogical to berate her stricken arm for 'uselessness'. My father, I think, judged his own life and travails of comparatively little interest—to others, and perhaps even to himself. For a long time I used to surmise that not asking what was wrong with you showed a lack of courage, and also of mere human curiosity. Now I see that it was—perhaps it only ever is—a strategy of usefulness.

I cannot think of my parents as self-stuff-lacking bundles of genetic material for more than a moment. What's useful—and therefore in practical terms what's true—is to think of them in a commonsense, stone-kicking way. But Bundle Theory suggests another possible death stratagem. Rather than preparing to lament an old-fashioned, constructed-through-life self, one if not loveable at least essential to its owner, consider the argument that if this *I* does not really exist as I imagine and feel it, then why am I, or *I*, mourning it in advance?

This would be an illusion mourning an illusion, a mere chance bundle needlessly distraught about unbundling. Might this argument convince? Might it prove able to pass through death like a neutrino passing through a rock? I wonder; I shall have to give it time. Though naturally I think at once of a counter-argument, based on 'People tell me it's a cliché, but it doesn't feel like a cliché to me.' Theorists of mind and matter may tell me that my death is, if not exactly an illusion, at least the loss of something more inchoate and less personally marked than I pretend and desire it to be; but I doubt that this is how it will feel to *me* when the time comes. How did Berkeley die? With the full consolation of religion, rather than the theoretical consolation that it was all just private images anyway.

*   *   *

My brother points out that, had I persisted with the study of philosophy, I might know that Bundle Theory 'was invented by one D. Hume'; further, that 'any Aristotelian' could have told me that there was no self-stuff, no ghost in the machine, 'and no machine either'. But then, I know things that he does not: for instance, that our father suffered from Hodgkin's disease. I was astonished to discover that my brother has no knowledge, or at least no memory, of this. 'The story I tell myself (in part as a warning) is that he was in full health and vigour until he was seventy or seventy-two, and that once the quacks got their hands on him, it was downhill and rapidly.'

In this variant version—or rather, completely

fanciful reinvention—the much-travelled Aristotelian joins hands with his local Creuse peasant. One of the most persistent French rural myths is the story of the fellow in perfect health who comes down from the hills one day and makes the mistake of wandering into a doctor's surgery. Within weeks—days sometimes, even hours, depending on the narrator—he is fit only for the cemetery.

Before he left England to live in France, my brother went to have his ears syringed. The nurse offered to test his blood pressure while she was about it. My brother declined. She pointed out that it was free. He replied that this might very well be the case, but that he didn't *want* to be tested. The nurse, clearly not knowing what manner of patient she had in front of her, explained that at his age he might have high blood pressure. My brother, putting on a joke voice from a radio show transmitted long before the nurse had been born, insisted, 'I don't wish to know that.'

'Nor did I,' he tells me. 'Suppose my blood was OK, then the test would have been a waste of time; suppose it wasn't OK, then I wouldn't do anything about it (wouldn't take the pills, wouldn't change my diet) but from time to time I'd worry about it.' I reply that surely, 'as a philosopher', he ought to have considered the matter in the terms of a Pascalian wager. Thus, there were three possible outcomes: 1. Nothing wrong with you (good). 2. Something wrong with you but we can fix it (good). 3. Something wrong with you but, Sorry, mate, we can't (bad). However, my brother resists this optimistic reading of the odds. 'No, no. "Something wrong but we can fix it" = bad (I don't like being fixed). And "wrong and unfixable" is far worse if you know than if you don't.' As my friend G. put it, 'the evil is knowing it's going to happen'. And in his preferring of ignorance, my brother for once resembles our father more than I do.

I was once talking to a French diplomat and trying to explain my brother to him. Yes, I said, he is a professor of philosophy, who was at Oxford until the age of fifty, but now lives in the middle of France and teaches in Geneva. 'The thing about him,' I went on, 'is that he has an ambition—a philosophical ambition, you could say—to live nowhere. He is an anarchist, not in the narrow political sense, but in the wider philosophical one. So he lives in France, has his bank account in the Channel Islands, and teaches in Switzerland. He wants to live nowhere.' 'And where does he live in France?' asked the diplomat. 'The Creuse.' There was a Parisian chortle in reply. 'Then he has already achieved his ambition! He lives nowhere!'

Do you have a clear enough picture of my brother? Do you need more basic facts? He is three years older than me, has been married for forty years, and has two daughters. The first complete sentence uttered by his elder daughter was 'Bertrand Russell is a silly old man.' He lives in what he tells me is a *gentilhommière* (I had mistakenly called it a *maison de maître*: verbal gradations of house-type in France are as complex as those formerly applied to women of easy virtue.) He has half a dozen acres, with six llamas in a paddock: possibly the only llamas in the Creuse. His special area of philosophy is Aristotle and the pre-Socratics. He once told me, decades ago, that he had 'given up embarrassment'—which makes it easier to write about him. Oh yes, and he often wears a kind of eighteenth-century costume designed for him by his younger daughter: knee breeches, stockings, buckle shoes on the lower half; brocade waistcoat, stock, long hair tied in a bow on the upper. Perhaps I should have mentioned this before.

He collected the British Empire, I the Rest of the World. He was bottle-fed, I breastfed, from which I deduced the bifurcation of our natures: he cerebral, I soppy. As adolescent schoolboys, we used to leave our house in Northwood, Middlesex, each morning, and set off on a journey of an hour and a quarter, by three different Underground lines, to our school in central London; in the late afternoon, we returned by the same route. In our four years of making this joint journey (1957–61), my brother would not only never sit in the same compartment as me; he would never even take the same train. It was an older/younger brother thing; but also, I subsequently felt, something more.

Does any of this help? Fiction and life are different; with fiction, the writer does the hard work for us. Fictional characters are easier to 'see', given a competent novelist—and a competent reader. They are placed at a certain distance, moved this way and that, posed to catch the light, turned to reveal their depth; irony, that infrared camera for filming in the dark, shows them when they are not aware that anyone is looking. But life is different. The better you know someone, the less well you often see them (and the less well they can therefore be transferred into fiction). They may be so close as to be out of focus, and there is no operating novelist to dispel the blur. Often, when we talk about someone very familiar, we are referring back to the time when we first properly saw them, when they were held in the most useful—and flattering—light at the correct focal distance. Perhaps this is one reason why some couples stay in manifestly impossible relationships. The usual factors—money, sexual power, social position, fear of abandonment—doubtless apply; but the couple might also simply have lost sight of one another, be still working on an outdated vision and version.

Journalists occasionally ring me up when profiling someone I know. What they want are, first, a pithy character description, and secondly, some illustrative anecdotes. 'You know him/her—what's he/she really like?' Simple-sounding; but increasingly I don't know where to begin. If only a friend were a fictional character. So you start, for instance, with a string of approximate adjectives, like a gunner seeking to bracket a target; but you immediately feel the person, the friend, beginning to disappear, from life into mere words. Some anecdotes illustrate; others remain freestanding and inert. A journalist profiling me a few years ago rang an obvious source in the Creuse. 'I know nothing about my brother,' was the response he got. I don't think this was fraternal protectiveness; maybe it was irritation. Or perhaps, philosophical truthfulness. Though my brother might disagree that it was 'as a philosopher' that he denied knowing me.

An anecdote about my brother and me. When we were little, he used to put me on my tricycle, blindfold me, and push me as fast as possible into a wall. I was told this by my niece C., who had it from her father. I have absolutely no memory of it myself, and am not sure what, if anything, to deduce from it. But let me dissuade you from an immediate conclusion. It sounds to me like the sort of game I would have enjoyed. I can imagine my yelp of pleasure as the front tyre hit the wall. Perhaps I even suggested the game, or pleaded for it to be replayed.

I asked my brother what he thought our parents were like, and how he would describe their relationship. I have never asked him such things before, and his first reponse is quite typical: 'What were they like? I really don't have much idea: when I was a boy, questions like that didn't seem to arise; and later was too late.' Nonetheless, he addresses the task: he thinks they were good parents, 'reasonably fond of us', tolerant and generous; 'in their moral characters highly conventional—better, typical of their class and period'. But, he continues, 'I suppose their most remarkable characteristic—tho' not at all remarkable at the time—was the complete, or almost complete, lack of emotion, or at any rate, lack of public expression of emotion. I don't recall either of them being seriously angry, or frightened, or delirious with joy. I incline to think that the strongest feeling Mother ever allowed herself was severe irritation, while Father no doubt knew all about boredom.'

If asked to draw up a list of Things Our Parents Taught Us, my brother and I would be at a loss. We were given no Rules for Life, yet expected to obey intuited ones. Nothing of sex, politics or religion was mentioned. It was assumed we would do our best at school, then university, get a job and, probably, marry, and, perhaps, have children.

When I search my memory for specific instructions or advice laid down by my mother—for she would have been the lawgiver—I can only recall dicta not specifically aimed at me. For instance: only a spiv wears brown shoes with a blue suit; never move the hands of a clock or watch backwards; don't put cheese biscuits in the same tin as sweet ones. Hardly urgent copy for the commonplace book. My brother cannot remember anything explicit either. This might seem the odder, given that our parents were both teachers. Everything was supposed to happen by moral osmosis. 'Of course,' my brother adds, 'I think that *not* offering advice or instruction is a mark of a good parent.'

*   *   *

In childhood we have the self-satisfied delusion that our family is unique. Later, the parallels we discern with other families tend to be tied to class, race, income, interests; less often to psychology and dynamics. Perhaps because my brother lives only eighty miles from Chitry-les-Mines, where Jules Renard grew up, certain similarities now present themselves. Renard *père et mère* sound like an extreme, theatrical version of our parents. The mother was garrulous and bigoted; the father silent and bored. François Renard's vow of trappism was such that he would stop speaking in the middle of a sentence if his wife entered the room, and resume only after she had left; with my father, it was more that he was obliged to be silent because of my mother's loquacity and assertion of primacy.

The Renards' younger son Jules—my name too—could hardly stand his mother's presence; he was able to greet her and allow himself to be kissed (though would never kiss back), but could not bear to say more than the minimum, and used every excuse not to visit her. Though I put in more consecutive hours with my mother than Renard did with his, it was achieved only by switching to a mode of absence and reverie; and while I felt sorry for her in her widowhood, I could never, on those later visits, bear to stay the night. I couldn't face the physical manifestations of boredom, the sense of my vital spirits being drained away by her relentless solipsism, and the feeling that time was being sucked from my life, time that I would never get back, before or after death.

I remember from my adolescence a very small incident whose emotional resonance was preternaturally large. One day, my mother told me that Dad had been prescribed reading glasses, but was self-conscious about them, and so it would help if I were to comment approvingly. I nerved myself, and duly ventured the uninvited opinion that he looked 'distinguished' in his new specs. My father glanced at me ironically, and didn't bother to reply. I knew at once that he had seen through the ploy; I also felt that I had in some way betrayed him, that my false praise would make him more self-conscious, and that my mother had exploited me. It was, of course, no more than a homeopathic dose compared to the toxic pharmacology of some families' lives; and in message-bearing it was nothing to what the young Jules Renard was once obliged to do. He was still a boy when his father— unwilling to break his silence even in extreme circumstances—sent Jules to his mother with a simple request: to ask, on his behalf, if she wanted a divorce.

Renard said: 'To have a horror of the bourgeois is bourgeois.' He said: 'Posterity! Why should people be less stupid tomorrow than they are today?' He said: 'Mine has been a happy life, tinged with despair.' He records being hurt when his father didn't say a single word to him about his first book. My parents managed a little better, even if they seemed to have taken inspiration from Talleyrand's maxim about not exhibiting too much zeal. I sent them the novel not called *No Weather* as soon as it was published. Complete silence for two weeks. I rang up; my father didn't even mention having received the book. A day or two later, I went down to visit them. After an hour or so of small talk—i.e. listening to my mother—she asked me to drive Dad to the shops: a highly untypical, indeed unique, request. In the car, now that eye contact was no longer possible, he told me, sideways, that he thought the book well-written and funny, though he'd found the language 'a bit lower-deck'; he also corrected a gender mistake in my French. We kept our eyes on the road, shopped, and returned to the bungalow. My mother was now in a position to give her view: the novel 'made some points', she conceded, but she hadn't been able to bear the 'bombardment' of filth (in this, she agreed with the South African board of censors). She would show friends the cover of the book, but not allow them to look inside.

'One of my sons writes books I can read but can't understand, and the other writes books I can understand but can't read.' Neither of us wrote 'what she would have wanted'. When I was about ten, I was sitting with her on the top deck of a bus and unspooling one of those whirls of mild fantasy that come so easily at that age, when she told me I had 'too much imagination'. I doubt I understood the term, though it was clear that what was being referred to was a vice. Years later, when I started using that denigrated faculty, I deliberately wrote 'as if my parents were dead'. Yet the paradox remains that there is, behind most writing, at some level, a vestigial desire to please your parents. A writer might ignore them, might even seek to offend them, might knowingly write books he would expect them to hate; yet some part of him still suffers disappointment when he fails to please them. (Though if he did please them, a different part of him would be disappointed.) This is a common occurrence, if a matter of frequent surprise to the writer. It may be a cliché, but it didn't feel like one to me.

I remember a curly-haired boy who definitely had 'too much imagination'. He was called Kelly, lived further down the road from us, and was a bit weird. One day, when I was six or seven, and on my way home from school, he stepped out from behind a plane tree, stuck something into the middle of my back, and said, 'Don't move or I'll plug you.' I froze, being correctly terrified, and stayed there, in his power, wondering if he would release me, not knowing what was pressed hard into my back, for an unguessable length of time. Were any further words uttered? I don't think so. I wasn't being robbed: it was the purest form of hold-up—one in which the hold-up itself is the entire point. After a sweaty couple of minutes, I decided to risk death, and fled, turning as I did so.

Kelly was holding in his hand an (old-style, round-pinned, fifteen-amp) electric plug. So why did I become a novelist rather than he?

Renard, in his *Journal*, expressed the complicated wish that his mother had been unfaithful to his father. Complicated, not just in its psychology, but also in its weighting. Did he think this would have been a fair revenge for his father's punitive silences; did he imagine it would have made her a more relaxed and companionable mother; or did he want her to be unfaithful so that he could have an even lower opinion of her? During my mother's widowhood, I wrote a short story set in the recognizable ground plan of my parents' bungalow (a 'superior chalet' in estate agents' terminology, I later discovered). I also used the basic ground plan of my parents' characters and modes of interaction. The elderly father (quiet, ironic) is having an affair with a doctor's widow in a neighbouring village; when the mother (sharp-tongued, irritating) finds out, she responds—or so we are invited to believe, though we may not be quite certain—by assaulting him with heavy French saucepans. The action—the suffering—is seen from their son's point of view. Though I based the story on a septuagenarian dégringolade I heard about elsewhere, which I then grafted on to my parents' home life, I didn't deceive myself about what I was up to. I was retrospectively—posthumously—giving my father a bit of fun, of extra life, of air, while exaggerating my mother into a demented criminality. And no, I don't think my father would have thanked me for this fictional gift.

I saw my father for the last time on 17 January 1992, thirteen days before his death, at a hospital in Witney, some twenty minutes' drive from where my parents lived. I had agreed with my mother that we should visit him separately that week: she would go on the Monday and Wednesday, I on the Friday, she on the Sunday. So the plan was for me to drive down from London, have lunch with her, go and see Dad in the afternoon, then drive back to town. But when I got home (as I continued to call my parents' house long after I had a home of my own), my mother had gone back on the arrangement. It was something to do with laundry, and also fog, but mainly it was to do with being absolutely bloody typical of my mother. In all my adult life I can't remember a single occasion—apart from that set-up literary drive to the shops—when my father and I were alone together for a stretch of time. My mother, even when out of the room, was always there. I doubt it was fear of being talked about behind her back (in any case, she was the last topic I would have wanted to discuss with my father); it was more that no event in the house, or outside it, was validated without her presence. And so she was always there.

When we got to the hospital, my mother did something—again entirely typical—which made me cringe at the time, and rage ever since. As we approached my father's room, she said she would go in first. I assumed this was to check that he was 'decent', or for some other unspecified wifely purpose. But no. She explained that she hadn't told Dad I'd be coming that day (why not? control,

control—of information, if nothing else) and that it would be a nice surprise. So in she went. I hung back, but could see Dad slumped in his chair, head on chest. She kissed him and said, 'Raise your head.' And then, 'Look who I've brought.' Not, 'Look who's come to see you,' but 'Look who *I've brought.*' We stayed about half an hour, and my father and I had two shared minutes about an FA Cup match (Leeds 0 Manchester United 1—a Mark Hughes goal) we'd both seen on television. Otherwise, it was like the previous forty-six years of my life: my mother always present, nattering, organizing, fussing, controlling, and my relationship with my father reduced to an occasional wink or glance.

The first thing she said to him in my presence that afternoon was, 'You look better than you did when I last came, you looked terrible then, terrible.' Next she asked him, 'What have you been doing?' which seemed a pretty daft question to me—and to my father, who ignored it. She followed this with subsidiaries about TV watching and newspaper reading. But something had been ignited in my father, and five minutes later, exasperated—and doubly so by his impaired speech—he gave her his reply. 'You keep asking me what I've been doing. *Nothing.*' It was uttered with a terrible mixture of frustration and despair ('The word that is the most true, the most exact, the most filled with meaning, is the word "Nothing".'). My mother chose to ignore the remark, as if Dad had lapsed into bad manners.

When we left, I shook his hand as I always did, and put my other hand on his shoulder. As he said goodbye, twice, his voice cracked into an eerie

197

alto croak, which I took for some laryngeal malfunction. Later, I wondered if he knew, or strongly suspected, that he would never see his younger son again. In all my remembered life, he never told me that he loved me; nor did I reply in kind. After his death, my mother told me that he was 'very proud' of his sons; but this, like much else, had to be osmotically deduced. She also said, to my surprise, that he was 'a bit of a loner', adding that his friends had become her friends, and that by the end she was closer to them than he was. I do not know if this was true, or a monstrous piece of self-importance.

A couple of years before his death, my father asked if I had a copy of Saint-Simon's *Mémoires*. I did—a rather poncey, twenty-volume edition, bound in scarlet leather, which I had never opened. I brought him the first volume, which he read in a spine-breaking manner; and then, on subsequent visits, as requested, the following ones. Sitting in his wheelchair, while cooking duties briefly spared us my mother's presence, he would recount some piece of cut-throat politicking from the court of Louis XIV. At a certain point in his final decline, another stroke skewed some of his intellectual faculties: my mother told me that she had three times found him in the bathroom trying to pee into his electric razor. But he carried on with Saint-Simon, and when he died, he was in the middle of volume sixteen. A red silk bookmark still shows me the last page he read.

According to his death certificate, my father died of a) stroke; b) heart trouble; and c) abscess on the lung. But these were the things he was treated for in the last eight weeks of his life (and the time before that), rather than what he died of. He died—in unmedical terms—of being exhausted and giving up hope. And 'giving up hope' isn't a moral judgement on my part. Or rather, it is, and an admiring one: his was the correct response of an intelligent man to an irrecoverable situation. My mother said she was glad I hadn't seen him towards the very end: he was shrunken, had stopped eating and drinking, and didn't speak. Though on her final visit, when asked if he knew who she was, he had replied with what were perhaps his last words: 'I think you're my wife.'

* * *

On the day my father died, my sister-in-law, calling from France, insisted that my mother not be left alone in the house that night. Others urged the same, and advised me to get some sleeping pills (for sleep, that is, not suicide or murder). When I arrived—with some reluctance—my mother was robustly derisive: 'I've been alone in the house every night for eight weeks,' she said. 'What's different now? Do they think I'm going to . . .' She stopped, looking for the end of her sentence. I suggested, '. . . top myself?' She accepted the words: 'Do they think I'm going to top myself, or burst into tears, or do something stupid like that?' She then expressed a lively contempt for Irish funerals: for the number of mourners, the public wailing, and the widow being supported. (She had never been to Ireland, let alone to a funeral there.) 'Do they think I'll have to have somebody to hold me up?' she asked scornfully. But when the undertaker came to discuss her requirements—the simplest coffin, just a spray of roses, with no ribbon and absolutely no cellophane—she interrupted him at one point to say, 'Don't think I grieve any the less for him because . . .' This time, her sentence didn't need completing.

In widowhood, she said to me, 'I've had the best of life.' There would have been no point in the politeness of contradiction, of offering her a 'Yes, but.' Some years before, she had said to me, in Dad's presence, 'Of course, your father's always preferred dogs to humans,' to which my father, challenged, gave a sort of confirming nod which I took—perhaps wrongly—as a strike against her. (I also reflected that, despite knowing this, she would not have another dog in the forty or so years since the disappearance of *Maxim: le chien*.) And many, many years before that, when I was an adolescent, she said, 'If I had my time again, I'd paddle my own canoe,' which I then took merely as a strike against my father, failing to consider that any such rescheduled paddling would have obliterated her children as well. Perhaps I am putting together quotes to which I am giving false coherence. And the fact that my mother did not die of grief, but was left for five years in her own canoe when least equipped to paddle it, does not signify either.

Some months after my father's death, I was talking to my mother on the phone. I told her that friends were coming to supper, and it emerged that I was cooking one course and my wife the other. With something as close to wistfulness in her voice as I had ever heard, she said, 'How nice it must be for the two of you to cook.' And then, adopting a much more typical tone, 'I couldn't even trust your father to lay the table.' 'Really?' 'No, he'd throw things down any old how. Just like his mother.' His mother! My father's mother had died nearly half a century previously, while Dad was in India during the war. Granny Barnes was rarely mentioned in our household; my mother's family, alive or dead, had primacy. 'Oh,' I said, trying to keep the intense curiosity from my voice. 'Was she like that?' 'Yes,' my mother replied, disinterring a fifty-year-old snobbery, 'She used to lay the knives the wrong way round.'

I imagine my brother's mental life proceeding in a sequence of discrete and interconnected thoughts, whereas mine lollops from anecdote to anecdote. But then, he is a philosopher and I am a novelist, and even the most intricately structured novel must give the appearance of lolloping. Life lollops. And these anecdotes of mine should be treated with suspicion because they come from me. Another anecdotalist, recording my parents' last years, might comment on how devotedly and efficiently my mother looked after my father, how coping with him wore her out, but how impressively she still managed the house and the garden all that time. And this would be true too, even if I could not help noticing a grammatical change in the way she ran the garden. During the final months Dad was in hospital, the tomatoes, the beans, and everything else in greenhouse and ground, were renamed 'my tomatoes', 'my beans', and so on, as if Dad had been dispossessed of them even before he was dead.

That other anecdotalist might complain how unfair this son is on his entirely crime-free mother by writing a short story in which he turns her into a battering wife. (Renard discovered an edition of

201

Poil de Carotte being passed round Chitry-les-Mines with the anonymous inscription: 'Copy found by chance in a bookshop. A book in which he speaks ill of his mother in order to take revenge on her.') Further, how indecent it is for a son to describe his father's physical decline; how this contradicts the affection he claims to feel; and how the son can only face unpleasant truths by looking for something undignified or risible, like the story of a confused old man trying to pee into his electric razor. And some of this might be true too. Though the business with the electric razor is more complicated, and I would like to defend my father's behaviour here as almost rational. Throughout his life, he had shaved with razor and brush, the lather coming over the decades from bowl, stick, tube and can. My mother never liked the mess he made in the basin—'Mucky pup' being the term of disapproval in our dogless household—so when electric razors came in, she kept trying to persuade Dad to get one. He always refused: this was one territory where he would not be ruled. I remember, during one of his first spells in hospital, my mother and I arriving to catch him in hopeless mid-shave: attempting, with weakened wrist, blunt blade and inadequate foam, to spruce himself up for our visit. But at some point in his closing years, her campaign must have succeeded—perhaps because his legs failed and he could no longer stand at the basin. So I can imagine his resentment at this electric razor (which I also imagine her buying). It must have seemed both a reminder of his lost physique, and proof of a final defeat in a lengthy marital argument. Why would you not want to pee into it?

'I think you're my wife.' Yes, remaining in character: this we hope for, this we cling to, as we look ahead to everything collapsing. So—and this has been a long way round to an answer—I doubt that when my time comes I shall look for the theoretical comfort of an illusion farewelling an illusion, a chance bundle unbundling itself. I shall want to remain in what I shall obstinately think of as my character. Francis Steegmuller, who had attended Stravinsky's funeral in Venice, died at the same age as the composer. In the last weeks of his life, he asked his wife, the novelist Shirley Hazzard, how old he was. She told him he was eighty-eight. 'Oh God,' he replied. 'Eighty-eight. Did I know about this?' That sounds exactly like him—the 'did' so different from a 'do'.

*　　　*　　　*

'If I were a scribbler,' wrote Montaigne—though whether he accounted himself more, or less, than one is not clear—'I would produce a compendium of the various ways in which men have died. (Anyone who taught men how to die would teach them how to live.) Dicearchus did write a book with such a title, but for another and less useful purpose.'

Dicearchus was a Peripatetic philosopher, and his book, *The Perishing of Human Life*, has, with complete appropriateness, failed to survive. The short version of Montaigne's scribblerish anthology would be a collection of famous last words. Hegel, on his deathbed, said, 'Only one man ever understood me,' then added, 'and he didn't understand me.' Emily Dickinson said, 'I must go in. The fog is rising.' The grammarian Père Bouhours said: '*Je vas, ou je vais mourir: l'un ou l'autre se dit.*' (Loosely, 'Soon I shall, or soon I will die: both are correct.') Sometimes a last word might be a last gesture: Mozart's was to mouth the sound of the timpani in his *Requiem*, whose unfinished score lay open on his bedspread.

Are such moments proof of dying in character? Or is there something inherently suspicious about them: something of the press release, the AP wire, the prepared impromptu? When I was sixteen or seventeen, our English master—not the one who later killed himself, but one with whom we studied *King Lear* and thus learnt that 'Ripeness is all'— told the class, with more than a touch of self-satisfaction, that he had already scripted his own last words; or rather, word. He was planning to say, simply, 'Damn!'

This master had always been sceptical about me. 'I hope, Barnes,' he once challenged me, after an unsatisfactory lesson, 'that you're not one of those bloody back-row cynics.' Me, sir? Cynic, sir? Oh no—I believe in baa-lambs and hedgerow blossom and human goodness, sir. But even I thought this planned self-farewelling pretty stylish, as did Alex Brilliant. We were a) impressed by the wit; b) surprised that this old loser of a school-master should have such self-knowledge; and c) determined that we wouldn't live our own lives so that they came to the same verbal conclusion. I hope that Alex had forgotten this by the time he was killing himself, with pills, over a woman, a decade or so later.

At around the same time, by a strange social coincidence, I heard about the end of this master's

204

life. He had suffered a stroke which left him paralysed and speechless. Every so often he would be visited by an alcoholic friend who—believing, as alcoholics do, that everyone else is also much better with a drink inside them—used to smuggle a bottle of whisky into the residential home and pour it into the old schoolmaster's mouth while the eyes goggled back at him. Had there been time for that last word before the stroke hit, or was he able to bring it to mind then, as he lay there, having booze slopped into him? It's enough to make a bloody back-row cynic out of you.

Modern medicine, by extending the period of dying, has rather done for famous last words, given that their utterance depends upon the speaker knowing it is time to deliver them. Those determined to go out on a phrase could, I suppose, pronounce it and then lapse into a deliberate, monastic silence until it is all over. But there was always something heroic about famous last words, and given that we no longer live in heroic times, their loss will not be much lamented. We should celebrate instead ungrandiose, yet still characterful, last words. Francis Steegmuller, a few hours before dying in a Naples hospital, said (presumably in Italian) to a male nurse who was cranking up his bed, 'You have beautiful hands.' A last, admirable catching at a moment of pleasure in observing the world, even as you are leaving it. A.E. Housman's last words were to the doctor giving him a final—and perhaps knowingly sufficient—morphine injection: 'Beautifully done.' Nor need solemnity rule. Renard recorded in his *Journal* the death of Toulouse-Lautrec. The painter's father, a known eccentric, came to visit his son and instead of concerning himself with the patient immediately started trying to catch the flies circulating in the sick room. The painter, from his bed, remarked, 'You stupid old bugger!', then fell back and died.

*   *   *

Historically, the French state admitted only two kinds of human being on its territory: the living and the dead. Nothing in between. If you were alive, you were allowed to ambulate and pay taxes. If you were dead, you had to be either buried or cremated. You might think this a typically bureaucratic, not to say otiose, categorization. But about twenty years ago its legal truth became a matter of challenge in the courts.

The case arose when a woman in early middle age, about to die of cancer, was cryonically frozen and placed in a refrigeration plant by her husband. The French state, refusing to accept that she was anything other than dead, required him to bury her or burn her. The husband took the case through the courts, and was eventually granted permission to keep his wife in his cellar. A couple of decades later, he also not-quite-died, and was also cryonically frozen to await the marital reunion he profoundly anticipated.

To thanato-liberals, looking for a middle position between the free market use-it-then-junk-it approach to life, and the socialist utopia of eternity for all, cryonics might seem to offer an answer. You die, but you don't die. Your blood is drained, your body frozen, and you are kept alive, or at least not totally dead, until such time as your

206

disease has become curable, or life expectancy stretched so that you awake with many new, long years ahead. Technology reinterprets religion— and delivers man-made resurrection.

The French story ended recently in a grimly familiar way: some electric malfunction raised the temperature of the bodies to a level which made the return to life impossible, and the couple's son was left with every freezer-owner's nightmare. What struck me more than the story itself, however, was the newspaper photograph accompanying it. Taken in the cellar of the French house, it showed the husband—then a 'widower' for many years—sitting beside the shabby unit containing his wife. On top of the freezer was a jug of flowers and a framed photograph of the woman in her glamorous prime. And there, next to this cabinet of absurd hopefulness, sat a haggard and depressed-looking old man.

It was never going to work, was it? And we should be grateful for them that it didn't. Stop time? Rewind the clocks (or move the hands backwards—something my mother would never have allowed)? Imagine that you are a vibrant young woman, 'dying' in your thirties; imagine waking up and discovering that your faithful husband has fulfilled his natural span before being frozen in his turn, and that you are now married to someone who has aged twenty, thirty, forty years in your absence. You then pick up where you left off? Imagine the best-case scenario: that you both 'die' at more or less the same age, say in your fifties, and are resuscitated when there is a cure for your diseases. What exactly has happened? You have been brought back to life only to die all over again, without even re-experiencing youth this time round. You should have remembered, and followed, the example of Pomponius Atticus.

To have your youth again, to cheat not just your second death, but the first one as well—the one Montaigne judged the harder of the two: this is the real fantasy. To dwell in Tir-na-nog, the mythical Celtic land of the ever-young. Or to step into the fountain of youth: the medieval world's popular, materialistic short cut to paradise. As you soaked in its waters your skin instantly pinkened, your bags lifted, and those chickeny bits grew taut. None of the bureaucracy of divine judgement and soul-weighing first. The technological magic of rejuvenating water, delivering youth where clunky cryonics can only deliver a delayed old age. Not that cryonophiles will give up: those currently being frozen will doubtless be counting on stem-cell technology to rewind the biological clock by the time they get their different kind of *réveil mortel*: 'O rational creature / Who wishes for eternal life.'

I was too quick to judgement on Somerset Maugham. 'The great tragedy of life is not that men perish, but that they cease to love.' Mine was a young man's objection: yes, I love this person, and believe it will last, but even if it doesn't there will be someone else for me, and for her. We shall both love again, and perhaps, schooled by unhappiness, do better next time. But Maugham was not denying this; he was looking beyond it. I remember a didactic story (perhaps from Sir Thomas Browne) of a man who followed a succession of his friends to the grave, each time feeling a little less sorrow, until the point where he

208

could stare down into the grave with equanimity, and think of it as his own. The moral was not that pit-gazing works, that philosophizing will teach us how to die; the story was rather a lament for the loss of the ability to feel, first about your friends, then about yourself, and finally about even your own extinction.

This would indeed be our tragedy, from which death might well offer the only relief. I have always mistrusted the idea that old age brings serenity, suspecting that many of the old were just as emotionally tormented as the young, yet socially forbidden to acknowledge it. (This was the objective reason for awarding my father a septuagenarian affair in that story.) But what if I was wrong—doubly so—and this required appearance of serenity masked not a roil of feelings but its opposite: indifference? At sixty, I look around at my many friendships, and can recognize that some of them are not so much friendships any more as memories of friendships. (There is still pleasure in memory, but even so.) New friendships come, of course, but not so many as to deflect the fear that some terrible cooling-off—the emotional equivalent of planet death—might lie in wait. As your ears get bigger, and your fingernails split, your heart shrinks. So here's another would-you-rather. Would you rather die in the pain of being wrenched away from those you have long loved, or would you rather die when your emotional life has run its course, when you gaze out at the world with indifference, both towards others and towards yourself? 'No memory of having starred / Atones for later disregard / Or keeps the end from being hard.' Turgenev, having just turned sixty, wrote to Flaubert: 'This is the start of the tail-end of life. A Spanish proverb says that the tail is the hardest part to flay . . . Life becomes completely self-centred—a defensive struggle with death; and this exaggeration of the personality means that it ceases to be of interest, even to the person in question.'

It is not just pit-gazing that is hard work, but life-gazing. It is difficult for us to contemplate, fixedly, the possibility, let alone the certainty, that life is a matter of cosmic hazard, its fundamental purpose mere self-perpetuation, that it unfolds in emptiness, that our planet will one day drift in frozen silence, and that the human species, as it has developed in all its frenzied and over-engineered complexity, will completely disappear and not be missed, because there is nobody and nothing out there to miss us. This is what growing up means. And it is a frightening prospect for a race which has for so long relied upon its own invented gods for explanation and consolation. Here is a Catholic journalist rebuking Richard Dawkins for poisoning the hearts and minds of the young: 'Intellectual monsters like Hategod Dawkie spread their despairing gospel of nihilism, pointlessness, vacuity, the emptiness of life, the lack of significance anywhere at any time and, in case you don't know this useful word, floccinaucinihilipilification.' (It means 'estimating as worthless'.) Behind the excess, and the misrepresentation, of the attack, you can smell the fear. Believe in what I believe—believe in God, and purpose, and the promise of eternal life—because the alternative is fucking terrifying. You would be like those children walking fearfully through the Austrian forest at night. But instead of nice Herr Witters urging you to think only of God, there would be beastly Old Dawks the science master scaring you with tales of Bears and Death, and ordering you to take your mind off things by admiring the stars.

*   *   *

Flaubert asked: 'Is it splendid, or stupid, to take life seriously?' He said we should have 'the religion of despair' and be 'equal to our destiny, that's to say, impassive like it'. He knew what he thought about death: 'Does the *self* survive? To say that it does seems to me a mere reflection of our presumptuousness and pride, a protest against the eternal order! Death has perhaps no more secrets to reveal to us than life.' But while he distrusted religions, he had a tenderness towards the spiritual impulse, and was suspicious of militant atheism. 'Each dogma in itself is repulsive to me,' he wrote. 'But I consider the feeling that engendered them to be the most natural and poetic expression of humanity. I don't like those philosophers who have dismissed it as foolishness and humbug. What I find there is necessity and instinct. So I respect the black man kissing his fetish as much as I do the Catholic kneeling before the Sacred Heart.'

Flaubert died in 1880, the same year as Zola's mother. Uncoincidentally, this proved to be the year in which Zola received *le réveil mortel*. He was then forty (so in this respect I can pull rank on him). In memory, I had always pictured him being catapulted, like me, from sleep into wailing fear. But this was a proprietorial assimilation. In fact, he

211

would be awake at the time: he and his wife Alexandrine, each unable to sleep from mortal terror, and each too embarrassed to confess it, would lie there side by side, with the flicker of a night light keeping utter darkness at bay. Then Zola would find himself projected from the bed—and the deadlock would be broken.

The novelist also developed an obsession with a particular window in his house at Medan. When his mother died, the staircase had proved too narrow and twisty for her coffin, so the undertakers had been obliged to lower her out through the window. Zola would now stare at it every time he passed, wondering whose corpse would be the next to travel by this route—his own or his wife's.

Zola confessed these effects of *le réveil mortel* on Monday 6 March 1882, when he dined with Daudet, Turgenev and Edmond de Goncourt, who wrote it all down. That evening the four of them—reduced from the original *Dîner des Cinq* by the loss of Flaubert—talked about death. Daudet started them off by admitting that for him death had become a kind of persecution, a poisoning of his life, to such an extent that he could no longer move into a new apartment without his eyes automatically seeking out the place where they would stand his coffin. Zola made his confessions, and then it was Turgenev's turn. The suave Muscovite was as familiar with the thought of death as the rest of them, but had a technique for dealing with it: he would brush it away like *this*—and he demonstrated a little gesture of the hand. Russians, he explained, knew how to make things disappear into a 'Slav mist', which they summoned up to protect themselves from logical yet unpleasant trains of thought. Thus, if you were caught in a blinding snowstorm, you would deliberately not think about the cold, otherwise you would freeze to death. The same method could be successfully applied to the larger subject: you avoided it like *this*.

Twenty years later, Zola died. He did not achieve the *belle mort* he had once lauded—that of being suddenly crushed like an insect beneath a giant finger. Instead he showed that, for a writer, 'dying in character' contains an extra option. You may die in your personal character, or in your literary character. Some manage to do both, as Hemingway proved when he pushed two shells into his favourite Boss shotgun (made in England, bought at Abercrombie & Fitch), then placed the barrels into his mouth.

Zola died in literary character, in a scene of psycho-melodrama worthy of his early fiction. He and Alexandrine had returned to Paris from the house with the threatening window. It was a chilly day in late September, so they ordered a fire to be lit in their bedroom. While they were away, work had been done on the roof of the apartment building, and here the narrative offers the reader a choice of interpretations. The chimney leading from their bedroom had been blocked, either by incompetent artisans or—so the conspiracy theory runs—by murderous anti-Dreyfusards. The Zolas retired to bed, locking the door as was their superstitious habit; the smokeless fuel in the grate gave off carbon monoxide. In the morning, when servants broke down the door, they found the writer dead on the floor, and Alexandrine—spared the killing concentration of fumes by a few extra feet—unconscious on the bed.

Zola's body was still warm, so the doctors tried reviving him with the procedure employed five years previously on Daudet: rhythmic traction of the tongue. If this made slightly more sense in Zola's case—the technique had been developed for victims of poisoning by sewer-gas—it was no more effective. Alexandrine, when she recovered, told of how the couple had woken in the night, troubled by what they took to be indigestion. She had wanted to call the servants, but he overruled her with what turned out to be his (modern, unheroic) last words: 'We shall feel better in the morning.'

Zola was sixty-two when he died, exactly the same age as I shall be when this book is published. So let's start again. LONDON MAN DIES: NOT MANY HURT. A London man, aged anything from sixty-two upwards, died yesterday. For most of his life, he enjoyed good health, and had never spent a night in hospital until his final illness. After a slow and impecunious professional start, he achieved more success than he had expected. After a slow and precarious emotional start, he achieved as much happiness as his nature permitted ('Mine has been a happy life, tinged with despair'). Despite the selfishness of his genes, he failed—or rather, declined—to hand them on, further believing that this refusal constituted an act of free will in the face of biological determinism. He wrote books, then he died. Though a satirical friend thought his life was divided between literature and the kitchen (and the wine bottle), there were other aspects to it: love, friendship, music, art, society,

214

travel, sport, jokes. He was happy in his own company as long as he knew when that solitude would end. He loved his wife and feared death.

That doesn't sound so bad, does it? The world throws up far worse lives and (I am guessing here) far worse deaths, so why the fuss about his departure? Why the fuss from him, that is? Surely this is committing the cardinal English sin of drawing attention to oneself. And does he not imagine that others fear death just as much as he does?

Well, he—no, let's go back to I—I know many people who don't think about it as much. And not thinking about it is the surest way of not fearing it—until it comes along. 'The evil is knowing it's going to happen.' My friend H., who occasionally rebukes me for morbidity, admits: 'I know that everybody else is going to die, but I never think *I* am going to die.' Which generalizes into the commonplace: 'We know we must die but we think we're immortal.' Do people really hold such heaving contradictions in their heads? They must, and Freud thought it normal: 'Our unconscious, then, does not believe in our own death; it behaves as if it were immortal.' So my friend H. has merely promoted her unconscious to take charge of her conscious.

Somewhere, between such useful, tactical turning away and my appalled pit-gazing there lies—there must lie—a rational, mature, scientific, liberal, middle position. So here it is, enunciated by Dr Sherwin Nuland, American thanatologist and author of *How We Die*: 'A realistic expectation also demands our acceptance that one's allotted time on earth must be limited to an allowance

215

consistent with the continuity of our species . . . We die so that the world may continue to live. We have been given the miracle of life because trillions and trillions of living things have prepared the way for us and then have died—in a sense, for us. We die, in turn, so that others may live. The tragedy of a single individual becomes, in the balance of natural things, the triumph of ongoing life.'

All of which is not just reasonable but wise, of course, and rooted in Montaigne ('Make room for others, as others have made room for you'); yet to me quite unpersuasive. There is no logical reason why the continuity of our species should depend upon my death, or yours, or anybody else's. The planet may be getting a bit fullish, but the universe is empty—LOTS AVAILABLE, as the cemetery placard reminds us. If we didn't die, the world wouldn't die—on the contrary, more of it would still be alive. As for the trillions and trillions of living things that 'in a sense'—a phrase of giveaway weakness—died for us: I'm sorry, I don't even buy the notion that my grandfather died 'in a sense' that I might live, let alone my 'Chinese' great-grandfather, forgotten forebears, ancestral apes, slimy amphibia and primitive swimming items. Nor do I accept that I die in order that others may live. Nor that ongoing life is a triumph. A triumph? That's far too self- congratulatory, a bit of sentimentalism designed to soften the blow. If any doctor tells me, as I lie in my hospital bed, that my death will not only help others to live, but be symptomatic of the triumph of humanity, I shall watch him very carefully when next he adjusts my drip.

Sherwin Nuland, whose sympathetic good sense

I am declining to accept, comes from a profession that is—to this lay person's surprise—even more death-fearing than my own. Studies indicate that 'of all the professions, medicine is the one most likely to attract people with high personal anxieties about dying'. This is good news in one major sense—Doctors are Against Death; less good in that they may unwittingly transfer their own fears on to their patients, over-insist on curability, and shun death as failure. My friend D. studied at one of the London teaching hospitals, which traditionally double as rugby-playing institutions. Some years previously, there had been a student who, despite regularly failing his exams, had been allowed to stay on and on because of his prowess on the pitch. Eventually, this skill began to decline and he was told—yes, we must make way for others—to leave both desk and training field. So instead of becoming a doctor, he made a career switch too implausible for any novel, and became a gravedigger. More years passed, and he returned to the hospital, this time as a cancer patient. D. told me how he was put in a room at the top of the hospital, and no one would go near him. It was not just the appalling stink from the necrotic flesh of his pharyngeal cancer; it was the wider stink of failure.

'Do not go gentle into that good night,' Dylan Thomas instructed his dying father (and us); then, repeating his point, 'Rage, rage against the dying of the light.' These popular lines speak more of youthful grief (and poetic self-congratulation) than wisdom based on clinical knowledge. Nuland states plainly that 'No matter the degree to which a man thinks he has convinced himself that the process of

217

dying is not to be dreaded, he will yet approach his final illness with dread.' Gentleness—and serenity—are unlikely to be options. Further, there are 'overwhelming odds' against death occurring as we hope (the cabbage-planting scenario): the manner, the place, the company will all disappoint us. Further still, and in contradiction to Elisabeth Kübler-Ross's famous five-step theory—according to which the dying pass successively through Denial, Anger, Bargaining and Depression to final Acceptance—Nuland observes that in his experience, and that of every clinician he knows, 'Some patients never, at least overtly, progress beyond denial.'

Maybe all this Montaignery, this pit-gazing, this attempt to make death, if not your friend, at least your familiar enemy—to make death boring, even to bore death itself with your attention—maybe this is not the right approach after all. Perhaps we would do better to ignore death while we live, and then go into strict denial as life approaches its end; this might help us, in Eugene O'Kelly's grotesque phrase, to ' "succeed" at death'. Though of course by 'do better', I mean 'help our lives pass more easily' rather than 'discover as much truth about this world before we leave it'. Which is the more useful to us? Pit-gazers may well end up feeling like Anita Brookner heroines—those dutiful, melancholy truth-adherents perpetually losing out to jaunty vulgarians who not only extract more brash pleasure from life but rarely end up paying for their self-delusions.

*   *   *

I understand (I think) that life depends on death. That we cannot have a planet in the first place without the previous deaths of collapsing stars; further, that in order for complex organisms like you and me to inhabit this planet, for there to be self-conscious and self-replicating life, an enormous sequence of evolutionary mutations has had to be tried out and discarded. I can see this, and when I ask 'Why is death happening to me?' I can applaud the theologian John Bowker's crisp reply: 'Because the universe is happening to you.' But my understanding of all this has not evolved in its turn: towards, say, acceptance, let alone comfort. And I don't remember putting in to have the universe happen to me.

Non-death-fearing friends with children occasionally suggest that I might feel differently were I a parent myself. Perhaps; and I can see how well children function as 'worthwhile short-term worries' (and long-term ones) of the kind recommended by my friend G. On the other hand, my awareness of death struck long before children were a consideration in my life; nor did having them help Zola, Daudet, my father, or the thanatophobic G., who has produced twice his demographic quota. In some cases, children can even make things worse: for instance, mothers may feel their mortality more acutely when the children leave home—their biological function has been fulfilled, and all that the universe now needs of them is to die.

The main argument, however, is that your children 'carry you on' after your death: you will not be entirely extinguished, and foreknowledge of this brings consolation at a conscious or

219

subconscious level. But do my brother and I carry on our parents? Is this what we think we're doing—and if so, is it in a fashion remotely close to 'what they would have wanted'? No doubt we are bad examples. So let's assume that the proposed intergenerational portage occurs in a manner satisfactory to all, that you are part of a rare stack of reciprocally loving generations, each seeking to perpetuate its predecessor's memory, virtue, and genes. How far does such 'carrying on' go? One generation, two, three? What happens when you reach the first generation born after you are dead, the one with no possible memory of you, and for whom you are mere folklore? Will you be carried on by them, and will they know that this is what they are doing? As the great Irish short story writer Frank O'Connor put it: folklore 'can never get anything right'.

Did my mother question the manner in which I might carry her on when I published the 'bombardment' of filth that was my first novel? I doubt it. My next book was a pseudonymous thriller of significantly higher filth-content, so I advised my parents against reading it. But my mother was undeterrable, and duly reported back that parts of it 'made my eyes stand out like chapel hatpegs'. I reminded her of the health warning. 'Well,' she replied, 'you can't just leave a book on a shelf.'

I doubt she viewed her two sons as the future hod-carriers of family memory. She herself preferred retrospection. She liked us best—as she did most children—between the ages of about three and ten. Old enough not to be 'mucky pups', but still to acquire the insolent complications of adolescence, let alone the equality and then surpassingness of adulthood. There was nothing, of course, that my brother and I could do—short of a tragic early death—to prevent ourselves committing the banal sin of growing up.

*　　*　　*

On the radio, I heard a specialist in consciousness explain how there is no centre to the brain— no location of self—either physically or computationally; and that our notion of a soul or spirit must be replaced by the notion of a 'distributed neuronal process'. She further explained that our sense of morality comes from belonging to a species which has developed reciprocal altruism; that the concept of free will, as in 'making conscious decisions from a little self inside' must be discarded; that we are machines for copying and handing on bits of culture; and that the consequences of accepting all this are 'really weird'. To begin with it means, as she put it, that 'these words coming out of this mouth at this moment, are not emanating from a little me in here, they are emanating from the entire universe just doing its stuff'.

Camus thought that life was pointless—'absurd' was indeed the better word to choose, richer in characterization of our lonely position as beings 'without a reasonable reason for being'. But he believed that nonetheless we must, while here, invent rules for ourselves. He further said that 'what I know most surely about morality and the duty of man I owe to sport'—specifically to football, and his time as a goalkeeper for Racing

221

Universitaire in Algiers. Life as a game of football, its rules arbitrary yet necessary, since without them the game simply couldn't be played, and we would never have those moments of beauty and joy which football—and life—can bring.

When I first discovered this comparison, I applauded it like a fan from the terraces. I was also, like Camus, a goalkeeper, if a less distinguished one. My last ever game was for the *New Statesman* against the Slough Labour Party. The weather was miserable, the goalmouth a mudpatch, and I lacked proper boots. After letting in five goals I was too ashamed to return to the dressing room, so drove, sodden and dispirited, straight back to my flat. What I learnt that afternoon about social and moral behaviour in a godless universe came from two small boys who wandered round behind my goal and briefly studied my flailing attempts to keep the Slough Labour Party at bay. After a few minutes, one observed cuttingly, 'Must be a stand-in goalie.' Sometimes we are not just amateurs in our own lives, but made to feel like substitutes.

Nowadays, Camus' metaphor is outdated (and not just because sport has become a zone of increasing dishonesty and dishonour). The air has been let out of the tyres of free will, and the joy we find in the beautiful game of life is a mere example of cultural copying. No longer: out there is a godless and absurd universe, so let's mark out the pitch and pump up the ball. Instead: there is no separation between 'us' and the universe, and the notion that we are responding to it as a separate entity is a delusion. If this is indeed the case, then the only comfort I can extract from it all is that I shouldn't have felt so bad about letting in five goals against the Slough Labour Party. It was just the universe doing its stuff.

The expert in consciousness was also asked how she viewed her own death. This was her reply: 'I would view it with equanimity, as just another step, you know. "Oh, here's this—I'm in this radio studio with you—what a wonderful place to be. Oh, here I am on my deathbed—this is where I am . . ." Acceptance I would say is the best that could come out of this way of thinking about things. Live life fully now, here—do the best you can, and if you ask me why I should do that—I don't know. That's where you hit the question of ultimate morality—but still, that's what this thing does. And I expect it to do it on its deathbed.'

Is this properly philosophical, or strangely blithe, the assumption that Acceptance—Kübler-Ross's fifth and final mortal stage—will be available when required? Skip Denial, Anger, Bargaining and Depression, and just head straight for Acceptance? I am also a little disappointed by 'Oh, here I am on my deathbed—this is where I am' as the Last Words of the future (still preferring, for instance, my brother's 'Make sure that Ben gets my copy of Bekker's Aristotle'). Nor am I quite sure I entirely trust someone who calls a radio studio 'a wonderful place to be'.

'That's what this thing does. And I expect it to do it on its deathbed.' Note the demise here of the personal pronoun. 'I' has mutated to 'it' and 'this thing', a switch both alarming and instructive. As human character is being re-thought, human language must be re-thought with it. The newspaper profiler's world of character description—a

223

fixed spectrum of adjectives, illustrated by some gamey anecdotes—occupies one end of the spectrum; the philosopher's and the brain scientist's—no submarine captain in the turret, and all around a sea of loose associativeness—the other. Somewhere in between lies the everyday world of doubting common sense, or common usefulness, which is also where you find the novelist, that professional observer of the amateurishness of life.

In novels (my own included) human beings are represented as having an essentially graspable, if sometimes slippery, character, and motivations which are identifiable—to us, if not necessarily to them. This is a subtler, truer version of the profiler's approach. But what if it isn't, actually, at all the case? I would, I suppose, proffer Automatic Defence A: that since people imagine themselves with free will, built character and largely consistent beliefs, then this is how the novelist should portray them. But in a few years this might seem the naive self-justification of a deluded humanist unable to handle the logical consequences of modern thought and science. I am not yet ready to regard myself—or you, or a character in one of my novels—as a distributed neuronal process, let alone replace an 'I' or a 'he' or a 'she' with an 'it' or 'this thing'; but I admit the novel currently lags behind probable reality.

*   *   *

Flaubert said: 'Everything must be learnt, from talking to dying.' But who can teach us to die? There are, by definition, no old pros around to

224

talk—or walk—us through it. The other week, I visited my GP. I have been her patient for twenty years or so, though am more likely to run into her at the theatre or concert hall than in her surgery. This time, we are discussing my lungs; the previous time, Prokofiev's Sixth Symphony. She asks what I am up to; I tell her I am writing about death; she tells me she is too. When she e-mails through her paper on the subject, I am at first alarmed: it is full of literary references. Hey, that's *my* territory, I think, in a sub-murmur of rivalrous apprehension. Then I remember that this is normal: 'When faced with death, we turn bookish.' And happily her points of reference (Beckett, T.S. Eliot, Milosz, Sebald, Heaney, John Berger) rarely overlap with mine.

At one point she discusses Fayum portraits, those Coptic images which strike the modern eye as intensely realistic representations of individual presences. So they doubtless were; but they were not painted to decorate the walls of this life. Like those Cycladic figurines, their purpose was entirely practical and funerary: they were to be attached to a mummified corpse, so that in the next world the spirits of the dead would be able to recognize the new arrival. Except that the next world has turned out, disappointingly, to be the same world, with a few more centuries added on, and its presiding spirits and portrait-scrutinizers have turned out to be us—a very junior version of eternity.

It must have been a strange collaboration, between a sitter preparing for death and an artist elaborating his or her only representation. Was it practical and businesslike, or edged with lachrymose fearfulness (not just about dying; also

225

about whether the image would be accurate enough for the sitter to be recognized)? But it suggests to my GP a parallel, modern, medical transaction. 'Is this,' she asks, 'what is required of doctor and [dying] patient? If so, how does one find the moment to start?' At which point I realize that, perhaps to our mutual surprise, she and I have already started. She, by sending me her reflections on death, to which I shall respond with this book. If she proves to be my death-doctor, we shall at least have had a long preliminary conversation, and know our areas of disagreement.

Like me, she is a non-believer; like Sherwin Nuland, she is appalled at the over-medicalization of dying, at how technology has shunted out wise thoughtfulness, so that death is viewed as shameful failure by patient as well as doctor. She argues for a reconsideration of pain, which is not necessarily a pure enemy, but something the patient can turn to use. She wants more room for 'secular shriving', a time for a drawing-up of accounts, for expressions of forgiveness and—yes—remorse.

I admire what she has written, but (just to get our terminal conversation going early) disagree with her on one key subject. She, like Sherwin Nuland, sees life as a narrative. Dying, which is not part of death but part of life, is the conclusion to that narrative, and the time preceding death is our last opportunity to find meaning in the story that is about to end. Perhaps because my professional days are spent considering what is narrative and what isn't, I resist this line of thought. Lessing described history as putting accidents in order, and a human life strikes me as a reduced version of this: a span of consciousness during which certain

226

things happen, some predictable, others not; where certain patterns repeat themselves, where the operations of chance and what we may as well for the moment call free will interact; where children on the whole grow up to bury their parents, and become parents in their turn; where, if we are lucky, we find someone to love, and with them a way to live, or, if not, a different way to live; where we do our work, take our pleasure, worship our god (or not), and watch history advance by a tiny cog or two. But this does not in my book constitute a narrative. Or, to adjust: it may be a narrative, but it doesn't feel like one to me.

My mother, whenever exasperated by the non-arrival or malfeasance of some goofy handyman or ten-thumbed service engineer, would remark that she could 'write a book' about her experiences with workmen. So she could have done; and how very dull it would have been. It might have contained anecdotes, scenelets, character portraits, satire, even levity; but this would not add up to narrative. And so it is with our lives: one damn thing after another—a gutter replaced, a washing machine fixed—rather than a story. Or (since I meet my GP in concert halls) there is no proper announcement of theme, followed by development, variation, recapitulation, coda, and crunching resolution. There is an occasional heart-lifting aria, much prosaic recitative, but little through-composition. 'Life is neither long nor short—it merely has longueurs.'

So if, as we approach death and look back on our lives, we 'understand our narrative' and stamp a final meaning upon it, I suspect we are doing little more than confabulating: processing strange, incomprehensible, contradictory input into some kind, any kind, of believable story—but believable mainly to ourselves. I do not object to this atavistic need for narrative—not least since it is how I make my living—but I am suspicious of it. I would expect a dying person to be an unreliable narrator, because what is useful to us generally conflicts with what is true, and what is useful at that time is a sense of having lived to some purpose, and according to some comprehensible plot.

Doctors, priests and novelists conspire to present human life as a story progressing towards a meaningful conclusion. Dutifully, we divide our lives into sections, just as popular historians like to divide a century into decades and affix a spurious character to each of them. When I was a boy, adulthood seemed an inaccessible condition—a mixture of unattainable competences and unenviable anxieties (pensions, dentures, chiropodists); and yet it arrived, though it did not feel from within how it looked from without. Nor did it seem like an achievement. Rather, it felt like a conspiracy: I'll pretend that you're grown up if you pretend that I am. Then, as acknowledged (or at least unrumbled) adults, we head towards some fuller, maturer condition, when the narrative has justified itself and we are expected to proclaim, or shyly admit, 'Ripeness is all!' But how often does the fruit metaphor hold? We are as likely to end up a sour windfall or dried and wizened by the sun, as we are to swell pridefully to ripeness.

*   *   *

A man writes a book about death. Between the

time he thinks of his opening line—'Let's get this death thing straight'—and the time he types his actual and different opening line, approximately 750,000,000 people in the world will have died. During his writing of the book, a further 75,000,000 or so die. Between his delivering the book to publishers and its appearance, a further 45,000,000 die. When you look at those figures, Edmond de Goncourt's argument—about any divine bookkeeper being far too overworked if He accorded us all some further existence—feels almost plausible.

In one of my novels I had a character imagine that there must be other possibilities beyond the brute either/or, the ultimate would-you-rather, of 1. God exists, or 2. God doesn't exist. So there were various alluring heresies, like: 3. God used to exist, but doesn't any more; 4. God does exist, but has abandoned us; 8. God did exist, and will exist again, but doesn't exist at the moment—He is merely taking a divine sabbatical (which would explain a lot); and so on. My character got up to number 15 (there is no God, but there is eternal life) by the time he, and I, reached the end of our imagining powers.

One possibility we didn't consider was that God is the ultimate ironist. Just as scientists set up laboratory experiments with rats, mazes and pieces of cheese placed behind the correct door, so God might have set up His own experiment, with us playing rat. Our task is to locate the door behind which eternal life is hidden. Near one possible exit we hear distant ethereal music, near another smell a whiff of incense; golden light gleams around a third. We press against all these doors, yet none of them yields. With increasing urgency—for we know that the cunning box we find ourselves in is called mortality—we try to escape. But what we don't understand is that our non-escaping is the whole point of the experiment. There are many fake doors, but no real one, because there is no eternal life. The game thought up by God the ironist is this: to plant immortal longings in an undeserving creature and then observe the consequences. To watch these humans, freighted with consciousness and intelligence, rushing around like frantic rats. To see how one group of them instructs everyone else that *their* door (which even they can't open) is the only correct one, and then perhaps starts killing anyone who puts money on a different door. Wouldn't that be fun?

The experimenting, ironic, games-playing God. Why not? If God made man, or man made God, in His or his own image, then *homo ludens* implies *Deus ludens*. And the other favourite game He gets us to play is called Does God Exist? He gives various clues and arguments, drops hints, appoints agents provocateurs on both sides (didn't that Voltaire do a good job?), then sits back with a beatific smile on His face and watches us try to work it out. And don't think that a quick and craven acceptance—Yes, God, we always knew you were there from the start, before anyone else said so, You're the man!—will cut any ice with this fellow. If God were a class act, I suspect He would approve of Jules Renard. Some of the faithful confused Renard's typically French anti-clericalism with atheism. To which he replied:

You tell me that I am an atheist, because we

do not each of us seek God in the same way. Or rather, you believe that you've found Him. Congratulations. I am still searching for Him. And I'll carry on searching for the next ten or twenty years, if He grants me life. I fear not finding Him, but I'll carry on searching all the same. He might be grateful for my attempt. And perhaps He will have pity on your smug confidence and your lazy, simple-minded faith.

The God-game and the Death-maze fit together, of course. They make a three-dimensional puzzle of the sort which attracts those tired of the mere simplicities of chess. God, the vertical game, intersects with Death, the horizontal one, making up the biggest puzzle of all. And we scurry squeakingly up ladders that end in mid-air, and rush round corners which lead only to cul-de-sacs. Does that feel familiar? And you can almost believe that God—this kind of God—was reading that journal entry of Renard's: 'And I'll carry on searching for the next ten or twenty years, if He grants me life.' Presumptuous man! And so God granted him six and a half years: neither niggardly nor indulgent; just about fair. Fair in God's eyes, that is.

If as a man I fear death, and if as a novelist I professionally seek the contrary view, I should learn to argue in favour of death. One way of doing so is to make the alternative—eternal life—seem undesirable. This has been tried before, of course. That's one of the problems with death: almost everything's been tried before. Swift had his Struldbruggs, born with a red mark on their foreheads; Shaw, in *Back to Methuselah*, his Ancients, born from eggs and attaining adulthood at four. In both cases the gift of eternity proves wearisome and the ever-continuing lives are thinned to emptiness; their owners—their endurers—yearn for the comfort of death and are cruelly denied it. This seems to me a skewed and propagandist take, rather too evidently designed to console the mortal. My GP points me to a subtler version, Zbigniew Herbert's poem 'Mr Cogito and Longevity'. Mr Cogito 'would like to sing / the beauty of the passage of time'; he welcomes his wrinkles, he refuses life-extending elixirs, 'He is delighted by lapses of memory / he was tormented by memory'—in short, 'immortality since childhood / put him in a state of trembling fear.' Why should the gods be envied, Herbert asks, and answers wryly, 'for celestial draughts / for a botched administration / for unsatiated lust / for a tremendous yawn'.

The stance is appealing, even if most of us can imagine improving the administrative workings of Mount Olympus, and wouldn't be too bored either by celestial draughts or a little more lust-satisfying. But the attack on eternity is—as it has to be—an attack on life; or at least, a celebration of, and expression of relief at, its transience. Life is full of pain and suffering and fear, whereas death frees us from all this. Time, Herbert says, is Eternity's way of showing us mercy. Think of all this stuff going on ceaselessly: who wouldn't pray for an end to it? Jules Renard agreed: 'Imagine life without death. Every day you'd want to kill yourself from despair.'

Leaving aside the problem of eternity's eternalness (which could, I think, be fixed—given

232

time), one of the attractions of old-fashioned, God-arranged death-survival—apart from the obvious, spectacular one of *not dying*—is our underlying desire and need for judgement. This is surely one of religion's gut appeals—and its attraction for Wittgenstein. We spend our lives only partially seeing ourselves and others, and being partially seen by them in return. When we fall in love, we hope—both egotistically and altruistically—that we shall be finally, truly seen: judged and approved. Of course, love does not always bring approval: being seen may just as well lead to a thumbs-down and a season in hell (the problem, and the paradox, lies in the lover having enough of a sense of judgement to choose a beloved with such a reciprocal sense of judgement as to approve of the lover). In the old days, we could comfort ourselves that human love, even if brief and imperfect, was but a foretaste of the wonder and perfect vision of divine love. Now it's all that we've got, and we must make do with our fallen status. But still we long for the comfort, and the truth, of being fully seen. That would make for a good ending, wouldn't it?

So perhaps we could put in for just the Judgement, and skip the heaven part—which in any case might contain that upbraiding God of Renard's imagination: 'You aren't here to have *fun*, you know!' Perhaps we don't need the full deal. Because—possible God scenario number 16b—consider for a moment any sensible God's response to the dossier of our life. 'Look,' He might say, 'I've read the papers, and I've listened to the pleas of your most distinguished divine advocate. You certainly tried to do your best (and by the way, I did grant you free will, whatever those provocateurs have been telling you). You were a dutiful child and a good parent, you gave to charity, you helped a blind dog across a road. You did as well as any human being can be expected to, given the material from which you're made. You want to be seen and approved? Here, I put my SEEN & APPROVED stamp on your life, your dossier, and your forehead. But really, let's be honest with one another: do you think you deserve eternal life as a reward for your human existence? Doesn't that strike you as a gross jackpot to win for such a trifling fifty-to-a-hundred-year investment? I'm afraid Somerset Maugham was right about your species not being cut out for it.'

It would be hard to disagree with this. If arguments about the tedium of eternity and the pain of life fail to convince, the Argument from Unworthiness remains persuasive. Even granted a Merciful—not to say, Soppy—Deity, can we objectively claim there would be much point to our perpetuation? It might be flattering to make the occasional exception—Shakespeare, Mozart, Aristotle, over there, behind the velvet rope, the rest of you down this trapdoor—but it wouldn't make much sense, would it? There's a one-size-fits-all thing about life, and no going back on the specifications.

*   *   *

My parents' ashes were blown by the Atlantic wind gusting in on the French coast; my grandparents were dispersed at the crematorium—unless they were urned and mislaid. I have never visited the grave of a single member of my family, and doubt I ever shall unless my brother obliges me (he plans to be buried in his garden, within the sound of cropping llamas). Instead, I have visited the graves of various non-blood relatives: Flaubert, Georges Brassens, Ford Madox Ford, Stravinsky, Camus, George Sand, Toulouse-Lautrec, Evelyn Waugh, Degas, Jane Austen, Braque . . . Quite a few of them were hard to find, and there was hardly a queue or a flower at any of their tombs. Camus would have been unlocatable except for the presence of his wife in a better-tended plot beside him. Ford took an hour and a half to track down in a vast clifftop cemetery in Deauville. When I eventually found his low, simple slab, the name and dates were almost illegible. I squatted down and cleaned out the lichened chisel-cuts with the keys to my rental car, scraping and flicking until the writer's name stood clear again. Clear, yet odd: whether it was the French mason's fault for leaving inadequate gaps, or something in the way I had spruced it up, but the triple name now seemed to split differently. FORD, it began correctly, but then continued MAD OXFORD. Perhaps my perception was influenced by remembering Lowell's description of the English novelist as 'an old man mad about writing'.

I should like to grow into (though by some bureaucratic reckonings I already am) an old man mad about writing; nor would I mind being visited. I like the idea—a desire my brother might deem illegitimate, being the future want of a dead person, or the want of a future dead person—of someone reading a book of mine and seeking out my grave in response. This is literary vanity in the main; but there's brute superstition lurking underneath. Just as it's hard to shake entirely the lingering memory of God, and the fantasy of judgement (as long as it's fair—i.e. deeply indulgent), and the hopeful, hopeless dream that there's some celestial fucking point to it all, so it's hard to hold constantly to the knowledge that death is final. The mind still seeks an escape from mortality's box, can still be tempted by a little science fiction. And if God is no longer there to help, and cryonics is a sad old man sitting by a leaky fridge hoping that a tragedy can have a happy ending, then we must look elsewhere. In my first novel the (at times all too convincingly autobiographical) narrator considers the possibility of some kind of cloning. Naturally, he imagines it in terms of things going wrong. 'Suppose they find a way, even after you are dead, of reconstituting you. What if they dig up your coffin and find you're just a bit too putrefied . . . What if you've been cremated and they can't find all the grains . . . What if the State Revivification Committee decides you're not important enough . . .' And so on—up to and including the scenario in which you've been approved for a second incarnation, and are about to be brought back to life, when a clumsy nurse drops a vital test tube, and your clearing vision hazes over eternally.

'The want of a future dead person.' My brother points out wryly that 'Alas, all our wants are wants of future dead people.' But anyway, for what it's worth, yes, burial. Visit me and scrape the lichen from my name with the key of your rental car; then propose me for secular resurrection from a chunk of my DNA, though not—I hope you don't mind

236

my insisting on this point—before the technical process really has been perfected. And then we shall see if my consciousness is the same as the first time round, whether I remember anything of this previous life (recognize this sentence as my own), and whether I sit down at the nearest typewriter and with laborious excitement produce the same books all over again—in which case there will, apart from anything else, be some interesting copyright problems.

No, that's all a bit desperate. I know they've dug butcher's cuts of woolly mammoth out of the permafrost and are planning to regrow one of those tusky trundlers in a laboratory. But pleading novelists would come pretty low down any list, I imagine (perhaps in the future, writers will seek to make resuscitation a term of contract, like having their books printed on acid-free paper). Better to agree with the French state's either/or: either you're alive, or you're dead, and nothing in between. Better to make it a definite adieu than a chance-in-a-billion au revoir, and to say, with Daudet, 'Farewell wife . . . family, the things of the heart.' And then 'Farewell me, cherished me, now so hazy, so indistinct.' That's wiser, isn't it?

*   *   *

Wisdom consists partly in not pretending any more, in discarding artifice. Rossini wrote his *Petite Messe solennelle* after coming out of a thirty-eight-year retirement. He called his late works 'the sins of my old age' and the Mass 'the last of these sins'. At the end of the manuscript, he wrote a dedication in French: 'Dear God, well, here it is, finished at last, my Little Solemn Mass. Have I really written sacred music, or is it just more of my usual damn stuff? I was born for opera buffa, as You well know. Not much skill there, just a bit of feeling, that's the long and the short of it. So, Glory be to God, and please grant me Paradise. G. Rossini—Passy, 1863.'

This inscription is childlike in its hopefulness. And there is something infinitely touching when an artist, in old age, takes on simplicity. The artist is saying: display and bravura are tricks for the young, and yes, showing off is part of ambition; but now that we are old, let us have the confidence to speak simply. For the religious, this might mean becoming as a child again in order to enter heaven; for the artist, it means becoming wise enough, and calm enough, not to hide. Do you need all those extravagances in the score, all those marks on the canvas, all those exuberant adjectives? This is not just humility in the face of eternity; it is also that it takes a lifetime to see, and say, simple things.

'Wise enough'. Sometimes my coevals say, in a puzzled fashion, 'The funny thing is, I don't feel any older.' I certainly do, and if I am in any doubt, there is a stark calculation available when passing, say, a twelve-year-old lolling outside the school gates with a precocious cigarette in hand. I reflect that I, as a sixty-year-old in 2006, am closer in age to the oldest surviving soldier of the First World War than I am to that kid. Do I feel wiser? Yes, a little; certainly, less foolish (and perhaps wise enough to lament the loss of some folly). Wise enough to be simple? Not quite yet, O Lord.

Wisdom is the virtuous reward for those who patiently examine the workings of the human heart and the human brain, who process experience and thus acquire an understanding of life: isn't it? Well, Sherwin Nuland, wise thanatologist, has something to say on the matter. Would you like the good news first, or the bad? A sound tactic always to choose the good—you might die before you get to hear the bad. The good news is that we do indeed sometimes become wiser as we grow older. And here's the (longer) bad news. We know all too well that our brains wear out. However frantically their component parts renew themselves, the cells of the brain (like the muscles of the heart) have a limited shelf life. For every decade of life after the age of fifty, the brain loses two per cent of its weight; it also takes on a creamy-yellow tinge—'even senescence is colour-coded'. The motor area of our frontal cortex will lose twenty to fifty per cent of its neurons, the visual area fifty per cent, and the physical sensory part about the same. No, *that*'s not the bad part. The bad part comes enclosed in a comparatively good part—the news that the higher intellectual functions of the brain are much less affected by this widespread cellular morbidity. Indeed, 'certain cortical neurons' seem to become more abundant after we reach maturity, and there is even evidence that the filamentous branchings— the dendrites—of many neurons continue to grow in old people who don't suffer from Alzheimer's (if you *do* have Alzheimer's, forget it). From this, 'Neurophysiologists may actually have discovered the source of what wisdom we like to think we can accumulate with advancing age.' Weigh that 'like to think we can accumulate' and grieve. A friend who occasionally seeks my ear nicknames me 'The Advice Centre'—a tag which, even allowing for

239

irony, gives me absurd pleasure. But it turns out that I've just got this bushy growth of filamentous branchings—nothing I can do about it.

Wisdom, philosophy, serenity: how will they stack up against mortal terror, eleven on a scale of one to ten? As an example, I give you Goethe. One of the wisest men of his age, who lived into his eighties with his faculties intact, his health excellent and his fame universal. He had always been impressively sceptical about the notion of survival after death. He thought a concern for immortality the preoccupation of idle minds, and those who believed in it far too self-congratulatory. His amused and practical position was that if, after this life, he were to discover that there was another one, he would of course be pleased; but he ardently hoped he wouldn't run into all those bores who had spent their terrestrial time proclaiming their belief in immortality. To hear them crowing 'We were right! We were right!' would be even more intolerable in the next life than it had been in this.

What could appear saner and wiser than this? And so Goethe continued working deep into old age, completing the second part of *Faust* in the summer of 1831. Nine months later, he fell ill, and took to his bed. He had one final day of extreme pain, though even after losing the power of speech he continued to trace letters on the rug over his knees (still taking his usual care over punctuation—a wonderful example of dying in character). Friends loyally claimed that he had died nobly, even Christianly. The truth, as revealed by his doctor's diary, was that Goethe was 'in the grip of a terrible fear and agitation'. The reason for the 'horror' of that final day was evident to the doctor: Goethe, the wise Goethe, the man who had everything in perspective, could not avoid the dread that Sherwin Nuland promises us.

*   *   *

Turgenev had that little hand gesture, which made the unbearable subject vanish into a Slav mist. Nowadays, the gesture and the mist are available pharmaceutically. When my mother had her initial stroke, the doctors, as a matter of medical routine—and without mentioning it to her family—whacked in the antidepressants. So though she was angry, and deeply frustrated, and at times 'completely bonkers', she was probably not depressed. My father, preceding her down this route, often struck me as depressed, and would sit with his head in his hands. I took this for a natural and logical response, given a) what had happened, b) his temperament, and c) that he was married to my mother. Perhaps medicine will develop a procedure allowing us to master that part of the brain which considers its own death. As with the patient-operated morphine drip, we might, at a thumb-click, be able to control our own death-mood and death-feelings. Denial *click* Anger *click click* Bargaining—ah, that's better. And perhaps we shall be able to click ourselves beyond mere Acceptance ('Oh, here I am on my deathbed—this is where I am') to Approval: to finding the whole business reasonable, natural, even desirable. We shall feel comforted by the Law of the Conservation of Energy, by the knowledge that nothing is ever lost in the universe. We shall feel

241

gratitude for our lucky lives when so many trillions and trillions of potential people went unborn. We shall acknowledge that ripeness is all, and think of ourselves as a fruit happy to drop from the twig, a crop serene about its harvesting. We shall be proud to make room for others as others have made room for us. We shall feel convinced and consoled by that medieval image of the bird flying into the lighted hall and flying out the other side. And what, after all, could be more useful to us as dying animals? Welcome to the Euphoria Ward.

We shall probably die in hospital, you and I: a modern death, with little folklore present. In Chitry-les-Mines the peasants used to burn the straw from a dead person's mattress, while saving the cloth. When Stravinsky died, his widow Vera made sure that all the mirrors in the room were covered; she also avoided touching his corpse, believing that the spirit lived on within it for another forty days. In many cultures, doors and windows would be opened so that the soul might escape and fly free; and you didn't lean over, or stand in front of a dying person, for the same reason. Hospital dying has done away with such customs. In place of folklore, we have bureaucratic procedure.

At the Witney registry of Births and Deaths it said KNOCK AND WAIT on the door. As my mother and I waited, a larky couple came down the corridor past us from the direction of Marriages. The registrar was a woman in her late thirties, with two Cabbage Patch dolls pinned to the wall and a fat paperback by Maeve Binchy beside her. Spotting a reader, my mother remarked that her son was also a writer (I died a little death): 'Julian

242

Barnes, have you heard of him?' But the registrar had not; and instead we found common literary ground by discussing the television adaptation of Melvyn Bragg's *A Time to Dance*. The questions and the silent form-filling took place. Then, at the very end, the registrar won my mother's approval without even knowing that she was doing so. Ma leaned forward to sign her husband's death certificate, and the official exclaimed, 'Oh, *don't* you keep your nails in perfect condition!' As she always had. Her nails: the reason she hoped to go deaf rather than blind.

Five years later, registering my mother's death, I was dealt with by a different woman, one with a metronomic delivery and no skill—or luck—in human contact. All the details had been given, the signatures provided, the duplicate copies obtained, and I was rising to leave when she suddenly uttered four soullessly otiose words in a dead voice: 'That completes the registration.' She used the same mechanical tone employed by the humanoid bosses of the Football Association, when the last of the ivory balls has been drawn from the velvet bag, and they announce, 'That completes the draw for the quarter-final round of the FA Cup.'

And that completes the folklore of my family. I would like a little more myself. I wouldn't mind you standing over my deathbed—a friendly face would be welcome, even if I doubt its availability at two in the morning in an understaffed hospital. I don't expect doors and windows to be left open after I'm dead, not least because the insurance company would decline to pay out in the event of burglary. But I wouldn't mind that headstone. In the last year of his life, when he knew himself

243

condemned, Jules Renard took to visiting cemeteries. One day he went to see the Goncourt Brothers in their Montmartre tomb. The younger brother had been buried there in 1870; the elder, Edmond, in 1896, after a graveside eulogy from the death-fearing Zola. Renard noted in his *Journal* how the brothers' literary pride was such that they disdained mention of their profession. 'Two names, two sets of dates, they thought that was enough. *Hé! hé!*' Renard comments, in that curious French transcription of a cackle. 'That's not anything you can rely upon.' But did such plainness denote vanity—the assumption that everyone would know who they were—or its very opposite, a proper avoidance of boastfulness? Also, perhaps, a sober awareness that, once released into history, no writer's name is guaranteed? I wonder what it says on Renard's tomb.

*　　　*　　　*

'We shall probably die in hospital, you and I.' A foolish thing to write, however statistically probable. The pace, as well as the place, of our dying is fortunately hidden from us. Expect one thing and you will likely get another. On 21 February 1908, Renard wrote: 'Tomorrow I shall be forty-four. It's not much of an age. Forty-five is when you have to start thinking. Forty-four is a year lived upon velvet.' On his actual birthday, he was a little more sombre: 'Forty-four—the sort of age at which you must give up hope of ever doubling your years.'

To admit that you might not make it to eighty-eight seems a modest calculation rather than a declaration of defiance. Even so, by the following year, Renard's health had declined so sharply that he was unable to walk from one end of the Tuileries to the other without sitting down for a chat with the old women selling lilies of the valley. 'I shall have to start taking notes on my old age,' he concluded, and wrote ruefully to a friend, 'I'm forty-five—that wouldn't be old if I were a tree.' Once, he had asked God not to let him die too quickly, as he wouldn't mind observing the process. How much observation did he now think he would need? He made it to forty-six and three months.

When his mother fell backwards into the well, creating 'the soft eddy familiar to those who have drowned an animal', Renard commented, 'Death is not an artist.' Its virtues are at best artisanal: diligence, stubborn application and a sense of contradictoriness which at times rises to the level of irony; but it doesn't have enough subtlety, or ambiguity, and is more repetitive than a Bruckner symphony. True, it has complete flexibility of location, and a pretty array of encircling customs and superstitions—though these are our doing, rather than its. Renard noted one detail certainly unknown to my folklorically impoverished family: 'As death approaches, one smells of fish.' Now that's something to look out for.

Though why should Death care if we join Renard in snootily excluding it from the guild of artists? When has it ever looked for Art's approval? With its co-worker Time, it just goes about its business, a cheerless commissar reliably fulfilling a quota of 100 per cent. Most artists keep a wary eye on death. Some see it as a hurry-up call;

some optimistically trust that posterity's hindsight will bring their vindication (though 'Why should people be less stupid tomorrow than they are today?'); for others, death is the best career move. Shostakovich, noting that the fear of death is probably the deepest feeling we have, went on: 'The irony lies in the fact that under the influence of that fear people create poetry, prose and music; that is, they try to strengthen their ties with the living and increase their influence on them.'

Do we create art in order to defeat, or at least defy, death? To transcend it, to put it in its place? You may take my body, you may take all the squidgy stuff inside my skull where lurks whatever lucidity and imagination I possess, but you cannot take away what I have done with them. Is that our subtext and our motivation? Most probably— though *sub specie aeternitatis* (or even the view of a millennium or two) it's pretty daft. Those proud lines of Gautier's I was once so attached to— everything passes, except art in its robustness; kings die, but sovereign poetry lasts longer than bronze—now read as adolescent consolation. Tastes change; truths become clichés; whole art forms disappear. Even the greatest art's triumph over death is risibly temporary. A novelist might hope for another generation of readers—two or three if lucky—which may feel like a scorning of death; but it's really just scratching on the wall of the condemned cell. We do it to say: I was here too.

* * *

We may allow Death, like God, to be an occasional

246

ironist, but shouldn't nevertheless confuse them. The essential difference remains: God might be dead, but Death is well alive.

Death as ironist: the *locus classicus* is the 1000-year-old story I first came across when reading Somerset Maugham. A merchant in Baghdad sends his servant out to buy provisions. In the market the man is jostled by a woman; turning, he recognizes her as Death. He runs home pale and trembling, and pleads for the loan of his master's horse: he must go at once to Samarra and hide where Death will never find him. The master agrees; the servant rides off. The master himself then goes down to the market, accosts Death and rebukes her for threatening his servant. Oh, replies Death, but I made no threatening gesture—that was just surprise. I was startled to see the fellow in Baghdad this morning, given that I have an appointment with him in Samarra tonight.

And here is a more modern story. Pavel Apostolov was a musicologist, composer for brass band, and lifelong persecutor of Shostakovich. During the Great Patriotic War he had been a colonel commanding a regiment; afterwards, he became a key member of the Central Committee's music section. Shostakovich said of him: 'He rode in on a white horse, and did away with music.' In 1948, Apostolov's committee forced the composer to recant his musical sins, and drove him close to suicide.

Twenty years later, Shostakovich's death-haunted 14th Symphony was given a 'closed premiere' in the Small Hall of the Moscow Conservatoire. This was in effect a private vetting by Soviet musical experts, with no danger of the

247

new work infecting the greater public. Before the concert Shostakovich addressed the audience. The violinist Mark Lubotsky remembered him saying: 'Death is terrifying, there is nothing beyond it. I don't believe in life beyond the grave.' Then he asked the audience to be as quiet as possible because the performance was being recorded.

Lubotsky was sitting next to a female administrator of the Composers' House; beyond her was an elderly, bald man. The symphony had reached its intensely quiet fifth movement when the man jumped up, banged his seat loudly, and rushed out of the hall. The administrator whispered, 'What a bastard! He tried to destroy Shostakovich in 1948, but failed. He still hasn't given up, and he's gone and wrecked the recording on purpose.' It was, of course, Apostolov. What those present didn't realize, however, was that the wrecker was himself being wrecked—by a heart attack which was to prove fatal. The 'sinister symphony of death', as Lubotsky called it, was in fact grimly playing him out.

The Samarra story shows how we used to think of death: as a stalker on the prowl, watching and waiting to strike; a black-clad figure with scythe and hourglass; something out there, personifiable. The Moscow story shows death as it normally is: what we bear within us all the time, in some piece of potentially berserk genetic material, in some flawed organ, in the time-stamped machinery of which we are made up. When we lie on that deathbed, we may well go back to personifying death, and think we are fighting illness as if it were an invader; but we shall really just be fighting ourselves, the bits of us that want to kill the rest of us. Towards the end—if we live long enough—there is often a competition among our declining and decaying parts as to which will get top billing on our death certificate. As Flaubert put it, 'No sooner do we come into this world than bits of us start dropping off.'

The bit of Jules Renard that did for him was his heart. He was diagnosed with emphysema and arteriosclerosis, and began his last year *au lit et au lait* (bed and milk—two and a half litres a day). He said: 'Now that I am ill, I find I want to make some profound and historic utterances, which my friends will subsequently repeat; but then I get too over-excited.' He teasingly gave his sister responsibility for having his bust erected in the little square in Chitry-les-Mines. He said that writers had a better, truer sense of reality than doctors. He felt his heart was behaving like a buried miner, knocking at irregular intervals to signal that it was still alive. He felt that parts of his brain were being blown away like a dandelion clock. He said: 'Don't worry! Those of us who fear death always try to die as stylishly as possible.' He said: 'Paradise does not exist, but we must nonetheless strive to be worthy of it.' The end came in Paris, on 22 May 1910; he was buried at Chitry four days later, without benefit of clergy, like his father and brother before him. At his writerly request, no words were spoken over his body.

Too many French deaths? Very well, here's a good old British death, that of our national connoisseur of mortal terror, Philip Larkin. In the first decades of his life, Larkin could sometimes persuade himself that extinction, when it eventually came, might prove a mercy. But by his

249

fifties, his biographer tells us, 'The dread of oblivion darkened everything'—and then, 'As he entered his sixties his fears grew rapidly.' So much for my friend G.'s reassurance that things get better after sixty. In the year that was to contain his death, Larkin wrote to a fellow poet, 'I don't think about death *all* the time, though I don't see why one shouldn't, just as you might expect a man in a condemned cell to think about the drop all the time. Why aren't I screaming?' he wondered, referring back to his poem 'The Old Fools'.

Larkin died in hospital in Hull. A friend, visiting him the day before, said, 'If Philip hadn't been drugged, he would have been raving. He was that frightened.' At 1.24 a.m., a typical deathing hour, he said his last words, to a nurse holding his hand: 'I am going to the inevitable.' Larkin was hardly a Francophile (though more cosmopolitan than he affected); but you could, if you wished, take this as an allusion to, and correction of, Rabelais' supposed deathbed utterance; 'I am going to seek a Great Perhaps.'

Larkin's death can do nothing but chill. Pit-gazing led not to calm, but to increased terror; and though he feared death, he did not die stylishly. Did Renard? Given the discretion of French biography, there are no specific details; however, one friend, Daudet's son Léon, wrote that he showed 'wonderful courage' in his last illness. Daudet concluded; 'Good writers, like good soldiers, know how to die, whereas politicians and doctors are afraid of death. Everyone can corroborate this remark by looking around them. Though there are, of course, exceptions.'

Here is the old argument, as phrased by Renard

when he was young and in good health: 'Death is sweet; it delivers us from the fear of death.' Is this not a comfort? No, it is a sophistry. Or rather, further proof that it will take more than logic, and rational argument, to defeat death and its terrors.

* * *

After we die, the hair and the fingernails continue spookily to grow for a while. We all know that. I've always believed it, or half-believed it, or half-assumed there must be 'something in it': not that we turn into shock-heads with vampiric fingernails as we lie in our coffins, but, well, perhaps a millimetre or two of hair and nail. Yet what 'we all know' is usually wrong, in part if not whole. As my friendly thanatologist Sherwin Nuland points out, the matter is simple and incontrovertible. When we die, we stop breathing; no air, no blood; no blood, no possible growth. There might be a brief flicker of brain activity after the heart ceases to beat; but that's all. Perhaps this particular myth springs from our fear of live burial. Or perhaps it's based on honest misobservation. If the body appears to shrink—indeed, does shrink—after death, then the flesh of the fingers might pull back, giving the illusion of nail growth; while if the face looks smaller, this might have the effect of giving you bigger hair.

Being wrong: my brother in error. After our mother's death, he took our parents' ashes to the Atlantic coast of France, where they had often holidayed. He and his wife scattered them on the dunes with the help of J., our parents' closest French friend. They read 'Fear no more the heat o' the sun' from *Cymbeline* ('Golden lads and girls all must / As chimney-sweepers, come to dust') and Jacques Prévert's poem *'Les Escargots qui vont à l'enterrement'*; my brother pronounced himself 'strangely moved' by the event. Later, over dinner, conversation turned to our parents' annual visits to that part of France. 'I remember being staggered,' my brother told me, 'when J. described how every night Father had kept them up to the early hours with his anecdotes and lively conversation. I can't remember him ever speaking after they moved to that frightful bungalow, and I had imagined that he had forgotten how to be amusing. But evidently I was quite mistaken.' The best explanation I can offer is that our father's French, being superior to our mother's, enabled him for those few weeks of the year to gain linguistic and social primacy; either that, or our mother, when abroad, might deliberately have become a more conventionally listening wife (however unlikely that sounds).

Being wrong: an error of my own in return. I was breastfed, my brother bottle-fed: from this I once deduced the bifurcation of our natures. But one of my last visits to my mother produced an uncharacteristic moment of near-intimacy. There had been a report in the newspapers concluding that breastfed children were more intelligent than bottle-fed ones. 'I read that as well,' said Ma, 'and I laughed. Nothing wrong with *my two*, I thought.' And then—under cross-examination— she confirmed that I had no more been breastfed than my brother. I didn't ask her reason: whether a determination to give us an equal start in life, or a squeamishness at a potentially messy business ('Mucky pup!'). Except that it was still not exactly the same start, for she mentioned that we had been fed on different formulae. She even told me the names on the bottles, which I promptly forgot. A theory of temperament based on different brands of commercial baby-milk? That would be pretty tendentious, even I would admit. And nowadays I don't consider my brother's bringing of tea to our mother's sickbed any less warm-hearted than my own self-indulgent (and perhaps lazy) blanket-snuggling.

And here is a more complicated error, if equally long-term. P., the French *assistant* who told tales of Mr Beezy-Weezy, never came back to England; but his year with us was memorialized by the two small, unframed landscapes he gave my parents. They had a rather dark, Dutch feel to them: one showed a tumbledown bridge across a river, with foliage cascading from the parapet; the other, a windmill against a rowdy sky with three white-headdressed women picnicking in the foreground. You could tell they were artistically done because of the thick brushstrokes used in river, sky and meadow. During my childhood and adolescence, these two paintings hung in the sitting room; later, at the 'frightful bungalow', they presided over the dining table. I must have glanced at them regularly for fifty years and more, without ever asking myself, or my parents, where exactly P. had set up his box of oils. France—his native Corsica, perhaps—Holland, England?

When I was house-clearing after my mother's death, I found in a drawer two postcards showing exactly the same two views. My first instinct was to assume that they had been specially printed for P. to advertise his work: he always had a beretful of theoretically money-making schemes. Then I turned them over and realized that they were commercially produced art cards of typically Breton scenes: *'Vieux Moulin à Cléden'* and *'Le Pont fleuri'*. What I had all my life imagined to be competent originality was merely competent copying. And then there was a further twist. The cards were signed 'Yvon' in the bottom right-hand corner, as if by the artist. But 'Yvon' turned out to be the name of the card company. So the pictures had been produced in the first place solely in order to be turned into postcards—whereupon P. had turned them back into the 'original' paintings they had never been. A French theorist would have been delighted by all this. I hastened to tell my brother of our fifty-year error, expecting him to be equally amused. He wasn't at all: for the simple reason that he had a clear memory of P. painting the pictures, 'and of thinking how much cleverer it was to copy than to make something up out of your own head'.

Such factual corrections are easily made, and may even feel mentally refreshing. It will be harder to face error about perceptions and judgements you have come to look upon as your own achievements. Take death. For most of my sentient life I've known the vivid dread, and also felt fully able—despite what Freud maintained—to imagine my own eternal non-existence. But what if I am quite wrong? Freud's contention, after all, was that our unconscious mind remains doggedly convinced of our immortality—a thesis irrefutable by its very nature. So perhaps what I think of as pit-gazing is only the illusion of truth-examination because deep down I do not—cannot—believe in the pit;

and this illusion may even continue until the very end if Koestler is right about our consciousness splitting when we are *in extremis*.

And there's another way of being wrong: what if the dread we feel in advance—which seems to us so absolute—turns out to be as nothing compared to the real thing? What if our void-imaginings are but the palest rehearsal for what we experience—as Goethe found out—in the final hours? And what, further, if the approach of death overwhelms all known language, so that we cannot even report the truth? A sense of having been wrong all the time: well, Flaubert did say that contradiction is the thing that keeps sanity in place.

And beyond death, God. If there were a games-playing God, He would surely get especial ludic pleasure from disappointing those philosophers who had convinced themselves and others of His non-existence. A.J. Ayer assures Somerset Maugham that there is nothing, and nothingness, after death: whereupon they both find themselves players in God's little end-of-the-pier entertainment called Watch the Fury of the Resurrected Atheist. That's a neat would-you-rather for the God-denying philosopher: would you rather there was nothing after death, and you were proved right, or that there was a wonderful surprise, and your professional reputation was destroyed?

'Atheism is aristocratic,' Robespierre declared. The great twentieth-century British embodiment of this was Bertrand Russell—helped, no doubt, by the fact that he *was* aristocratic. In old age, with his unruly white hair, Russell looked, and was treated, like a wise man halfway to godhead: a one-man

Any Questions? panel in himself. His disbelief never wavered, and friendly provocateurs took to asking him how he would react if, after a lifetime of propagandizing atheism, he turned out to be wrong. What if the pearly gates were neither a metaphor nor a fantasy, and he found himself faced by a deity he had always denied? 'Well,' Russell used to reply, 'I would go up to Him, and I would say, "You didn't give us enough evidence".'

*　　*　　*

Psychologists tell us we exaggerate the stability of our past beliefs. Perhaps this is a way of asserting our shaky selfhood; also, of congratulating ourselves, as on a greater achievement, when we re-think those beliefs—just as we take pride in our acquisition of wisdom after those extra dendrites start sprouting. But apart from the constant, if unmonitored, flux of our self, or our selfness, there are times when the whole world, which we like to imagine so solid around us, suddenly lurches: times when 'getting it wrong' hardly covers the cosmic shift. The moment of that first, personal *réveil mortel*; the moment—not necessarily contemporaneous—when we grasp that everyone else will die too; the realization that human life itself will end, as the sun boils away the oceans; and then, beyond that, planet death. All this we take on board, trying to keep our balance as we do.

But there is something else, even more vertiginous, to consider. We are, as a species, inclined to historical solipsism. The past is what has led to us; the future is what is being created by us. We claim ownership, triumphantly, of the best of times, and also, self-pityingly, of the worst of times. We tend to confuse our scientific and technological progress with moral and social progress. And we forget a little too easily that evolution is not just a process which has brought the race to its current admirable condition, but one which logically implies evolution away from us.

Yet how far, on a practical basis, do we look back, and how far ahead? I think I can see with reasonable clarity and breadth back to about the middle of the nineteenth century (in my own Western European culture, of course). Beyond that there are individual geniuses, moral and artistic exemplars, key ideas, intellectual movements, and pieces of historical action, but only here and there, rarely part of a continuum; and my reverse-looking runs out at, say, those Cycladic figurines of 3000–2000 BC. My forward looking certainly goes no further than the same basic hundred and fifty years or so; it is cautious, unfocused, and low in its expectations of posterity.

Chekhov was the great understander, and dramatizer, of our two-directional gaze. He specialized in defeated idealists who once dreamed of a better life, but are now becalmed in the present and fearful of the future. As a Chekhov play nears its end, a character will timidly express the hope that posterity may enjoy a less painful life and look back with tenderness on such forlorn predecessors. Knowing chuckles and superior sighs can sometimes be heard from the posterity that makes up the audience: the soft sound of forgiveness cut with an ironic recognition of what has actually happened in the intervening century—Stalinism, mass murder, gulags, brutal

257

industrialization, the felling and poisoning of all those forests and lakes so mournfully invoked by Dr Astrov and his soulmates, and the handing-over of music to the likes of Pavel Apostolov.

But as we look back at the tunnel-vision dupes of yesteryear, we tend to forget about our successors looking back at us, and judging our self-absorption for what it is worth—worth to them, not to us. What understanding, what tenderness, what forgiveness for us? What about *our* posterity? If we consider the question at all, our timescale is likely to be Chekhovian: a generation or two, perhaps a century. And those we imagine judging us will not, we presume, be so very different from us, because from now on the planet's future is going to be about fine-tuning the human animal: improving our moral and social senses, tamping down our aggressive habits, defeating poverty and disease, outwitting climate change, extending the human lifespan, and so on.

Yet from an evolutionary viewpoint, these are mere politicians' dreams, incredibly short-term. Not long ago, scientists in various disciplines were asked to describe the single idea they wished were more generally understood. I have forgotten all the others, so reorienting was the impact of a statement by Martin Rees, Astronomer Royal and Professor of cosmology and astrophysics at Cambridge:

I'd like to widen people's awareness of the tremendous timespan lying ahead—for our planet, and for life itself. Most educated people are aware that we're the outcome of nearly 4bn years of Darwinian selection, but

258

many tend to think that humans are somehow the culmination. Our sun, however, is less than halfway through its lifespan. It will not be humans who watch the sun's demise, 6bn years from now. Any creatures that then exist will be as different from us as we are from bacteria or amoebae.

Of course! WRONG—VERY WRONG—ALL THE TIME. And how amateurish not to have considered something so bluntly, intimidatingly consequential. 'We' shall not die out in six billion years. Something far beyond us—or at any rate, far different from us—will die out. For a start, we might have disappeared in another of the planet's great extinctions. The Permian Extinction took out ninety-nine per cent of all animals on earth, the Cretaceous two-thirds of all species, including the dinosaurs, making it possible for mammals to become the dominant land vertebrates. Perhaps a third Extinction will take us out in our turn and leave the world to . . . what? Beetles? The geneticist J.B.S. Haldane used to joke that if there were a God, He must have 'an inordinate fondness for beetles', given that He had created 350,000 species of them.

But even without a new Extinction, evolution will not unfold in the way we—sentimentally, solipsistically—hope. The mechanism of natural selection depends on the survival, not of the strongest, nor the most intelligent, but of the most adaptable. Forget the best and the brightest, forget evolution being some grand, impersonal, socially acceptable version of eugenics. It will take us where it wishes—or rather, not take 'us', since we shall soon prove ill-equipped for wherever it's heading; it will discard us as crude, insufficiently adaptable prototypes, and continue blindly towards new life forms which will make 'us'—and Bach and Shakespeare and Einstein—seem as distant as mere bacteria and amoebae. So much *a fortiori* for Gautier and art defeating death; so much for that pathetic murmur of *I was here too*. There is no 'too', as there will be nothing to which or to whom we can recognizably appeal, nothing that in turn will recognize us. Perhaps those future life forms will have retained and adapted intelligence, and will view us as primitive organisms of curious habit and faint historico-biological interest. Or perhaps they will be life forms of small intelligence but great physical adaptability. Imagine them munching away on the surface of the earth, while all the evidence of *homo sapiens*'s brief existence slumbers in the fossil record below.

At some point in that progress, Missing God will come to seem as delusionary a state as my mother's when imagining that I had stood her up on the tennis court. Not that the Amoeba Proposition necessarily sees God off. It would still be compatible with the experimenting God—for such a God, were He to exist, would scarcely be interested in an eternally stable group of research specimens. Just working with and on humans for the next six billion years would be immensely dull: it might make God want to kill Himself out of boredom. And then, if we avoid handing the planet over to beetles, and successfully evolve towards brainier and more complex beings, perhaps God Hypothesis number 72b. might come into play:

260

namely, that while we don't have immortal souls now, we shall have in the future. God is merely waiting until the Argument from Unworthiness no longer applies.

Two questions. Does realizing that, from the viewpoint of an evolving planet with six billion years still to run, we are not much more than amoebae, make it easier to accept that we do not possess free will? And if so (and even if not so), does this make it easier to die?

*　　　*　　　*

When I remember my father, I often think of how his nails used to curve over the flesh of his fingertips. In the weeks after his cremation, I used to imagine, not his face or his bones in the furnace, but those familiar fingernails. Beyond that, I think of the various insults his body showed towards the end. A stroke-damaged brain and tongue; a long scar up his belly which he offered to show me once but I lacked the guts to see; spreading bruises on the backs of his hands from the insertion of drips. Unless we are very lucky, our bodies will reveal the history of our dying. One small revenge might be to die and show no signs of having died. Jules Renard's mother was pulled from the well without a scratch or a scar on her. Not that Death—the ultimate bean counter—would care one way or the other. Any more than it cares whether or not we die in character.

We live, we die, we are remembered, we are forgotten. Not immediately, but in tranches. We remember our parents through most of their adult lives; our grandparents through their last third;

261

beyond that, perhaps, lies a great-grandfather with a scratchy beard and a rank odour. Perhaps he smelt of fish. And beyond that? Photographs, and a little haphazard documentation. In the future there will be a technological update of my shallow drawer: generations of ancestors will survive on film and tape and disc, moving, talking, smiling, proving that they too were here. As an adolescent I once hid a tape recorder under the table during dinner in an attempt to prove that, far from it being the 'social event' my mother decreed every meal should be, no one ever said anything remotely interesting and I should therefore be excused conversation and allowed to read a book if I preferred. I did not explain these personal aims, thinking they would become self-evident once the clatter of cutlery, banalities and non-sequiturs was played back. Annoyingly, my mother was enchanted by the tape, declaring that we all sounded just like a Pinter play (to my mind a mixed compliment, in both directions). And then we continued exactly as before; and I never kept the tape, so that my parents' voices are quite extinct in the world and play now only in my head.

I see (and hear) my mother in hospital, wearing a green dress, sitting canted over in a wheelchair by her bed. She was cross with me that day: not over tennis, but because I had been asked to discuss her treatment with the doctor. She resented every manifestation of incapacity, just as she resented the futile optimism of physiotherapists. When asked to name the hands on a watch, she declined; when instructed to open or close her eyes, she remained impassive. The doctors were unable to decide if it was a case of couldn't or wouldn't. My assumption was 'wouldn't'—that she was, in lawyer's terminology, 'mute of malice'—because in my company she was able to articulate whole sentences. Painfully—but then the sentences themselves were often filled with pain. For instance: 'You don't understand how difficult it is for a woman who has always controlled her life to be restricted like this.'

I spent some awkward minutes with her that afternoon, then went to find the doctor. His prognosis was very discouraging. As I returned to the ward, I told myself that my face must not betray his professional judgement that the next stroke would almost certainly kill her. But my mother was way ahead of me. Turning a corner, I saw, from twenty yards or more across a crowded ward, that she was beadily alert for my return; and as I progressed towards her, refining the semi-lie that I was about to tell, she stuck out her sole working forearm and delivered a thumbs-down sign. It was the most shocking thing I ever saw her do; the most admirable too, and the one occasion when she tore at my heart.

She thought the hospital ought to amputate her 'useless' arm; she thought, for some time, that she was in France, and wondered how I had found her; she thought a Spanish nurse came from her Oxfordshire village, and that all the other nurses came from the various parts of England where she had lived in the previous eighty years. She thought it 'stupid' not to have expired in a single go. When she asked, 'Do you have any trouble comprehending me?' she pronounced each syllable of the verb fastidiously. 'No, Ma,' I replied, 'I understand everything you say, but you don't

263

always get things completely right.' '*Ha,*' she retorted, as if I were some smiley physio. 'That's putting it mildly. I'm quite *loopy.*'

Her mixture of wild confabulation and lucid insight was constantly wrong-footing. In general, she seemed serene about whether she was visited or not, and took to saying, 'You must go now,' which was the complete bloody opposite of how she had been for decades. One day I looked down at the fingernails which the Witney registrar of births and deaths had admired five years previously. You could see how long it was since she had been able to do them; the heavily lacquered and lovingly shaped nails had continued to grow, pushing on to create an eighth of an inch of clear unvarnished whiteness below the cuticle. The nails she had once imagined herself still tending even if sunk in deafness. I looked upwards from the cuticles: the fingers of her dead arm had now swollen to the size, and to the outer texture, of carrots.

Driving back to London, the setting sun in my mirror, the Haffner Symphony on the radio, I thought: if this is what it's like for someone who has worked with her brain all her life, and can afford decent care, I don't want it. Then wondered if I was deluding myself, and would want it, when it came, on any terms; or whether I would have the courage or the cunning to circumvent it; or whether it just happens, and by happening condemns you to see it through, ragingly, dreadingly. However much you escape your parents in life, they are likely to reclaim you in death—in the manner of your death. The novelist Mary Wesley wrote: 'My family has a propensity—

it must be our genes—for dropping dead. Here one minute, gone the next. Neat. I pray that I have inherited this gene. I have no wish to linger, to become a bed-bound bore. A short sharp shock for my loved ones is what I want: nicer for them, lovely for me.'

This is a commonly expressed hope, but one my GP disapproves of. Citing this passage, she calls it 'perhaps another manifestation of the contemporary denial of death', and an attitude that 'attaches no value to the opportunities provided by a final illness'. I don't think either of my parents would have thought of their final illnesses as providing 'opportunities': for sharing memories, saying farewell, expressing remorse or forgiveness; while the funeral-planning—that's to say, their desire for an inexpensive and virtually mourner-free cremation—had been stated some time before. Would my parents have 'succeeded at death' if they had become emotional, confessional, soppy? Would they have found out that this was what they had always wanted? I rather doubt it. Though I regret my father never told me he loved me, I'm pretty sure that he did or had, and his melancholy silence on this and other key matters at least meant that he died in character.

When my mother was first in hospital, there was a comatose old woman in the next bed. She lay on her back, quite unmoving. One afternoon, with my mother in a fairly loopy state of mind, the woman's husband arrived. He was a small, neat, respectable working man, probably in his late sixties. 'Hello, Dulcie, it's Albert,' he announced in a ward-filling voice, with a rich, pure Oxfordshire accent which should have been recorded before it died out.

'Hello my darling, hello my love, are you going to wake up for me?' He kissed her echoingly. 'It's Albert, darling, are you going to wake up for me?' Then: 'I'll just turn you so I can put your hearing aid in.' A nurse arrived. 'I'm putting her hearing aid in. She didn't wake up for me this morning. Oh, it's fallen out. There, I'm going to turn you some more. Hello darling, hello Dulcie, hello my beautiful, it's Albert, are you going to wake up for me?' And so on, at intervals, for the next quarter of an hour, with a brief break of, 'You said something, didn't you, I know you said something, what did you say?' Then back to 'Hello darling, it's Albert, are you going to wake up for me?' interspersed with more kissing. It pierced the heart (and the head), and was only bearable by its edge of black comedy. My mother and I naturally pretended that nothing was going on, or if it was, nothing that we could hear; though the fact that my father's name had also been Albert was not, I suspect, lost on her.

The fingernails on my mother's useless arm continued to grow at exactly the same rate as the fingernails on the one with which she gave herself the thumbs-down; then she died and, contrary to popular belief, all ten nails stopped growing immediately. As had my father's, which curled round and over the flesh of his finger-pads. My brother's nails (and teeth) have always been stronger than mine, a detail I used to put down to the fact that he is shorter than me, and therefore his calcium is more concentrated. This may be scientific nonsense (and the answer lie in differing brands of commercial baby-milk). In any case, I have thinned my fingernails over the years by running them between my front teeth, automatically, when I am reading, writing, worrying, correcting this very sentence. Perhaps I should stop and find out if they will grow curvingly over my fingertips as my father comes to reclaim me.

*   *   *

Montmartre Cemetery is a green, cat-ridden place, cool and breezy even on a hot Parisian day; it is intimate, contoured and reassuring. Unlike the vast necropolis of Père-Lachaise, it creates the illusion—which a few graveyards do—that only those buried here have ever died; further, that they once lived quite close, perhaps in the very houses that rise at the cemetery's boundary; further still, that death is maybe not such a bad business after all. Jules Renard, five months before he died: 'As soon as you look it properly in the face, death is gentle to understand.'

Here lie some of my dead; most of them, being writers, in the lower and therefore cheaper section. Stendhal was buried here some thirty years after he had been 'seized with a fierce palpitation of the heart' outside Santa Croce, and felt as if 'the wellspring of life was dried up within me, and I walked in constant fear of falling to the ground'. We wish to die not just in character but in the manner of our own expectation? Stendhal was granted such fortune. After suffering a first stroke, he wrote, 'I find that there's nothing ridiculous about dropping dead in the street, as long as one doesn't do it deliberately.' On 22 March 1842, after dining at the Foreign Ministry, he got the non-ridiculous end he sought, on the pavement of the Rue Neuve-des-Capucines. He was buried as 'Arrigo Beyle, Milanese', a rebuke to the French who did not read him, and a tribute to the city where the smell of horse dung had moved him almost to tears. And as a man not unprepared for death (he made twenty-one wills), Stendhal composed his own epitaph: *Scrisse. Amo. Visse.* He wrote. He loved. He lived.

A few steps away lie the Goncourt Brothers. 'Two names, two sets of dates, they thought that was enough. *Hé! hé!'* But this is not how their tomb strikes me. For a start, it is a family grave: two children buried with their parents. They are sons first, writers second; and perhaps a family burial is like a family meal—a social occasion, as my mother used to insist. One at which certain rules apply: for instance, no boasting. So the only indicator of the brothers' fame is the pair of low-relief copper portraits on the tomb's upper surface, with Edmond and Jules facing one another in death as they did in their inseparable lives together.

The Goncourts have a new neighbour, as of 2004. An old grave, its concession expired, has been replaced by one with a gleaming black marble headstone, topped by a portrait bust of its occupant. The newcomer is Margaret Kelly-Leibovic, professionally known as Miss Bluebell, the Englishwoman who trained generations of athletic and beplumed six-footers to twirl and kick, twirl and kick for the lubriciously monocled. Just in case you doubt her importance, the four medals she was awarded—including the *légion d'honneur*—have been painted, life-size, though with an amateurish hand, on to the black marble. The fastidious, deeply conservative, Bohemia-hating aesthetes beside the parvenue troupe-trainer from the Lido (who didn't think her name was 'enough')? That must lower the tone of the neighbourhood: *Hé! hé!* Perhaps; but we shouldn't let death become an ironist (or let Renard's cackle succeed) too easily. The Goncourts discuss sex in their *Journal* with a candour which can still shock today. So what more appropriate—even if delayed by a century—than a posthumous *à trois* with Miss Bluebell?

When Edmond de Goncourt was buried here, and the family line died out, Zola gave the graveside address. Six years later, he was back in his own right, borne to a tomb as showy as the Goncourts' was simple. The poor boy from Aix who made the name of his immigrant Italian family resound across Europe was buried beneath a rich art nouveau swirl of reddish-brown marble. On top is a portrait bust of the writer so fierce that it seems to be defending not just his coffin and his oeuvre but the entire cemetery. Yet Zola's fame was too great for him to be granted posthumous peace. After only six years, the French state bodysnatched him for the Panthéon. And here we must allow death some irony. For consider the case of Alexandrine, who had survived that night of smoke inhalation from the blocked chimney. Her widowhood was to last twenty-three years. For six of these, she would have visited her husband in green and pleasant Montmartre; for the next seventeen, it was a trudge to the chilly, echoing Panthéon. Then Alexandrine herself died. But pantheons are only for the famous, not their relicts, so she was buried—as she must have known she would be—in that vacated tomb. And then in their turn, Mme Alexandrine's children joined her; and then her grandchildren, all stuffed into a vault that was missing its patriarch and the very reason for its splendour.

We live, we die, we are remembered,— 'misremember me correctly', we should instruct— we are forgotten. For writers, the process of being forgotten isn't clear-cut. 'Is it better for a writer to die before he is forgotten, or to be forgotten before he dies?' But 'forgotten' here is only a comparative term, meaning: fall out of fashion, be used up, seen through, superseded, judged too superficial—or, for that matter, too ponderous, too *serious*—for a later age. But *truly* forgotten, now that's much more interesting. First, you fall out of print, consigned to the recesses of the secondhand bookshop and dealer's website. Then a brief revival, if you're lucky, with a title or two reprinted; then another fall, and a period when a few graduate students, pushed for a thesis topic, will wearily turn your pages and wonder why you wrote so much. Eventually, the publishing houses forget, academic interest recedes, society changes, and humanity evolves a little further, as evolution carries out its purposeless purpose of rendering us all the equivalent of bacteria and amoebae. This is inevitable. And at some point—it must logically happen—a writer will have a last reader. I am not asking for sympathy; this aspect of a writer's living and dying is a given. At some point between now and the six-billion-years-away death of the planet, every writer will have his or her last reader. Stendhal, who in his lifetime wrote for 'the happy

270

few' who understood him, will find his readership dwindling back to a different, mutated, perhaps less happy few, and then to a final happy—or bored—one. And for each of us there will come the breaking of the single remaining thread of this strange, unwitnessed, yet deeply intimate relationship between writer and reader. At some point, there will be a last reader for me too. And then that reader will die. And while, in the great democracy of readership, all are theoretically equal, some are more equal than others.

My last reader: there is a temptation to be sentimental over him or her (if 'he' and 'she' still apply in that world where evolution is taking our species). Indeed, I was about to make some authorial gesture of thanks and praise to the ultimate pair of eyes—if eyes have not also evolved differently—to examine this book, this page, this line. But then logic kicked in: your last reader is, by definition, someone who doesn't recommend your books to anyone else. You bastard! Not good enough, eh? You prefer that trivial stuff which is all the rage in your superficial century (and/or that leaden stuff which makes you judge me trivial)? I was about to mourn your passing, but I'm getting over it fast. You're really not going to press my book on anyone else? You really are so mean-spirited, so idle-minded, so lacking in critical judgement? Then you don't deserve me. Go on, fuck off and die. Yes, *you*.

I shall myself long since have fucked off and died, though of what cause I cannot yet tell or, like Stendhal, predict. I had assumed that my parents, in a last controlling act, would determine my end; but you can't always rely on your parents, especially after they're dead. Mary Wesley, to the disapproval of my GP, was counting on her family's famed talent for conking out—dropping like a fly listening to Shostakovich's fifteenth quartet. But when the time came, she found that they had neglected to pass on this hereditary skill, or repeated luck. She died instead, more slowly than she would have wanted, from cancer—though still with admirable stoicism. One witness reported how 'She never complained about her uncomfortable bed, hard food and painful, bony body except for one occasional comment—"Bugger".' So, by the sound of it, she died in character, and at least was able to swear, unlike my stroke-struck, tongue-tied English master, who never got to utter the promised 'Damn!' as his famous last word.

*   *   *

Nowadays, it costs five euros to visit the church— or as the ticket prefers, the 'monumental complex'—of Santa Croce in Florence. You enter not by the west front, as Stendhal did, but on the north side, and are immediately presented with a choice of route and purpose: the left gate for those who wish to pray, the right for tourists, atheists, aesthetes, idlers. The vast and airy nave of this preaching church still contains those tombs of famous men whose presence softened up Stendhal. Among them now is a relative newcomer: Rossini, who in 1863 asked God to grant him paradise. The composer died in Paris five years later and was buried in Père-Lachaise; but as with Zola, a proud state came and body-snatched him for its pantheon. Whether God chose to grant Rossini paradise depends perhaps on whether or not God has read the Goncourt *Journal*. 'The sins of my old age'? Here is the *Journal*'s entry for 20 January 1876: 'Last night, in the smoking-room at Princesse Mathilde's, the conversation turned to Rossini. We talked of his priapism, and his taste, in the matter of love, for unwholesome practices; and then of the strange and innocent pleasures the old composer took in his final years. He would get young girls to undress to the waist and let his hands wander lasciviously over their torsos, while giving them the end of his little finger to suck.'

Stendhal wrote the first biography of Rossini in 1824. Two years later, he published *Rome, Naples and Florence*, in which he described how Henri, or Arrigo, Beyle had come to Florence in 1811. He descended from the Apennines one January morning, he saw 'from a far distance' Brunelleschi's great dome rising above the city, he got down from the coach to enter on foot like a pilgrim, he stood before paintings which thrilled him till he swooned. And we might still believe every word of his account if he had remembered to do one thing: destroy the diary he had kept of that original trip.

Stravinsky in old age wrote: 'I wonder if memory is true, and I know that it cannot be, but that one lives by memory nonetheless and not by truth.' Stendhal lived by the memory of 1826 whereas Beyle had written the truth of 1811. From the diary, we learn that he did indeed cross the Apennines by coach and descend into the city, but memory took one road and truth another. In 1811 he couldn't have seen Brunelleschi's dome from afar for the simple reason that it was dark. He

273

arrived in Florence at five in the morning, 'overcome with fatigue, wet, jolted, obliged to maintain a hold on the front of the mail wagon and sleeping while seated in a cramped position'. Unsurprisingly, he went straight to an inn, the Auberge d'Angleterre, and to bed. He left orders to be woken two hours later, but not for touristic purposes: he headed for the post-house and tried to book himself a seat on the next coach to Rome. But that day's coach was full, and so was the next day's—and this was the only reason he stayed in Florence for the three days in which he added to the history of aesthetic response. Another incompatibility: the book sets the visit in January; the diary dates it to September.

Still, he went to Santa Croce: memory and truth agree on that. But what did he see? The Giottos, presumably. That's what everyone goes for: the Giottos which, as *Firenze Spettacolo* reminds us, are in the Niccolini Chapel. But in neither account does Beyle/Stendhal actually mention Giotto, or, for that matter, any of the other starred masterpieces our modern guidebooks urge us towards: the Donatello crucifix, the Donatello Annunciation, the Taddeo Gaddi frescoes, the Pazzi Chapel. Tastes change over a couple of centuries, we conclude. And Beyle does mention the Niccolini Chapel. The only problem is, it doesn't contain the Giottos. Standing in front of the altar, he would—should—have turned right for the Bardi Chapel and the Peruzzi Chapel. Instead, he turned left, to the Niccolini Chapel in the far north-east corner of the transept. Here, the four paintings of sibyls which moved him to 'rapture' were by Volterrano. You may well ask; as I did.

274

(And found the answers: born Volterra 1611, died Florence 1690, follower of Pietro da Cortona, patronee of the Medici, decorator of the Pitti Palace.)

In the memory of 1826, the chapel was unlocked by a friar, and Stendhal sat on the step of a faldstool, his head thrown back against a desk, to gaze at the frescoed ceiling. In the truth of 1811, there is no friar and no faldstool; further, in both 1811 and 1826, and at any date previous or since, the sibyls have been located high on the walls of the chapel, but not on the ceiling. Indeed, the diary of 1811, after praising the Volterranos, continues: 'The ceiling of the same chapel is very effective, but my eyesight is not good enough to judge ceilings. It merely appeared to me to be very effective.'

Today the Niccolini Chapel isn't locked, but this famous location where art began to replace religion lies ironically in the roped-off section intended for the prayerful. Instead of a friar you need a uniformed official; instead of a folding stool, a pair of binoculars. I explained my secular purpose to a man in a suit; and perhaps in Italy the words 'I am a writer' carry a little more weight than in Britian. Sympathetically, he advised me to stuff my guidebook into my pocket and not to take it out while 'praying'; then he unhooked the rope.

In holiday clothes, I tried to look convincingly grave as I crossed this reserved corner of the church. Yet at 2.30 on a Thursday afternoon there was not a single believer—let alone a priest or a friar—in any of these sacred spaces. The Niccolini Chapel was also quite deserted. The four Volterranos, still neck-strainingly high on the walls,

275

have been recently cleaned, and show themselves even more plainly as competent yet routine expressions of the baroque. But then I would have wanted them to be: the more ordinary the paintings, the better the story. Also, of course, the stronger the implicit warning to our own contemporary taste. Just give it time, these sibyls seem to warn. Time may not reinstate Volterrano for Giotto, but it's bound to make you look foolish, fashionable, amateur. That is time's business, now that God has given up the job of judgement.

Apart from the Volterranos, there was one other painting in Santa Croce which excited Stendhal beyond measure. It showed Christ's descent into limbo—that place so recently abolished by the Vatican—and left him 'aflutter for two hours'. Beyle, then working on his history of Italian painting, had been told it was by Guercino, whom he 'worshipped from the bottom of my heart'; two hours later, a different authority ascribed it (correctly) to Bronzino, 'a name unknown to me. This discovery annoyed me a great deal.' But there was nothing equivocal about the picture's effect. 'I was almost moved to tears,' he wrote in his diary. 'They start to my eyes as I write this. I've never seen anything so beautiful . . . Painting has never given me so much pleasure.'

So much pleasure that he faints? And if not at the Giottos (which he never claimed, but which later wishful thinking foisted upon him), then at least at Volterrano and Bronzino combined? Well, here's a final problem. Stendhal's Syndrome, paraded and patented—if not named—in 1826, does not appear to have taken place in 1811. That famous episode in the porch of Santa Croce—the fierce palpitation of the heart, the wellspring of life drying up—was not deemed worthy of a diary entry at the time. The nearest approximation to it comes after the line 'Painting has never given me so much pleasure.' Beyle goes on: 'I was dead tired, my feet swollen and pinched in new boots—a little sensation which would prevent God from being admired in all His glory, but I overlooked it in front of the picture of limbo. *Mon Dieu*, how beautiful it is!'

So all reliable evidence for Stendhal's Syndrome effectively dissolves before our eyes. But the point is not that Stendhal was an exaggerator, a fabulator, a false-memory artist (and Beyle a truth-teller). The story becomes more, not less, interesting. It is a story instead about narrative and memory. Narrative: the truth of a novelist's story is the truth of its final form, not that of its initial version. Memory: we should believe that Beyle was equally sincere, whether writing at a few hours' distance from events, or fifteen years later. Note also that whereas Beyle was 'almost moved to tears' in front of the Bronzino, they 'started to his eyes' when he wrote about the sibyls a couple of hours later. Time brings not just narrative variation but emotional increase. And if forensic examination appears to diminish the story of Santa Croce, it remains, even in its original, unimproved version, about aesthetic joy being greater than religious rapture. Fatigue and tight boots would have distracted Beyle from God's glory, had he gone into the church to pray; but the power of art overcame pinched toes and rubbed heels.

*　　　*　　　*

My grandfather, Bert Scoltock, had only two jokes in his repertoire. The first referred to his and Grandma's wedding day, 4 August 1914, and so came with half a century of repetition (rather than honing): 'We were married the day war broke out,' (heavy pause) 'and it's been *war ever since*!!!' The second was a story drawn out as long as possible, about a chap who went into a café and asked for a sausage roll. He took a bite, then complained that there wasn't any sausage in it. 'You haven't reached it yet,' said the café's proprietor. The fellow took another mouthful and repeated his complaint. 'You've bitten right past it,' came the reply—a punchline my grandfather would then reprise.

My brother agrees that Grandpa was humourless; though when I add 'boring and a little frightening', he dissents. But then Grandpa did favour his first-born grandchild, and taught him how to sharpen a chisel. It's true, he never beat me for pulling up his onions, but his was a headmasterly presence in the family, and I can easily summon up his disapproval. For instance: every year, he and Grandma would come over for Christmas. Once, in the early sixties, Grandpa, looking for something to read, went to the bookshelves in my bedroom and, without asking, removed my copy of *Lolita*. I can see the Corgi paperback now, see how my grandfather's woodworking and gardening hands methodically broke the spine as he read. This was something Alex Brilliant also used to do—though Alex behaved as if breaking a book's spine showed you were engaging intellectually with its contents;

whereas Grandpa's (exactly similar) behaviour seemed to indicate disrespect for both the novel and its author. At every page—from 'fire of my loins' to 'the age when lads / Play with erector sets'—I expected him to throw it down in disgust. Amazingly, he didn't. He had started, so he would finish: English puritanism kept him doggedly ploughing through this Russian tale of American depravity. As I nervously watched him, I began to feel almost as if I had written the novel, and now stood revealed as a secret nymphet-groper. What *could* he be making of it? Eventually, he handed the book back to me, its spine a vertical mess of whitened cicatrices, with the comment, 'It may be *good literature*, but I thought it was SMUTTY.'

At the time, I smirked to myself, as any aesthete going up to Oxford would. But I did my grandfather a disservice. For he had accurately recognized *Lolita*'s appeal to me then: as a vital combination of literature and smut. (There was such a dearth of sexual information—let alone experience—around that a reworking of Renard obtained: 'It is when faced with sex that we turn most bookish.') I also did Grandpa a disservice earlier by suggesting that he left me nothing in his will. Wrong again. My brother corrects me: 'When Grandpa died, he left me his repro Chippendale desk (which I never liked) and he left you his gold half-hunter watch (which I had always coveted).'

An old press cutting in my archive drawer confirms that the desk was a retirement present in 1949, when Bert Scoltock, then sixty, left Madeley Modern Secondary School after thirty-six years as a head teacher in various parts of Shropshire. He also received an armchair—quite probably that

279

very Parker Knoll; also, a fountain pen, a cigarette lighter, and a set of gold cufflinks. Girls from the Domestic Science Centre baked him a two-tier cake; while Eric Frost, 'representing a group of boys from the Woodwork Centre' gave him 'a nut bowl and mallet'. I remember this last item well since it was always on display at my grandparents' bungalow, yet never used. When it finally came into my possession, I understood why: it was comically impractical, the mallet firing shell-shrapnel all over the room while reducing the nuts to powder. I always assumed that Grandpa must have made it himself, since almost every wooden object in house and garden, from trug to book trough to grandmother clock case, had been sawn and sanded and chamfered and dowelled by his own hands. He had a great respect for wood, which he took to its final conclusion. Shocked by the notion that coffins crafted from fine oak and elm were reduced to ashes a day or two later, he specified that his own be made from deal.

As for the gold half-hunter, it has been in my top desk drawer for decades. It comes with a gold fob-chain for waistcoat-wear and a leather strap if you prefer to dangle it from lapel buttonhole into top pocket. I open its back: 'Presented to Mr B. Scoltock, by Managers, Teachers, Scholars and Friends, after his leaving after 18 years as head teacher at Bayston Hill C of E School. June 30th 1931.' I had no idea my brother had ever coveted it, so I tell him that now, after forty-odd years of suffering this sinful emotion, the watch is his. 'As for the half-hunter,' he replies, 'I think he would have wanted you to keep it.' He *would have wanted*? My brother is winding me up with this hypothetical want of the dead. He goes on: 'More to the point, I now want you to keep it.' Yes, indeed, we can only do what *we* want.

I apply to my brother on the subject of Grandpa and Remorse. He has two explanations, 'the first perhaps too trivial': a running shame at having beaten his grandson for pulling up his onions. The second, more weighty, suggestion is this: 'When he used to tell me stories [about the First World War] they would run up to the time the boat left for France, and then start back again in hospital in England. He never said a word to me about the war. I suppose he was in the trenches. He didn't win any medals, I'm sure, nor was he wounded (not even a blighty). So he must have been invalided out for trench feet? Shell shock? Something less than heroic, in any case. Did he let his chums down? I once thought I'd try to find out what he actually did in the war—no doubt there are regimental records, etc. etc.; but of course I never got round to doing anything.'

In my archive drawer are Grandpa's birth certificate, his marriage certificate, and his photo album—that red cloth-bound book titled 'Scenes from Highways & Byways'. Here is Grandpa astride a motorbike in 1912, with Grandma perched on the back; roguishly laying his head on her bosom the following year, while grasping her knee with his hand. Here he is on his wedding day, hand around his bride's shoulder and pipe cocked in front of his white waistcoat, as Europe prepares to blow itself apart; on his honeymoon (a studio shot which has faded less); and with 'Babs'—as my mother was known before becoming Kathleen Mabel—born ten months after the wedding. There are pictures of him on home leave, first with two stripes up—Prestatyn, August 1916—and finally three. By this time Sergeant Scoltock is in the Grata Quies hospital outside Bournemouth, where he and the other inmates look remarkably perky as they pose in fancy dress for a concert party. Here is my grandfather in blackface, first with a certain Decker (cross-dressing as a nurse), and then with Fullwood (a Pierrot). And here again is that photo, the head-shot of a woman, still dated in pencil Sept 1915, but with the name (or perhaps the place) erased, and the face so scarred and gouged that only the lips and the Weetabixy hair remain. An obliteration that makes her more intriguing than 'Nurse Glynn', or even 'Sgt P. Hyde Killed in Action, Dec 1915'. An obliteration which seems to me a much better symbol of death than the ubiquitous skull. You only get down to bone after rotting through time; and when you do, one skull is much like another. Fine as a long-term symbol, but for the action of death itself, try just such a torn, gouged photograph: it looks both personal and instantly, utterly destructive, a ripping away of the light from the eye and the life from the cheek.

Formal investigation of my grandfather's war service is initially hampered by not knowing his regiment or date of enlistment. The first Scoltock to turn up is a box-maker invalided out with a medical statement that reads simply: 'Idiot'. (Oh to have an officially designated Idiot in the family.) But then here comes Private Bert Scoltock of the 17th Battalion, Lancashire Fusiliers, who enlisted on 20 November 1915, and two months later took that boat for France with the 104th Infantry Brigade, 35th Division.

My brother and I are surprised that Grandpa joined up so late. I had always imagined him getting fitted out in khaki just as Grandma was falling pregnant. But this must be a piece of back-imagining from our parents' lives: my father joined up and was sent out to India in 1942, leaving my mother pregnant with what turned out to be my brother. Did Grandpa not volunteer until November 1915 because of his daughter coming into the world? He was, as the inscription on his half-hunter confirms, then head teacher at a Church of England school, so perhaps he was in a reserved profession. Or did such a category not yet exist, given that conscription wasn't introduced until January 1916? Perhaps he saw it coming and preferred to volunteer. If Grandma was already a socialist by this time, he might have wanted to show that, despite having a politically suspicious wife, he was nonetheless patriotic. Did one of those smug women come up to him in the street and offer him a white feather? Did he have a close chum who joined up? Was he suffering from a recently married man's fear of entrapment? Is all this absurdly fanciful? Perhaps trying to trace his statement about remorse back to the First World War is misconceived, since it never came with any date attached. I once asked my mother why Grandpa never talked about the war. She replied, 'I don't think he thought it was very interesting.'

Grandpa's personal records (like those of many others) were destroyed by enemy action during the Second World War. The brigade diary shows that they reached the Western Front in late January 1916; there was heavy rain; Kitchener inspected them on 11 February 1916. In July, they finally saw

283

action (casualties 19th–27th: 8 officers wounded; Other Ranks, 34 killed, 172 wounded). The following month, the brigade was in Vaux, Montagne, and the front line at Montauban; Grandpa would have been in Dublin Trench, where the brigade complained of being shelled by their own under-aiming artillery; later in Chimpanzee Trench, at the south end of Angle Wood. In September and October they were in the line again (4th Sept–31st Oct, Other Ranks Casualties: 1 killed, 14 wounded—3 accidental, 3 at duty, 4 rifle grenade, 2 bombed, 1 aerial torpedo, 1 bullet). The brigade commander is listed as a certain 'Captain, Brigade Major B.L. Montgomery (later Alamein)'.

Montgomery of Alamein! We used to watch him on the dwarf's armoire—'ghastly little Monty poncing about in black and white', as my brother put it—explaining how he had won the Second World War. My brother and I used to mimic his inability to pronounce his *r*s. 'I then gave Wommel a wight hook', would be our mock summary of the Desert Campaign. Grandpa never told us he had served under Monty—never even told his own daughter, who would certainly have mentioned it as part of family history every time we tuned in.

The brigade's diary for 17 November 1916 notes: 'The Army Commander has lately seen a very short-sighted man in a Battalion of Infantry and a deaf man in another. These would be a danger in the front line.' (There's a novel would-you-rather: would you rather be deaf or blind in the First World War?) Another note from Command states: 'The number of courts martial held in the Division during the period 1st Dec.

1916 to date tend to show that the state of discipline in the Division is not what it should be.' Over that period the 17th Lancashire Fusiliers had 1 desertion, 6 Sleeping on Post and 2 'accidental' (presumably self-inflicted) injuries.

There is no evidence—there could be no evidence—that my grandfather featured in these statistics. He was an ordinary soldier who volunteered, was shipped out to France for the middle period of the war, and progressed from private to sergeant. He was invalided out with (as I have always understood it) trench foot or feet, 'a painful condition caused by prolonged immersion in water or mud, marked by swelling, blistering, and some degree of necrosis'. He returned to England at an unspecified date, and was discharged on 13 November 1917, along with twenty others from his regiment, as 'No longer physically fit for service.' He was then twenty-eight, and oddly—I assume mistakenly—listed as a private in the records of discharge. And despite my brother's memory, he did receive medals, if of the lowliest kind—the kind awarded for simply turning up: the British War Medal, given for entering a theatre of war, and the Victory Medal, given to all eligible personnel who served in an operational theatre. The latter reads, on its reverse, 'The Great War for Civilization 1914–1919.'

And there it all runs out, memory and knowledge. These are the available scraps; nothing more can be known. But since family piety is not my motivation, I am not disappointed. I give my grandfather's service, and its secrets, and his silence, as an example. First, of being wrong: thus I discovered that 'Bert Scoltock, so christened, so called, so cremated', in fact began life, in April 1889, at the register office of Driffield in the County of York, as Bertie; and was still Bertie in the census of 1901. Secondly, as an example of how much you can find out, and where that leaves you. Because what you can't find out, and where that leaves you, is one of the places where the novelist starts. We (by which I mean 'I') need a little, not a lot; a lot is too much. We begin with a silence, a mystery, an absence, a contradiction. If I had discovered that Grandpa had been one of the six Sleeping on Post, and that while he was slumbering the enemy had crept up and slaughtered some of his fellow Fusiliers, and that this had caused him great Remorse, a feeling he had carried to the grave (and if I were to discover all this from a hand-written affidavit—mark that remorsefully shaky signature—while clearing out an old bank-deposit box), I might have been satisfied as a grandson, but not as a novelist. The story, or the potential story, would have been spoilt. I know a writer who likes to linger on park benches, listening in to conversations; but as soon as his eavesdropping threatens to disclose more than he professionally requires, he moves on. No, the absence, the mystery, they are for us (him and me) to solve.

So in 'Scenes from Highways & Byways', my eye is drawn not to Great Uncle Percy in Blackpool or Nurse Glynn or Sgt P. Hyde Killed in Action Dec 1915 but to the lips and hair and white blouse of 'Sept 1915' and the erasure beside the date. Why was this photograph defaced, and its edges ripped as if by raging fingernails? And further, why was it not either removed from the album entirely, or at

286

least pasted over with another photograph? Here are some possible explanations: 1. It was a picture of Grandma, which Grandpa liked, but which she later took against. However, this wouldn't explain the seeming violence of the attack, which has dug through to the album page below. Unless, 1b., it was done after senility took hold, and Grandma had simply failed to recognize herself. Who is this woman, this interloper, this temptress? And so she scratched herself out. But if so, why this picture rather than any other? And why erase the scrap of information next to the date? 2. If this was another woman, was the gouging done by Grandma? If so, roughly when? Shortly after she was stuck into the album, as a dramatic marital strike? Much later, but in Grandpa's lifetime? Or after Grandpa's death, as a long-delayed act of revenge? 3. Could this, just possibly, be 'a very nice girl called Mabel', after whom my mother was named? What did Grandma once tell my mother—that there would be no bad men in the world if there were no bad women. 4. Grandpa might have done the gouging and attempted ripping himself. This seems highly unlikely as a) it was his album; b) he was experienced in handicrafts, leatherwork and bookbinding, and would certainly have made a better job of it; and c) photo-mutilation is, I suspect, a predominantly female crime. 5. But in any case, consider the dates. Bert (as he had become by 1914) and Nell were married the day war broke out; their daughter was conceived within a month, and born in June 1915. The mystery photograph is dated September 1915. My grandfather volunteered in November 1915, though conscription was to be introduced anyway

287

within a couple of months. Is this, perhaps, the reason he knew about remorse? And my mother, of course, was an only child.

A Bertie who changed into a Bert; a late volunteer; a mute witness; a sergeant discharged as a private; a defaced photograph; a possible case of remorse. This is where we work, in the interstices of ignorance, the land of contradiction and silence, planning to convince you with the seemingly known, to resolve—or make usefully vivid—the contradiction, and to make the silence eloquent.

*   *   *

My grandfather proposes, ' "Friday. Worked in garden. Planted potatoes." ' My grandmother retorts, 'Nonsense,' and insists, ' "Rained all day. Too wet to work in garden." ' He shook his head when his *Daily Express* told him of a Red Plot to Rule the World; she tut-tutted when her *Daily Worker* warned her about US Imperialist Warmongers Sabotaging People's Democracies. We all—their grandson (me), the reader (you), even my last reader (yes, you, you bastard)—are confident that the truth lies somewhere in between. But the novelist (me again) is less interested in the exact nature of that truth, more in the nature of the believers, the manner in which they hold their beliefs, and the texture of the ground between the competing narratives.

Fiction is made by a process which combines total freedom and utter control, which balances precise observation with the free play of the imagination, which uses lies to tell the truth and truth to tell lies. It is both centripetal and centrifugal. It wants to tell all stories, in all their contrariness, contradiction and irresolvability; at the same time it wants to tell the one true story, the one that smelts and refines and resolves all the other stories. The novelist is both bloody back-row cynic and lyric poet, drawing on Wittgenstein's austere insistence—speak only of that which you can truly know—and Stendhal's larky shamelessness.

A boy dives on to a leaky pouffe and through its broken seams squirt the torn-up love letters of his parents. But he will never be able to piece together the wonder and the mystery, or the routine and the banality, of their love ('People tell me it's a cliché, but it doesn't feel like a cliché to me'). Half a century on, the boy, now approaching old age, who has spent his adult life with stories, their meaning and their making, thinks of this as a metaphor of our lives: the energetic action, the torn-up clues, the unwillingness or inability to piece together a story of which we can know only fragments. What remains are blue scraps of paper, postcards with the stamps—and therefore postmarks—steamed off, and the tone of a Swiss cowbell as it ding-dongs stupidly down into a skip.

I have no memory of being that small boy who was pushed, blindfold, into a wall by his brother. Nor, without the kind of psychotherapeutic intervention of which I am suspicious, can I discover whether my non-memory comes from deliberate suppression (trauma! terror! fear of my brother! love of my brother! both!) or the unexceptionality of the event. My elder niece C. first described it to me, at the time she and I were dealing with my mother's final decline. She said that she and her sister were told it 'as a funny story' when they were little. But she did also remember concluding 'that it was not a particularly good way to behave, so perhaps he [her father, my brother] intended it as a cautionary tale of sorts'. If so, what might be the moral? Treat your younger sibling better than I did? Learn that life is like being pushed blindfold into a wall?

I apply to my brother for his version. 'The trike story,' he replies. 'I told it, or versions of it, to C. & C. to make them laugh—which, I fear, it did. (I can't recall ever telling them anything with a moral to it . . .).' Now, there's having a philosopher for a father. 'In my memory, it was a game we played in the back garden at Acton. An obstacle course was set up on the lawn—logs, tincans, bricks. The game was to tricycle round the course without serious injury. One of us steered the trike while the other one pushed. (I think the trike had lost its chain; but perhaps the pushing aspect added to the sadistic pleasures of the event.) The steerer was blindfolded. I'm pretty sure we took it in turns to steer and to push; but I suspect that I pushed you faster than you pushed me. I don't recall any major accident (nor even anyone being pushed into a wall—which in fact would not have been at all easy, given the layout of the garden). I don't recall your being frightened. I seem to think we thought it was fun, and rather naughty.'

My niece's initial summary of the game—my brother blindfolding me before pushing me into a wall—might be a child's shorthand memory, emphasizing what she herself would most have feared; or it might be a subsequent abbreviation or reimagining made in the light of her relationship with her father. What's more surprising is that my own memory is blindfold, especially given the elaborateness of the proceedings. I wonder how my brother and I can have acquired logs and cans and bricks from our very small, neat suburban garden, let alone laid out such a course, without it being known and noted, and permitted or forbidden. But my niece rejects this: 'I'm sure your parents never told me the story; in fact, I thought they never knew about it.'

I apply to her younger sister. She too remembers the obstacle course, the blindfolding, the frequency of the game. 'You were then pushed at breakneck speed through the obstacles and the race ended with you being rammed into the garden wall. It was billed as a Great Bit of Fun for both of you, with an undercurrent of doing something that was certainly disapproved of by Mother; I think not so much because of the damage inflicted on you but the misuse of garden tools and the soiling of washing hanging up to dry. I don't know why we were told this story (or why I remember it). I think it was the only story about you, in fact about the family at all, except for your grandmother vomiting on a boat into a series of yoghurt pots. I think it was supposed to prove to us that children should do whatever they please, in particular if it is silly and displeasing to adults . . . The story was told in a jokey way and we were certainly supposed to laugh and applaud the daring nature of the whole thing. I don't think we ever questioned the truth of it all.'

You see (again) why (in part) I am a novelist? Three conflicting accounts of the same event, one by a participant, two based on memories of subsequent retellings thirty years ago (and containing detail the original teller might himself have since forgotten); the sudden insertion of new material—'misuse of garden tools', 'soiling of washing'; the emphasis, in my nieces' versions, on a ritual climax to the game—me being pushed into a wall—that my brother denies; the forgetting of the whole episode by its second participant, despite his serfdom as a log-trundler and brick-gatherer; the absence, from my nieces' versions, of a return match in which I got to push the trike; and most of all, the moral variation between what my brother said he had been intending when he told the story (pure amusement), and what his daughters, separately and differently, concluded he was doing. My informants' replies might almost have been scripted to cast doubt on the reliability of oral history. And I am left with a new proposed definition of what I do: a novelist is someone who remembers nothing yet records and manipulates different versions of what he doesn't remember.

The novelist in the present instance would need to supply the following: who invented the game; how the trike lost its chain; how the pusher instructed the unseeing driver to steer; whether or not Mother Really Knew; which garden tools were used; how the washing got soiled; what sadistic and/or pre-sexual pleasures might have been involved; and why it was the main, almost the only story a philosopher told about his childhood. Also, if the novel were to be multi-generational, whether the two sisters who first heard it subsequently repeated it to their own daughters (and with what humorous or moral purpose)—whether the story dies out, or is changed again in the mouths and minds of a subsequent generation.

For the young—and especially the young writer—memory and imagination are quite distinct, and of different categories. In a typical first novel, there will be moments of unmediated memory (typically, that unforgettable sexual embarrassment), moments where the imagination has worked to transfigure a memory (perhaps that chapter in which the protagonist learns some lesson about life, whereas in the original the novelist-to-be failed to learn anything), and moments when, to the writer's astonishment, the imagination catches a sudden upcurrent and the weightless, wonderful soaring that is the basis for fiction delightingly happens.

These different kinds of truthfulness will be fully apparent to the young writer, and their joining together a matter of anxiety. For the older writer, memory and the imagination begin to seem less and less distinguishable. This is not because the imagined world is really much closer to the writer's life than he or she cares to admit (a common error among those who anatomize fiction) but for exactly the opposite reason: that memory itself comes to seem much closer to an act of the imagination than ever before. My brother distrusts most memories. I do not mistrust them, rather I trust them as workings of the imagination, as containing imaginative as opposed to naturalistic truth. Ford Madox Ford could be a mighty liar, and a mighty truth-teller, at the same time, and in the same sentence.

*   *   *

Chitry-les-Mines lies some twenty miles south of

Vézelay. A faded blue tin sign proposes a right turn off the main road to *Maison de Jules Renard*, where the boy grew up amid that silent parental war and, years later, the man broke down the bedroom door to find his suicided father. A second tin sign, and a second right turn, leads you to *Monument de Jules Renard*, whose erection he teasingly entrusted to his sister a few months before he died: 'We were wondering this morning who would see to setting up my bust on the little square in Chitry. We thought straight away that we could count on you . . .' The 'little square', a lime-planted triangle in front of the church, has inevitably become the Place Jules Renard. The writer's bronze bust is supported by a stone column, at the base of which sits a brooding Poil de Carotte, looking melancholy and mature for his age. A stone tree climbs up the other side of the column, bursting into leaf around the writer's shoulders: nature enclosing and protecting him, in death as in life. It is a handsome piece of work, and when unveiled in October 1913 by André Renard—pharmacist, former socialist deputy and distant cousin—it must have seemed the only monument this obscure village would ever require. Its size fits the square, and so renders the First World War memorial, only a few yards away, almost apologetic of its presence, its listed names somehow less important, and less of a loss to Chitry, than its arteriosclerotic chronicler.

There is not a shop, a café or even a grimy petrol pump in this straggly village; the only reason for an outsider to stop here is Jules Renard. Somewhere nearby must be the well, doubtless long since filled in, which claimed Mme Renard nearly a century ago. A tricolore on the building opposite the church identifies the *mairie* where both François Renard and his son performed their civic functions, where Jules was kissed on the lips by a bride he had just joined in matrimony ('It cost me 20 francs'). The tarmacked lane between *mairie* and *église* leads out of the village a few hundred yards to the cemetery, which still lies in open countryside.

It is a July day of canicular heat, and the square, sloping graveyard is as bleak and dusty as a parade round. A list of names and plot numbers is posted at the gate. Failing to realize that this refers to concessions about to expire, I look at first for the wrong Renard in the wrong plot. The cemetery's only other (living) occupant is a woman with a watering can, moving slowly among her favoured graves. I ask her where the writer might be found. 'He's down there on the left, next to the tap,' is her reply.

The village's most famous inhabitant is indeed tucked away in a corner of the graveyard. I remember that Renard *père* was the first person to be buried here without any religious ceremony. Perhaps that is why the family grave seems positioned a little below the salt, or next to the tap (if the tap was there then). It is a square plot, backed against the boundary wall, and protected by a low, green-painted iron railing; the little gate in the middle sticks from successive repaintings, and requires a certain force. Two stone planters sit just inside this gate. The squat tomb lies horizontally across the rear of the plot, and is surmounted by a large stonework book, open at a double page on which are inscribed the names of

295

those lying beneath.

And here they all are, six of them anyway. The father who didn't speak to his wife for thirty of their forty married years, who laughed at the notion that he might kill himself with a pistol, and used a shotgun instead. The brother who imagined that his mortal enemy was the central heating system in his office, who lay on a couch with the Paris telephone directory propping his inert head, and whose end made Jules angry at 'death and its imbecile tricks'. The mother, silenced at last after a garrulous life by an 'impenetrable' death. The writer who used them all. The wife who as a widow burnt a third of her husband's *Journal*. The daughter who never married and was buried here in 1945 under her nickname Baïe. This was the last time they opened the deep pit at whose edge Jules had seen a fat worm strutting on the day his brother Maurice was interred.

Looking at the vault, thinking of them all crammed in together—only the writer's sister Amélie and son Fantec escaped—and remembering their history of wrangling, hatred and silence, it strikes me that Goncourt would be justified in returning a *Hé! hé!* back at his younger colleague: for the company he is keeping, for that embarrassing sculptural cliché of the open stone book, for the naff planters. And then there is the inscription beneath which Renard lies. It begins, unsurprisingly, *'Homme de lettres'*, after which you might expect, in a filial echo, *'Maire de Chitry'*. Instead, the writer's subsidiary identification is as a member *'de l'Académie Goncourt'*. It feels like a tiny flicker of revenge for that diary entry: '. . . they thought that was enough'.

I look again at the stone planters. One is quite empty, the other contains a stunted yellow conifer, whose colour seems to mock any idea of keeping the memory green. This grave is no more visited than that of the Goncourts, though the proximity of the tap must bring a little passing traffic. I notice that there is still room on the stone book for a few more entries, so go back to the woman with the watering can and ask if there are any Renard descendants still in the village or its environs. She doesn't think so. I mention that no one has been added to the vault since 1945. 'Ah,' she replies, not entirely apropos, 'I was in Paris then.'

It doesn't matter what they put on your tomb. In the hierarchy of the dead it is visitor numbers that count. Is there anything sadder than an unvisited grave? On the second anniversary of his father's death, a mass was said for him in Chitry; only three old women from the village attended; Jules and his wife took a glazed earthenware wreath to the grave. In his *Journal*, he noted: 'We give the dead metal flowers, the flowers that last.' He went on: 'It is less cruel never to visit the dead than to stop going after a certain time.' Here we are less in the territory of 'What they would have wanted' than of 'How would they have reacted had they known?' What will happen to my brother in his garden grave when the cropping llamas and his widow are also dead and the house is sold? Who wants a decomposing Aristotle expert turning slowly into mulch?

There is something crueller than leaving the dead unvisited. You may lie in a *concession perpetuelle* for which you have paid, but if no one comes to see you, there is no one to hire a lawyer

297

to defend you when the municipality decides that perpetual doesn't always or necessarily mean perpetual. (So the Goncourts' neighbour was supplanted by 'Miss Bluebell'.) Then, even here, you will be asked to make way for others, to renounce finally the occupation of space on this earth, to stop saying, 'I was here too.'

So here's another logical inevitability. Just as every writer will have a last reader, so every corpse will have a last visitor. By whom I don't mean the man driving the earth-digger who scoops out your remnants when the graveyard is sold off for suburban housing. I mean that distant descendant; or, in my own case, that gratifyingly nerdy (or rather, charmingly intelligent) graduate student— still bibliophilic long after reading has been replaced by smarter means of conveying narrative, thought, emotion—who has developed a quaint and lonely (or rather, entirely admirable) attachment to long-forgotten novelists of the distant Print Era. But a last visitor is quite different from that last reader whom I told to fuck off. Grave visiting is not an emulative pastime; you do not swap suggestions like swapping stamps. So I shall thank my student in advance for having made the trip, and not ask what he or she really thinks of my books, or book, or anthologized paragraph, or of this sentence. Perhaps, like Renard when he went to Montmartre to see the Goncourts, my last visitor will have taken to cemetery-tramping after being given a death-warning, a Fayum moment, by the doctor; in which case, my sympathies.

Were I to receive such a diagnosis myself, I doubt I should start visiting the dead. I have done enough of that already, and shall have eternity (or

298

at least, until perpetuity no longer means what it says) in their company. I'd rather spend time with the living; and with music, not books. And in those last days I must try to verify a number of things. Whether I smell of fish, for a start. Whether dread takes over. Whether consciousness splits—and whether I shall be able to recognize it if it does. Whether my GP and I are going to make that journey of hers together; and whether I feel like forgiveness, memory-invoking, funeral planning. Whether remorse descends, and if it can be dispelled. Whether I am tempted—or deceived—by the idea that a human life is after all a narrative, and contains the proper satisfactions of a decent novel. Whether courage means not scaring others, or something considerably greater and probably out of reach. Whether I have got this death thing straight—or even a little straighter. And whether, in the light of late-arriving information, this book needs an afterword—one in which the *after* is stressed more heavily than usual.

So that's the view from here, now, from what, if I am lucky, if my parents are any sort of guide, might be three-quarters of the way through my life; though we know death to be contradictory, and should expect any railway station, pavement, overheated office or pedestrian crossing to be called Samarra. Premature, I hope, to write: farewell me. Premature also to scribble that graffito from the cell wall: I was here too. But not premature to write the words which, I realize, I have never put in a book before. Not here, anyway, on the last page:

THE END

Or does that look a little loud? Perhaps better in upper and lower case:

The End

No, that doesn't look . . . final enough. A last would-you-rather, but an answerable one.

Note to printer: small caps, please.

THE END

Yes, I think that's more like it. Don't you?

JB
London, 2005–7

300